LITERACY LESSONS

DESIGNED FOR INDIVIDUALS

PART TWO

Teaching
Procedures

You relate what you hear or see to things you already understand.

The moment of truth is the moment of input,
- *how you attend*
- *how much you care,*
- *how you encode,*
- *what you do with it*
- *and how you organise it.*

How well you access it depends on how well you stored it in the first place. How do you become more savvy about the way you remember things? Have a good system. Notice your errors and try to fix them.

The quote from Dr Larry Squire, of the University of California Medical School, can be found on the Dana Foundation video (1996) 'Your Brain: A Lifetime of Brain Fitness'. It is highly relevant to understanding many aspects of the recommendations in this book.

LITERACY LESSONS

DESIGNED FOR INDIVIDUALS

PART TWO
Teaching
Procedures

MARIE M. CLAY

Heinemann

Published by Heinemann Education, a division of Reed Publishing (NZ) Ltd, 39 Rawene Road, Birkenhead, Auckland, New Zealand. Associated companies, branches and representatives throughout the world.

In the United States: Heinemann, a division of Reed Publishing (USA) Inc., 361 Hanover Street, Portsmouth, NH 03801-3912.

ISBN-13: 978-1-86970-323-3 (NZ)
ISBN-10: 1-86970-323-5 (NZ)
© 2005 Marie M. Clay
First published 2005
Reprinted 2005, 2006 (x2)

Library of Congress Cataloging-in-Publication Data
Clay, Marie M.
Literacy lessons designed for individuals Part Two: Teaching Procedures / Marie M. Clay.
p. cm.
Includes bibliographical references and index.
ISBN 0-325-00917-1
1. Language arts (Early childhood). I. Title.
LB1139.5.L35C545 2005
372.6--dc22
2005029877

Cover design by Brenda Cantell

Printed in China

The pronouns 'she' and 'he' have often been used in this text to refer to the teacher and child respectively. Despite a possible charge of sexist bias it makes for clearer, easier reading if such references are consistent.

The author and publishers permit the following record sheets in the Part Two Appendices to be copied by teachers for use with children. The commercial use of any of these record sheets is strictly prohibited.

Contents

Introduction

Most children in classrooms make good progress in group teaching situations. However, the teaching procedures in this book are developed for children who, for different reasons, do not get off to a good start in the literacy instruction of their classrooms during their first year at school. (In New Zealand and the United Kingdom Reading Recovery is available for children who have received formal instruction for a year or more and in the United States they have received a year of formal preparation in kindergartens prior to Grade 1 instruction.) Day by day some children in each country find that their classmates pull ahead of them.

Selecting the lowest achievers at or around six years of age we ask, 'Can a series of carefully designed individual lessons take each child's idiosyncratic problems into account and turn the risk of failing into accelerated progress?'

We must consider all children in the age group, and not exclude any child for social or psychological or physical problems (unless the child has already been admitted to a special assistance programme with a trained professional). Reading Recovery operates as a pre-referral programme for children with many different kinds of developmental histories. The individual design of the lesson series allows us to make appropriate adjustments for a pre-existing condition or a developmental history of missed opportunities to learn. The preschool learning histories of all children have been extraordinarily varied.[1] (In this book the small numbers refer to Endnotes on pages 217–20.)

The lesson activities described in this guidebook have been progressively refined and revised over 30 years. Some changes arose as I tried to clarify points of ambiguity in the guidance I had offered to teachers; others were introduced as a result of new published research; and some became necessary because of changes in education systems. As new research has become available either the teaching procedures or the explanations or both have been modified in a succession of reprints and new editions. Changes are discussed with specially trained teachers in professional development sessions five to six times a year. This new manual consolidates the adjustments or changes that have been made in previous years. It also tries to look ahead in directions indicated by recent research in the field of literacy learning.

Children who enter an early literacy intervention are selected because they are well behind their average classmates. If they are to catch up they must learn at a rate that is faster than the pace of classroom learning. And the series of lessons must be as short as possible if the intervention is to serve all the children who need individually designed lessons. We are able to produce efficient results for a diverse population of learners because we are able to design a set of lessons for a particular child.

One teacher and one child work together in ways that allow a myriad of instructional adjustments to be made. From the recommended procedures a teacher selects those that she requires for a particular child with a particular problem at a particular moment in time. *There are no set teaching sequences: there is no prescription to learn this before that.* A highly appropriate recommendation for one child could be an unnecessary one for another child. The teacher must select the activities needed by a particular child after working with him, observing his responses, and thinking about what he needs to learn next. We do not want to see a child spending time on activities that are not moving him forward or lifting the complexity of what he can do.

If the teacher is to respond to individual differences in this way she cannot begin with the 'Early learning' sections in this book and then move to 'Intermediate' sections and finally to the 'Advanced learning' sections. For a particular child the teacher will need to work at different levels across many of the procedures. This book does not construct a beginning-to-end sequence of teaching. In any one lesson the teacher will need to draw upon ideas from different procedures, switching, for example, from something about learning to look at print to something about hearing sounds and finding out how to write them.

Early intervention teachers move flexibly around these procedures as they observe children and plan instructional opportunities. Hard-to-teach children do not follow predictable paths of progress so teachers will design a lesson sequence that is different for each child. Colleagues are invited to observe each other at work and to discuss the things that a teacher is finding difficult.

When a teacher expects a child to learn this before that she is forcing a child to move through her notion of the sequence in which change must occur. Reading and writing are too complex for that to happen. Preschoolers do not learn to speak in any set sequence! It is an essential feature of an early intervention which aims to accelerate learning that teachers remain responsive to the learning of a particular child, notice when it is possible to allow a leap forward, or act immediately on any confusions and regressions that emerge during the lesson. The teacher must be tentative, flexible and immediately responsive to the best opportunity for a particular learner to have at this moment.

The learning opportunity provided must draw upon the strengths this child has already demonstrated and relate to the new learning needs that have become apparent. Teaching is an immediate consequence of some prior behaviour. Through all the detail of these early literacy learning procedures teachers must remember that the child's ultimate resource for learning to read and write is his spoken language. New learning becomes linked with what he has already learned about language.

Further reading:
Lyons, C.A. (2003). 'Attention, movement, and learning', chapter 2, pp. 25–42, in *Teaching Struggling Readers: How to use brain-based research to maximise learning.* Portsmouth, NH: Heinemann.

1   Learning to look at print

Tutors and Teacher Leaders have asked me, 'How can we help teachers to understand *sooner* what it means for a child to learn how to look at print?' Reading begins with looking and ends when you stop looking. Reading begins with passing information through the eyes to the brain. But the eyes do not just take a snapshot of the detail of print and transfer it to the brain.

> *The child must learn to attend to some features of print,*
> *the child must learn to follow rules about direction,*
> *the child must attend to words in a line in sequence, and*
> *the child must attend to letters in a word left to right in sequence.*

In the first year of formal instruction children abandon diverse ways of scanning print and gradually learn to look at print in those controlled ways. This is not a naturally occurring set of learning; the rules of the code are arbitrary. In real life there are no fixed rules for the way your eyes scan an environment. When language is written down rules apply to the order in which we scan the print. Some children find this learning difficult or tedious. Others are carried along by their speech and pay as little visual attention to the detail of print as they can get away with. They must learn to give increased attention to visual perception.

Competent readers obey all the directional rules for the text they are reading and are unaware that they are doing so. Competent young readers pay close attention to 'which way to go, and what to attend to next', for a short time, but once the brain and eyes have been tutored to do this, children perform faultlessly. They coordinate body, hand and eye movements as they look at print. The learning is gradual and occurs across many trials while children are reading their first books and writing simple messages.[2]

There are many examples in the literature of young children who become confused about the messages in print. Lyons tells how David knew where to begin to write a sentence in a writing book and how to write from left to right across a page and yet he did not control directional movement when reading a book. His hand could control a movement that his eyes had yet to learn.[3]

Until a child attends to print in an organised way the teacher's moves or questions or comments will confuse him. Eyes, hands and brain have to attend to print according to the directional rules for recording the language in print, and this attending must occur with little effort and minimal attention. *Attending in a left-to-right sequence when reading English is not something already programmed in the brain. It must be learned.*

A study of children learning to read English and Hebrew at the same time showed that five-year-olds could cope with this, moving left to right for English and right to left for Hebrew.[4] Brain and body can manage this as long as the context of the activity makes it clear which code you are using.

Conversations with pre-literate children about print on a page can be very confusing to us because we take so many things about reading and writing for granted. Keep in mind that the young child you are talking to does not share your knowledge of the written code. Each of the ideas listed below is fundamental to coping with learning about the written code. None of them can be learned by just being told what to do.

- What is a letter? (This can be confused with what comes in the mail.)
- Some marks are letters but not all marks are letters.
- One letter may be linked to more than one sound.
- One sound may be linked to more than one letter.
- There are several letters in a name (or a word).
- What is 'a word' in your own speech?
- Why are there directional rules for reading and writing? (This was David's question; see Appendix, p. 209.)
- The orientation of a letter is very important: turn it around and it may become a different letter. This is not true of objects and toys which remain the same even when they are upside down or sideways.

So print presents a new kind of experience to the young child; the code is different from other things in his real world. A quick look at the code requires a child to bring together several pieces of information if he is to recognise something he has seen before. For a short period this is what he is learning to do — look at the print, consider several things he knows about it, and decide on a response.

Some children will have begun this learning before they begin formal literacy learning; others will begin as they try to read their names or first books in school. *Teachers must observe beginners closely and plan their encounters with print very carefully to ensure that confusions are minimal. And if something does confuse the child then the confusion should not be allowed to linger.*

All teachers of beginning readers need to foster these new understandings of the code. Children who have been at school a year may still not be consistent

- about where to begin the search for information,
- or how to control movement across a string of letters or a line of print,
- or where to go next.

When they direct their eyes to search for information within the directional rules of the printed page they will be able to link what they see to their own oral language responses.

> *Further reading:*
> Appendix, p. 198, for 'Mother is baking'. I have also written about these things in other books. *What Did I Write?* and *Writing Begins at Home* describe beginning writing behaviours and early ideas about the code. 'How to look at a code' is discussed in *Change Over Time in Children's Literacy Development*, pp. 145–47. How identical quadruplets learned about 'the open book' is reprinted in *Observing Young Readers*, pp. 76–82.

1 Learning about direction

Introduction

So how do the eyes learn to scan print? And how do we know which way the child's eyes are moving? 'Read it with your finger' is a direction given by the observer to get some impression of this. If the young child's finger cannot maintain the directional schema it is doubtful whether the brain will direct the eyes to pick up the information in the correct order.

Is this important? Absolutely! If the marks in print are going to be coordinated with the language understood by the brain then the eyes must attend visually in the same order, from left to right, and at the same time that the brain is hearing the sounds of language. This linking of seeing with hearing according to arbitrary rules must be learned.

We can scan objects, faces and pictures by moving the eyes in any direction. Little children have learned to scan the world like this without being aware of what they do. However, a printed message must be scanned in a different manner dictated by the arbitrary conventions for writing down a particular language. Readers can move left to right in one language and right to left in another. When the child is introduced to literacy in the English language he is usually exposed to the double-page spread of the open book and has to develop a consistent movement schema, left to right across lines, top to bottom down the page, and left page before a right page.

Although some young children have the linear directional movement pattern under control when they enter school others find it difficult to develop those disciplined movements. It is very different from what they needed to do when they were moving around their homes and communities. I have seen five-year-olds, obeying their own set of rules, moving their hands and eyes from the centre fold of the double page to the outside edge of every page, or from the bottom of a page to the top. When a child becomes confused it takes several weeks of good teaching to unpick the error learning and establish a left-to-right scanning pattern. On the other hand, once the directional rules have been learned, children rarely give conscious attention to them.

Letters come with special rules about what is up, what is down, what is left, what is right, and what is first, next, and last. Both reading and writing involve the same set of directional learning so the eyes and the muscles and hands can all reinforce this learning about direction.

A preschool child, watching a parent read a familiar storybook, can learn to turn the pages in a book. By the time he goes to school he may have learned to pay attention to lines of print one after the other, or to notice that print can be placed differently on some pages. A few children become more confused daily. They allow themselves to use a variety of approaches to print. They act as if they have taught themselves an idiosyncratic set of rules.

Children can experience problems with direction for different reasons. Some may have poor motor coordination; others may be quick and impulsive; some are timid about trying a new task; and some have been 'told what to do' and did not understand what they were told. Such children need more time than usual and sensitive teaching to help them to establish directional behaviour. The children who have practised bizarre or optional directional habits for a long time may find it hard to change their old habits and may resist change.

It is not just the young children who are confused. Some of the older children who have been at school longer have some of these confusions locked away, out of sight. Teachers should pay attention to the occasional lapse on directional rules when it occurs.

To learn these arbitrary rules the brain needs to experience a build-up of consistent events. Lapses must be kept to a minimum. This learning must occur early in the child's formal introductions to reading and writing. He has to become consistent as he attends to print so that everything else he learns falls into place. His eyes have to scan according to the serial order rules of the written language *without conscious attention. Demonstrations are recommended; talk may increase the confusions.*

We should not forget, however, that four-year-olds often 'catch on' to all of this without any problems, usually because some noticing adult gave them a couple of clear demonstrations and followed up with three or four checks. That may be all that it takes.

Complex movement patterns to be learned include

- attending to a left page before a right page
- moving from the top of the page downwards
- moving left to right across a line of print
- returning back to the left of the next line
- using the spaces to control attention to words
- attending left to right across a word
- knowing how and where to find what the teacher calls the 'first letter' or the 'last letter'
- and (ultimately) scanning every letter rapidly in sequence from first to last without lapses.

It is as complex as that. The movement patterns used by the eyes and brain in reading, and the hands, eyes and brain in writing, must become almost automatic, requiring only momentary attention.

Avoid talk about direction

Control over directional things can be taught by demonstration and with few words. Teacher talk can easily create confusions. One crisp demonstration might lead to learning after one trial but it is probable that the crisp demonstration will need to be repeated on other books and in other settings. The teacher must monitor these directional behaviours for a while and help the child to act consistently and correctly across all print activities. Before long the learner will come to control the directional schema and will allocate only a fraction of a second to any decision about direction.

Very rarely it may be necessary for a particular child to guide his own directional movements with words that remind him of what to do. This is not the best way to achieve the learning because talking himself through the movement is a temporary prop that has to be unlearned later. That will take time and will delay progress.

Be precise and consistent in your own movements during this period, and give deliberate, exaggerated demonstrations for a short period. You do not need to talk about the demonstration; just do it when you see the child is attending. Model the actions for children often. Avoid talking about the actions. Stop intruding when children show that they are becoming consistent. On the other hand *recurrent lapses, however infrequent, are danger signals, so do something about them.*

Some interesting issues

We recognise a familiar object in all its different views. How do we do that? A young child of five or six years is already an expert in object recognition so the brains of young school learners are tuned to this activity. How are the letters of a code different from familiar objects in the world? The letters of 'h', 'm' and 'n' are similar but different. They occur in various fonts and sizes. There are many exemplars of each letter.

We come to recognise that a certain string of letters can recur. The pattern for 'the' recurs in several places. I recently heard about a Spanish-speaking five-year-old given a Concepts About Print test in Spanish who was shown the page in which the order of letters within the word had been changed. Asked 'What is wrong on this page?' he replied, 'That word belongs in another book' (meaning, perhaps, that the pattern was most likely to come from an English book but it was wrong for a Spanish book).

In the study of visual perception it is widely accepted that our brains separate out different parts of a visual stimulus (colour, brightness, angles, form and movement) and that we process these things in different parts of the brain!

That is hard to think about. Imagine pulling all that information together in an instant.

What is particularly important about print is that the patterns are (typically) seen in an upright position that is orthogonal to the line of sight. So we orient the book, select a starting point, move consistently from left to right along a line (in English) and return back to the left end of the line. Why is this? *That way the letters will always look the same!* If we scanned back along the next line many letters would not look the same, viewed in a right-to-left perspective. You might accept some letters as identical that were not identical.

If you think about the learning task in that way, as a teacher, you will want to straighten up your letters on the magnetic board!

So, gaining control over the directional rules and orientation of letters in print will make it easier for the child to visually recognise letters and patterns of letters.

> *Further reading:*
> In *An Observation Survey of Early Literacy Achievement* (2005), pp. 37–48, the Concepts About Print task provides a standard way to observe directional learning. In *Becoming Literate: The construction of inner control*, directional learning was discussed extensively (pp. 94–95, 112–40, 141–44, 264, and some of chapter 7). You will find David's 'reading' of 'I am a dog' in the Appendices, p. 209.

Recording directional behaviours

A simple recording procedure can be used to capture what children actually do when they are just learning about how to move across print. A standard recording procedure is useful because it allows the records of an individual teacher to be understood and discussed by colleagues.

Select a book with simple text. Ask the child to read some pages or to read with you. Then, once the child is engaged with the task say 'Read it with your finger' for the next three to four pages.

- Show the horizontal direction with arrows. ⟶
- Show the vertical direction by numbering the lines.

  (3) ⟶
  (2) ⟶
  (1) ⟶

- Show whether the page was a left or right one (Lp/Rp).
- Show whether the child used a left or right hand (Lh/Rh).

A sample record from one child who does not yet control directional behaviours might look like this:

Teacher's record		Position on page

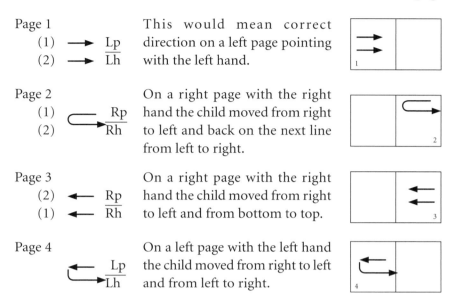

Page 1		This would mean correct	
(1) ——▶ Lp		direction on a left page pointing	
(2) ——▶ Lh		with the left hand.	
Page 2		On a right page with the right	
(1) ⊂—— Rp		hand the child moved from right	
(2) Rh		to left and back on the next line from left to right.	
Page 3		On a right page with the right	
(2) ◀—— Rp		hand the child moved from right	
(1) ◀—— Rh		to left and from bottom to top.	
Page 4		On a left page with the left hand	
◀—— Lp		the child moved from right to left	
Lh		and from left to right.	

A tentative interpretation of this record might be:

- the child had learned very little about the directional rules of English print,
- he used his left hand on a left page and his right hand on a right page (this will become more flexible),
- a starting position at the top left of a page had not been established,
- top to bottom direction was not consistent.

Reading Recovery procedures

Give clear demonstrations with few words. Give liberal praise for any attempts that move the behaviour closer to what is required.

Starting position

Check each new book you are selecting for the child to see that the starting position on a page is clear and uncluttered, and will not confuse this particular child.

- Accept either hand, whichever he chooses to use.
- Control the directional behaviour by pointing to the starting position on the page or line yourself. If you are too slow and he makes the wrong move you have given him an opportunity to get more confused.

- Provide opportunities for over-learning. (This means that the watchfulness continues well beyond the point where the teacher thinks the behaviour is learned.)
- Discreetly block the child from starting in the wrong place. Anticipate, to avoid intermittent practice of an old unwanted pattern. Use various devices like
  - — intercepting a false move,
  - — gently bringing the child's hand to the correct position,
  - — pointing yourself or showing appropriate alarm.

Starting signal

A more drastic measure is to mark the starting point. For example a green sticker (green light for go) may be placed to the left of the first line of text.

   I like pizza.

You may need to use this signal also in other places where the child is working during the lesson,

- on the blackboard
- on the table top
- on paper.

Teachers are sometimes surprised when they find that a child who controls direction in one place uses different directional responses in another place.

To assist orientation on more complex text a coloured line or margin can be placed on the left side of the page.

> I like pizza
> and ice cream
> and cola.

This provides the child with a prop, but later the teacher will have to help him work without the prop.

Do away with signals

The child should be encouraged to do away with signals (such as stickers and margin lines) as soon as he has gained some control over the top left starting position.

A helping hand

Teachers should not be afraid to encourage hand action to assist reading. Demonstration is an easy way to engage the child in the correct movements. For the most difficult cases, move the child's hand and arm through the

1

appropriate movements but let him control the movement as soon as he can manage it alone.

The child's pointing finger will guide his visual searching behaviour as it becomes easy for him to:

- find the top left starting point,
- move consistently left to right across lines, match words in speech to words in text, one after the other, moving left to right,
- locate the first letter of lines on request,
- locate the first letter of words.
- Eventually this will lead to using his eyes alone to do all these things.

A clear pointing finger (rather than a vague cluster of fingers) is helpful.

Later on, children find that pointing helps them to establish one-to-one matching of 'saying' with 'seeing'.

And how does it work in practice?

Carol Lyons provides an example. David knew where to begin to write a sentence in the writing book but did not control directional movement when reading. His teacher placed a green dot to indicate where to start on page 1, and he correctly identified the place to begin. She took hold of David's finger to demonstrate early strategies of directional movement and one-to-one matching of words read aloud to the words in print. She demonstrated left-to-right movement. This routine was repeated on two pages. On the third page she asked him where to start and which way to go. David said, 'I don't know.'

> *Further reading:*
> Lyons, C.A. (2003). *Teaching Struggling Readers,* pp. 160–61.

Do away with the helping hand

Sometimes a child's pointing covers the words he is trying to read.
Use a simple instruction like

> *You're covering up your words with your finger.*
> *Remember to point here, underneath the words.*

Be insistent.

> *Was your finger underneath the word? (Yeah!)*
> *No! It wasn't!*

If finger pointing is allowed to persist it may become a prop that gets in the way of fluent reading. So as soon as directional responding becomes consistent the teacher can begin to discourage pointing with the finger when reading familiar text.

A pointing finger, for a period, helps the eyes and brain attend to parts of a text. The child is only ready to discard the use of a finger if the eyes and the brain have learned how to search across print word by word in appropriate ways. To coordinate several skills while solving some new problem on a difficult text a child who has not needed to point for some time may begin doing so again. Even experienced readers can be seen using the finger to keep the place in small print, or to help them when the reading task is difficult for other reasons.

Voice pointing (Clay, 1991a) will often be heard, telling you that the reader is attending word by word. Before long the teacher can begin to require the child to read groups of words together, using the phrasing that is natural in normal speech and the intonation of normal conversation. At this time the child can be asked to drop the pointing (and strong encouragement may be necessary). Yet it is appropriate for the young learner, and adults too, to return to voice pointing temporarily, at a point of challenge. Both voice pointing and finger pointing are helpful at first to get attention focused on detail in print and to hold the place while other things are thought about. Both should occur less and less, making way for fast visual processing of print. Either may recur at difficulties in order to aid problem-solving.

A teacher may say

Sometimes we need to put a finger back in when it gets really tricky.

It follows that finger pointing might continue longer on the new text introduced in each lesson and would be discouraged when the child is rereading familiar books fluently at the beginning of the lesson.

Working left to right across a word — hand and eye

Because the child is moving his eyes and finger correctly across a line of print does not necessarily mean that the child is *attending left to right to the letters that make up the words*. This is how one teacher checked on her pupil.

From his first lessons I asked my student to say a word he knew slowly. I taught him to locate the word on the page of print, to say it slowly, and to move his finger underneath it from left to right while he was looking at the word. I referred to this as a 'slow check'. I made sure he was looking at the word as he moved his finger and said the word slowly.

It is important for children to learn directionality on the page of a book in the broad sense and teachers should not interrupt that learning by stopping too often to make a slow check on words. If special attention to left to right through a word is necessary, the phrase 'a slow check' could be useful when words are being studied in isolation. Used too often it could get in the way of learning fast recognition of words.

The eyes scan from left to right across a word, consistently

Consistent visual survey of the letters across a word from left to right is a further refinement of the left-to-right survey of a line of print. It can be developed in similar ways. Deliberate demonstrations by the teacher when appropriate without verbal explanations will produce good results. Children mimic well.

For a little more help during reading, or rereading after writing, or during work on words in isolation, the teacher might say things like

> *Say it slowly and move your finger under it, this way. Make a slow check while you move your finger under the word. Now show me how you can do it just with your eyes!*

The aim is to establish a fast visual scan that consistently works left to right across words.

Choice of texts

For the early stages of learning about direction select texts that use strong clear print that is well-differentiated from the pictures and with several words to a line. Preferably the text begins towards the top left of the page and the punctuation is normal. As the child gains control over direction some variations in layout can help the child to become flexible enough in his approach to print to deal with later variations he will encounter. But get the rule-governed behaviour firmly established before introducing opportunities for the child to cope with more variation. (See also pp. 18–19 for a school principal's comments.)

The end goal

The goal is a particular movement pattern suited to books, blackboards/whiteboards, paper and almost all print. The movement pattern discussed here is specific to English, Spanish, French and some other languages, but not to all written languages.

Signs that may indicate that a child has directional movement under control are that he can

- use either hand to point to print
- on either page
- without lapse in direction
- or by self-correcting after a lapse.

Different children will reach this goal in different ways. Most (but not all) will use an index finger and most will prefer to use a particular hand for a period. Say to the child 'Read this page with your finger.' Most children show how much control they have in response to that question. In the less secure child the response might be to use the dominant hand only and that is fine.

When the end goal is reached the child should be able to use either hand on either page. It seems as if the learner anticipates correctly the directional movements he needs to use. The brain will have learned that, faced with printed English, the eyes will need to move across print in certain ways. When the designer of the message has played some tricks on the reader, then the brain will have to give particular attention again to how to move across the print.

Check the more competent beginners too

Check on each child entering an early literacy intervention. Even if a child knows many letters and some words and seems to be under way with learning to read *the teacher cannot take the child's control of the directional schema for granted*. Beneath what seems to be the child's strengths there may be some well-established habits of fast perceptual survey that do not follow the directional rules of English. The eyes may be fixating on words in a line or letters in a word in intricate and unhelpful ways. The teacher must observe and demonstrate for the child in both reading and writing the most efficient way to move across print. Further checks should be made from time to time to see that the child scans left to right across the letters in a word.

Publishers can design layouts that might send any of us searching for where to begin, so an occasional lapse is not a problem. There are, however, two shifts that clearly call upon the reader to adjust his expectations about direction. The first is when the page of print in beginning books changes from one line to two or three lines, and the other is a later change that book designers make, when sentences do not finish at the end of a line but run on to the next line.

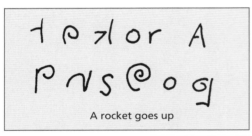

A rocket goes up

We have to help the beginning reader to learn how to attend to the correct starting place and how to move around the page of print.

This is a big assignment for any child who has given little attention to print or books before coming to school. It must be learned early, otherwise the block of print may be treated as if it were a whole beautiful piece of artwork full of detail to be scanned in any order.

Mirror writing is quite common

Some beginning writers, for a short period, show us that they can copy print quite easily moving from right to left and actually reversing most of the letters. What they write is hard for us to read. Their flexibility is working against establishing consistent left-to-right scanning with the eyes. Researchers studying visual perception report this but I have seen no convincing explanation for why this puzzling behaviour occurs. Insistence on a left-hand starting point for each line in writing seems to establish the preferred behaviour.

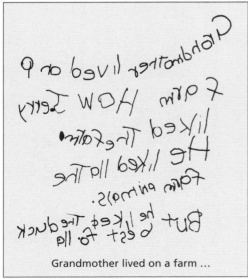

Grandmother lived on a farm ...

2 Locating what to attend to in print

Introduction

This section is about another early learning task. As the child looks at the blur of a page of print he scans for something to attend to. What can he recognise? Children like to locate things in the print of their favourite books. Beginners in Reading Recovery often delight in finding the 'No! No! No!' sequence in *Where's Spot?* When someone is reading to them it could be a phrase from a Seuss book like 'green eggs and ham!' that excites them.

The shape of a letter and its features may catch a child's attention; the lines, curves, tails, angles, or critical size of some part, the dot over the 'i', or the cross on the 't' — these things help to distinguish one letter from another. It is fair to assume that at first only a few details are recognised, among other mostly meaningless squiggles.

The white spaces separate patterns of letters. This is not obvious to some children. They have to learn that the spaces help us to see the words.

The few words that a child knows will stand out as a pattern that recurs, separated by white spaces on either side.

Put yourself in the child's position by looking at print in a book that uses a different script. Do you know whether to move from left to right or right to left? (See Clay, *Change Over Time*, p. 161.) How long would it take you to work out how many different symbols the printer is using? How are the symbols different one from the other? What should you attend to first, and where should your eyes move next? Did you scan skipping over the 'hard symbols', and did you search for the ones you recognise? Can you find a recurring pattern of several symbols that might be a word?

לִפְנוֹת עֶרֶב הִגִּיעַ סַבָּא.
"הַגָּרִי, הֵבֵאתִי לְךָ מַתָּנָה"
אָמַר סַבָּא.
מָה זֶה יָכוֹל לִהְיוֹת?

Sequence

Psychologists have pointed to a prior problem in some young children that we should consider before we think about letters and words. Can the child point to a line of blocks, counters or coins one after the other? Young preschool children have difficulty pointing to a row of objects in sequence. This is recognised as important in early mathematics lessons but few have noted that this is also a limitation for reading. If they cannot control the simple movement of pointing to a line of objects in sequence it will be hard to attend to each printed letter or word in sequential order.

Check this out with a new pupil. Ask him to point to each object in a row of objects, left to right. Then get him to point to each word in one line of large print. Many school entrants can do this or will quickly learn to do this in the first weeks of school. A few children will need special help in learning to do this. A child might fail this task for several reasons: only one is considered here. He seems unable to attend to, or focus on, or point to one after another across a line of blocks, or counters or words.

Recent research suggests that the concept of a word in text and the ability to point word by word while reading, both interact with phonemic awareness in early reading.[5] That makes a lot of sense. Having the eyes pick up the visual information from left to right across a word should be matched up with saying the word from the first through to the last sound!

Further reading:
Check relevant items in the Concepts About Print task of *An Observation Survey*. See also *Change Over Time in Children's Literacy Development*, pp. 146–47, 158–61.

Reading Recovery procedures

Early learning

Put down two objects in a row, placing them one after the other. Call the child's attention to them and point to the left one first and then the next one. Don't count them.

Ask the child to point to a row of three objects; four objects; five objects or more in sequence one after the other from left to right. Keep a record of

- the starting point
- the direction
- any difficulties.

Intermediate steps

Repeat the task with objects and sequences like felt dots, geometric shapes, pencil dots, two-letter words (same and different), four- or five-word sentences. It is probably wise to avoid using single letters at this point. Keep a record as before of: the starting point, the direction, and any difficulties.

Demonstrate the behaviour you want the child to copy and provide practice on print. The goal is a controlled movement with one-to-one correspondence. If you used objects or miniature toys ask the child to tell you about the objects in sequence. Without pointing do one of the following.

- '*I can name these.*' Name each one moving left to right.
- '*I can tell you the colour of the dots.*' Give the colour of each dot left to right.

Then ask the child to do those things.

Advanced learning

The task now is to have the child point to the words while reading using the spaces as signals on one line per page. Watch carefully when the child has to transfer this achievement to two lines per page, and again to more than two lines per page.

If the child needs help to see the words and the spaces between words,

- write out a line or two of the text of the book in large print exaggerating the spaces,

- or cut up a sentence into single words as the child watches,

- or you can over-emphasise the spaces by spreading out the words at first, and then gradually reduce these to normal spacing,

- or the child can remake the sentence and reread it several times, pointing carefully.

To develop an accurate locating response on text reading for the few children who still have difficulties:

- use two-finger framing (with two index fingers)
- use a long pointer (because it requires more effort to control the movement)
- encourage deliberate voice pointing for a short time.

The extra control needed to accomplish these more difficult motor tasks slows down speech so that the child feels the pauses between the spoken words while his fingers show the boundaries of the written words.

> *Further reading:*
> Carol Lyons writes about Collin in *Teaching Struggling Readers*, pp. 100–102.

Work for flexibility

Once good locating responses have been established on a familiar book and the child can show one word and can demonstrate the concept with two-finger framing, get the child to read fluently but pointing with one finger.

Select a message this child wrote. Write the message out, cut it up, and then get the child to help you reassemble it in more than one way to foster flexibility — in other words play with it.

- I went to the zoo.   • I went
                                to the zoo.   • I went
                                                       to the
                                                       zoo.

You could ask the child to read a word or two of the story on each rearrangement.

A more advanced task is to vary the size of the space that the child uses to reassemble his cut-up story:

- Large line space | I am a big girl |

- Progressively smaller space | I am
a big girl |

Children who have the most difficulty with learning about direction tend to have problems with this type of task.

Too many breaks

Over-segmenting on multisyllable words can cause difficulties with one-to-one correspondence. For example:

A	way	we	go
Away	we	go	to

Deal with this patiently and to overcome a bad case of too many breaks exaggerate the syllable segments with magnetic letters spatially and also by shouting or singing, then gradually rejoin the syllables again.

  A — way   Away

Caution

For many children the activities described in this section will be unnecessary. They learn these things incidentally while exploring books in a more enjoyable way. A child's progress should not be delayed by undue attention to locating problems. If such problems exist, fix them early. It would interrupt progress if you had to come back and attend to this again four weeks later.

One demonstration might be enough to give the child the idea that locating the words in the print is what is required. On the other hand the learning might need to be demonstrated or 'refreshed' every now and again. From time to time emphasise the left-to-right order of words in a line of print and the left-to-right construction of letters in a word.

3 Spatial layout

Introduction

I received this comment from an observant school principal.

> In most books printed for our youngest readers the spacing between words is not sufficient. Adults can discriminate between where one word ends and another begins; children cannot. They are learning the basics of left-to-right sequence, retaining the movement from one line to the next,

and often coping with confusing background shading and colouring. I believe that there should be four spaces between words, or even more on the early reading books.

Beginning readers are often helped if the word spacing and line spacing are increased until they have gained control over the directional rules of printed language and have developed reliable eye movements for attending to print.

Most of the examples in this section come from writing. It is important to remember that when the child is learning about the ways in which print is laid out on a page he uses this learning when he is reading *and* when he is writing. I think of this as *seeing print from two vantage points*. As they try to write stories children demonstrate for us what they know about using the space on the page. If a teacher notices confusions in writing this should make her observe very carefully what the child is attending to when reading from a page of print. She may notice that the relationships of letters and words are somewhat confused.

Further reading:
Chapter 7 in *Becoming Literate: The construction of inner control* provides more background. Refer also to *An Observation Survey of Early Literacy Achievement* (2005), pp. 21–22, 47–48.

Reading Recovery procedures

Breaking letters out of words

After letter identification work, quickly make a word that the child knows with magnetic letters. (This is not a demonstration of construction: it just appears in front of the child.) Demonstrate with deliberate movements breaking out the letters, sliding them from first to last,

- above
- or below
- or to his left (with the child on your left, see p. 42).

Then get the child to do this. And repeat with another word or two that he knows.

Delay the constructing of words by the child until he has gained a good control over breaking words into letters, and has a preference for attending to them from left to right. Provide the models of left-to-right construction for some time before you begin to ask the child to 'make' a word by himself.

If you need to demonstrate something about constructing a word, pull down the beginning letter(s) from one of your own examples and then pull down the last part, that is, all the other letters. Sometimes it is helpful to exaggerate the spaces between the letters of a word the child knows, laid out in the right order, and ask him to put the word together, working left to right.

During writing and cut-up stories

Pay attention to words from left to right in the writing part of the lesson or during work on the cut-up story. Help the child to leave a finger space between words, saying, 'It is easier for us to read.' The child will have to learn to do without this finger prop as soon as possible.

When the child writes his story and reassembles the cut-up story he rehearses the construction of words and lines of text from left to right.

Without too much talk about it, help the child to use the space on the page appropriately when spacing out his sentences. The teacher might point to a definite starting position in the top left-hand corner and indicate the way to go. She might suggest when and where to start a new line. She ought to anticipate when a word is too big for the space available.

The child will learn from this help how to organise his text on the page rather than from your talk. Gradually the learner learns to work within the directional and coding rules of the language.

During reading

Teachers are often surprised when they shift a child from one line of print per page to two lines of print. Why is it so difficult for some children to make that shift? Is it a hesitation over where to go next? Could it be a shake-up for the whole directional schema?

Help the child to organise his approach to any variations of space he encounters in written language. The order in which he attends to print is vital for success in reading and writing. He has to learn the rules and become able to handle any variations. Props should be used only as long as they are essential.

An important note   We have not found lined paper supportive of early writing for the child who is finding space and direction a problem. It imposes many constraints on his performance that he may not be ready for. It does not allow the teacher to begin with what the child can do.

The teacher may add cues and prompts to the blank unlined paper if these seem to help but only for a brief period of time. Having learned to work with the props the child then has to learn to work without them. The child who gradually learns to organise his production within the conventions of the printer's code on blank pages transfers easily to lined paper.[6]

Can we tell when children have learned to find their way around print? The teacher gets evidence of this as the child reads his books. She has another opportunity to observe aspects of layout during the cut-up story. The child projects his understanding of spatial layout on to the blank page in his writing book during every lesson.

4 Seeing something he recognises

Introduction

So we have discussed how to help children find their way around print. As quickly as possible the learner should also be expanding a meagre knowledge of print so that there are many opportunities for him to find letters and words he knows in the print he is trying to read. Temporarily the teacher has placed high value on correct left-to-right responses to lesson tasks.

Theorists may argue over whether adult readers look at all the print detail or only sample some of it. Expert readers can afford to engage a range of sampling from a rapid skimming to a careful examination of the fine print. For the beginning reader not much is recognisable among the squiggles, lines and dots. There may be only a few letters or features that the child can recognise. He does not have many visual signposts to guide him. Locating the visual information that he can recognise is a skill he will learn.

This old report from a century ago captures what happened on the first day of school for a child with little exposure to print. Initially the symbols were meaningless.

> The teacher must have been waiting for her. As she hesitated at the door, he came over, took her by the arm, and walked her rapidly to a desk where two other little girls were sitting. He … pushed a pencil and a piece of paper in front of her. He was a thin, sour-faced young man with cold unsympathetic eyes. She could not understand what he said to her before he turned away. One of the girls whispered to her, 'Make marks like the ones he makes.' The marks the teacher made on the blackboard spelled 'cat' but Polingayski did not know it. She copied them as best she could, filling her paper on both sides.[7]

So all the letters of the alphabet must change from being just squiggles to having multiple alternative identities and uses!

Many teachers who think of reading and writing as language activities find it difficult to think about what a child has to learn when he first begins to look at print. A rough early guide is that a child is likely to be scanning print in the way he scans a picture — looking here, there, and everywhere for one or two letters that he knows.

Sometimes we can tell what children might have been looking at from their writing. At other times it is what they say that alerts us to what they are looking at, or perhaps to what they are not looking at. Most of the time we really do not know what the beginning reader is attending to in print.

Most children adapt easily to the task and attack it as if they had a huge appetite to satisfy. A few children take a passive approach to print. They need a teacher who prompts them to explore print, and make their brains search the page for signals that they can locate, use, and recognise another time.

What should the learner attend to? Is the 'unit' a letter or a word? Is it a line of print or could it be two lines? These things are not obvious to the beginner and learning what to do with different kinds of units takes time.

The child's own name (or some other name) is often the first word recognised, and with that comes an understanding that certain letters in a certain order make up a name. This is helpful. From reading simple text the child can learn that words are separated by spaces. And it is usually the publishers who control when a line of print is a full sentence, and when, at higher levels, sentences run on to more than one line.

For children who need an early literacy intervention it is advisable to let them *attend to what is easy for them* at first and work from there. These are the children who cannot work well with a teacher's preconceived sequence of what she wants to teach to her class. Be alert throughout the lesson series to notice what this child finds easy or hard to attend to.

Once the learner begins formal literacy instruction his visual perception provides information that helps him to read and write but it takes a year or two to learn to identify all the symbols of the alphabet quickly and accurately in their various fonts and sizes. Slowly the child learns to juggle a wealth of piecemeal, novel information about direction, layout, concepts about print, letters, words and especially the sounds in print *presented to his brain through the eyes*.

> **Messages require words**
>
> 'If my name is Jenny and my brother's name is Alan, and I have three dolls which have different names, and I am only four and haven't yet learned to write any words, perhaps I could make some names for my dolls. Make them in writing, that is, because they have names. Their names are Katrina, Sleepy-eye doll, and Debbie. I can use the signs I know, and I can copy some from books, I can use the same ones twice, and I can turn some around.'
>
> TONNμi
> 'This says Sleepy-eye doll.'
>
> AUUDO
> 'This says Katrina.'
>
> JOOiꙄ
> 'This says Debbie.'

The beginning reader is a little like the novice driver out in the car on the road for the third or fourth time, unsure of what to attend to first, and wondering how he will ever get all the information into the right decision-making sequence. How you use your eyes when driving is something to think about. It provides a useful analogy for how much you depend on your eyes in reading and writing.

This visual attention to print increases. Gradually the child pays more attention to fine detail and becomes sensitive to minor differences in clusters of letters. (Learning to write contributes to this also.) And the recognition of encounters with print. Psychologists refer to this fast pick-up of information by the eyes as visual perception.

> *Capture the child's attention,*
>
> *notice what the child is aware of,*
>
> *give clear demonstrations,*
>
> *and encourage fast recognition.*

Further reading:

For further reading see *By Different Paths to Common Outcomes*, pp. 41–56, 64, *What Did I Write?*, *Becoming Literate*, pp. 255, 258–64, and *Change Over Time*, pp. 123, 146, 148, 161, 166–67, 170, 173–74.

4

Reading Recovery procedures for extending letter identification

This is a short segment in the lesson in which children must learn fast identification of all the letter shapes and features. This knowledge must be learned so well that the recognition is accurate, based on attending to detail in the print. Our visual perception of the details needs to be totally reliable and rapid. It needs to catch the brain's attention but require minimal conscious attention.

Early learning

Early in the lesson series the teacher helps the child to gain footholds in print. The child learns some letters and begins to work with some simple words. The teacher asks herself 'What detail in print is this child already attending to?'

Look back at the child's Observation Survey results. Scan those records to discover what detail in print the child was attending to. Refer to the Concepts About Print (C.A.P.) items that highlight visual survey of direction. They provide hints as to whether the child pays attention to word order, to first or last letters, or to letter order within words. Does this child know what you are talking about when you ask about 'the first letter' in a word?

If at the end of a completed lesson series a child reads quite well but confuses the concepts of 'a letter' and 'a word' on the C.A.P. task, that should concern the teacher!

Learning to look at print

The critical distinction between any two words will be made at the level of letters. Two similar words are distinguished by comparing the letters in those words.

Fast recognition of letters allows the reader to make faster decisions about words. Children who know only a few letters will learn words very slowly.

When the child begins lessons the 'known' may be not more than:

- the child's name
- a few words which he can read and/or write
- one or two particular little books
- and his own dictated stories.

Begin with the words the child knows in reading or in writing and move slowly towards extending the child on each activity. Here is a first lesson in an early intervention built around the child's name. The teacher can use several ways of directing the child's attention to visual features of print. For example a teacher may say

- '*Make your name here*', but the child makes no response. The teacher begins to write the child's name.
- She pays attention to the first letter, saying '*We make it like this.*'
- She models the movements vertically in the air.

That teacher has already worked on three ways of remembering.

1	*Movement*	The teacher holds the child's hand and guides him. This identifies the letters by movement (kinaesthetic learning).
2	*Words*	'*Down and around,*' the teacher says. This is a verbal description of movement.
3	*Visual form*	The teacher writes the letter. This provides a visual model, and dramatises the sequence of construction. (She may ask the child to write it also.)

The teacher writes the rest of the child's name and he copies this. From this the child learns

- some specific letters
- how to put them in a set sequence
- several features of letters, usable in other letters
- several features of words.

If some of the words you explore are words he wants to know this often results in the child taking more notice of the things the teacher calls attention to.

Suggestions for extending a meagre knowledge of letters

Extend the child's control from slow identification of a few letters to rapid response to the entire set of letters. *Introduce new letters into an array of letters the child already knows.*

The beginning reader and writer has to learn how to attend to the particular features that help all of us to distinguish letters, one from another. For example

'S' is distinct (even when it is upside down).

'E' and 'F' catch the attention, but are confusable.

'a' is confused with 'e',

'm' with 'n', 'u' and 'w',

'n' with 'u',

'k' with 'y'.

Four very confusable items are 'I', 'l', 'L' and the numeral '1', and they must be distinguished from 'f', 't' and 'i'.

The 'b', 'd', 'p' set is notorious, together with 'g' and 'g', 'h', and 'q', because the learner must consider the vertical stick and the position of the ball when it is approached from left to right!

Talk does not help much in making these distinctions.

The learner must attend to familiar letter features until each letter can be rapidly distinguished from all similar letters.

This section has a focus on letters but this does not mean that letters should be the focus of all teaching at this time. The child should be developing new knowledge in many aspects of reading and writing *at the same time*. He will be learning new things about story texts, new concepts about print, new words, and new letters or clusters of letters. The child can begin to read words using only a limited knowledge of letters; he can read text with only a limited knowledge of words. Many whole text and whole word activities precede and follow the letter work in every Reading Recovery lesson.

Remember, the child can only make use of what he can recognise as familiar in some way.

You need to respect the learner's pace of learning but you need to get the entire set of letters known as soon as this can happen. That will make the child's decisions about words easier.

Manipulating magnetic letters adds the support of the hands

Magnetic letters are colourful and three-dimensional and easy to move. They lend themselves to feel and to fast movement.

In a Reading Recovery lesson there is only a short segment for letter work in isolation. Children learn to identify all the letters accurately and fast. One end goal is the rapid recognition of all letters at a glance. The hand is only used as an early support system. However, daily writing consolidates learning about letter forms.

One child asked, 'Is "r" down and over a little bit or down and over a lot?' (comparing 'r' with 'n').

The letter 'u' can be confused by a child with the pronoun 'you'. The letter 'y' has one sound in 'baby' or 'happy', and a different sound in 'yes' and 'you'. The name of the letter 'y' is also a word 'why'. Many young learners and their teachers get into real trouble when they are trying to attend to that kind of complexity. Letter-sound relationships are neither simple nor obvious.

A child was reading *Freddie the Frog*, a text with many instances of the letter 'g'. After several pages this interaction occurred.

T: Read this with just your eyes. *(she means drop the finger-pointing)*

C: *(reads)* 'Frogs cannot roar,' said the lion.
    'Only lions can roar.'
    Along came a dog.
    'Ruff,' said the dog.
    Freddie tried to bark.
    'Frogs cannot bark,' said the dog.
    'Only dogs can bark.'
    That's a different one. *(pointing to the 'g' in 'dog')*

T: That 'g' is a different one.
    It's got some extra curly things on it but you knew it still said 'dogs'.
Another quirky thing about letters is coming under control.

Movement   The movement of magnetic letters can be large and bold at first, and later become minimal. The teacher can demonstrate the movement. If she moves letters or writes in deliberate ways she can stress particular points in the construction process. The child can group and regroup letters. Teachers need a large magnetic board placed so that the child can stand in front of it, and work at eye level, moving the letters easily. The board should be cleared of distractions — a big, clear working space.

Making words   The child can build, dismember, and rebuild small collections of letters several times. Pairing and grouping are good activities. (Writing is a slower process.) Producing one or two words he knows, which are also dismembered and rebuilt (always left to right), aids the child's visual discrimination of letters, as well as a vague understanding of the ways in which letters come together to make words. The focus is fast recognition, not learning the word!

Variation   Varied positions, sizes, and means of making letters help the child to learn the constant features. Sometimes a child makes an unimportant feature of a letter his main signal. Watch for odd things like that. We do not need to become too fussy about font differences.

Many of the activities in the writing and cut-up story sections of the lesson will help the children to discriminate further which features of letters they must give close attention to.

What makes this easy?

Involving the hands helps. Think about how Mother is supporting Donna in the example on p. 27. Carol Lyons writes about this as 'the movement necessary to develop the processing system that will eventually help her learn ways of remembering the letter name and recalling how to form the letter'.

> *Further reading:*
> See Carol Lyons, in *Teaching Struggling Readers*, pp. 41–42.

At first use only the letters the child can already identify. Give him lots of practice with these. Introduce new letters into an array of letters the child already knows. Add easy-to-see letters first. Letters will be easier to identify in isolation and hard when embedded within words or within continuous text. However, children need, in the long run, to see and recognise every letter in any setting.

As the child works with letters think about the following points.

- Allow the child to label letters in any appropriate way — by name, by sound, or because it is in a word he knows. Beginning readers making good progress use any of these ways of identifying letters. It seems to be useful to have more than one way of labelling a letter. Don't insist on only one type of label being used.

- Have the child run over the new letter with his finger to feel the shape. Identify the letter by name. Talk about the similarity/dissimilarity of the capital and lower-case forms.

- Model the formation of the new letter on a whiteboard, write in large print and match your movements with talk. (See p. 30 for how difficult this is for a few children.)

> Mother: Let's write the first letter in your name, Donna. *(Taking the child's hand)* Start at the top and go down. *(Mother and child make a vertical line down)* Move the pencil up. *(Mother and child trace over the vertical line)* Now move the pencil around and touch the top of the line to the bottom of the line. *(Mother and child make a curved line to complete the D)* That's the first letter of your name, Donna. What is the name of the first letter in your name? What letter did we make?
>
> Donna: D.

4

- Give the child verbal instructions, and guide his hand if necessary. Have the child write the letter
  — in the air
  — on the blackboard
  — in sand.

- Point to a letter to help the child to recognise it in text when it is the first letter in a word and when you know he knows it. Use the term 'letter'.

  Say, '*See this letter.*'
  Or '*Look at this letter.*'
  Or '*Does this letter help?*'

Reading Recovery teachers develop many interesting activities for drawing children's attention to the features of letters, such as sticky coloured paper cut-outs, formation cards showing where to start letters, tracing paper activities, and so on. But do only what is essential to get new letters recognised. Do not get too focused on letters.

I have been asked, 'Should teachers be saying the sound of letters children are manipulating?' Not as a matter of habit, no. Value whatever knowledge this child shows you he has. Many letter names contain a sound that letter makes. Ask yourself 'Where is this child in his learning? Is he ready for using just the sounds?' If not, let him work with what he knows and find opportunities to feed into his learning the things he does not yet know. Does he

- recognise the shape,
- or use a key word as a prop,
- or give an alphabetic name,
- or does he usually give the sound?

The teacher will reinforce old learning or provide new input according to what the child needs to learn next. When the child is very confident the teacher may want to call for either sounds or names for letters, encouraging flexibility.

Things to enhance letter learning

- Involve the child in some movement along with the visual attention.
- Spatially separate things and bring them together again.
- Repeat things.
- Invite the child to be active — to say, to build, to break up whatever is the focus of attention. Come back to it several times before moving on to the same form in another context.
- Rediscover letters or words in new contexts.
- Then return to this until the recognition is reliable and speedy.

In other words the child must really 'know' the unit of print you have worked on whenever it occurs again.

Things to do with similarities

- Draw attention to similarities among only those letters the child already knows.
- Match, pair or group all the letters that are the same using only lower case.

Things to do with differences

- Draw attention to letter differences on letters the child knows.
- Say '*Find one that is not like the others*' (a harder task).
- Contrast the most different first.

Things to do with arbitrary categories

- Learn capital and lower-case pairs.

Things to do with variation

- Sort the same letters in different colours.

Work for flexibility

- Use vertical and horizontal surfaces.
- Use different markers — felt pen, chalk, magnetic letters.
- For a particular child use sandpaper or felt letters.
- Use different sizes of print.

- Look for a simple book that illustrates the new letter and read it for the child, having him find examples of the letter in the text, usually in the first letter position.

- Get the child to identify the new letter by an object that *he* identifies with it.

- Go to his alphabet book (see pp. 34–39) and show him where the new letter fits in sequence. Draw the key picture and the lower- and upper-case letter forms. Stop there!

- If appropriate teach one or two new words starting with that letter in the same lesson.

Each new thing learned should be revised in several other activities.

Extend the knowledge of letters so that the child gives some identity to each of the letters. Be cautious with published materials: most have been constructed with a different aim in mind — to have the children learn a sound for every letter symbol.

It is a feature of most languages that many letters consistently represent one sound *but* one letter may signal several different things. For example

'c' is often used for /k/ or /s/ in English.

Different letters may signal the same thing:

'c' and 'k' can both be used for /k/, and 'ck' is used for /k/.

The sound a letter represents can also change depending upon the other letters surrounding it, or whether the syllable is stressed or not. We know that the English language is less consistent than many other languages and learners have to live with that!

It is not the aim of Reading Recovery to have the child learn a sound for every letter symbol. It is more useful to learn (in English) that sometimes a letter has one sound and in other contexts it can have a different sound. This means that the child must know he has to make a choice, deciding which of several sounds this particular letter may have.

Always do a little letter work after taking the Running Record in the lesson. When most of the letters are known, and breaking words into parts (see next section) is easy, add work that requires the child to generate new words but still give a little attention to letters and fast recognition (see sections 10 to 13).

When children confuse the visual forms of letters

If children have confused any two letters repeatedly then relearning those letters will not be easy for them. One way to help them control and monitor these unwanted responses on the one hand, and develop desirable new responses on the other, is to bring the behaviour under verbal direction for a short time.

The child is writing 'in the water' as part of his story. He tries out 'in' and 'the' on his work page, writes them into his message, rereads the sentence and says 'water'.

T: How would you start water?

C: Y.

T: Are you sure? *(She shows him an alphabet card and he points to w. She shows him pictures and he names them.)*

C: Watermelon, wagon, watch, waffle.

T: Okay, 'w' is how watermelon starts.

C: *(volunteers)* Down, up, down, up.

Read the example. Verbal directions like that should be used with caution and only as a temporary device, a prop. If continued for too long they will become an unwanted response, slowing up fast responding.

- Attend to similarities and differences of letters.
- Use three-dimensional forms such as magnetic letters.
- Create clear demonstrations of any distinctions that the child should learn.
- Put four or five examples of the same letter onto the magnetic board. Jumble the forms with a few known letters and have the child find 'all the Es', and 'all the Rs', and 'all the Ts'.
- Call for fast responses.

Revise new learning frequently and in different contexts, because it takes children some time to distinguish letters. As some letters become familiar they are omitted from the array from which he is selecting.

Attend to the forming of letters that are confused

In many cases of letter confusion an appropriate strategy is to help the child *gain control of one of the confusing letters* before introducing the second. It does not help to put two letters that children confuse side by side.

Draw the child a model on the blackboard slowly, directing your movements verbally. Ask the child to try, and guide his hand if necessary. Talk about what you are doing.

'Make k down, and in and out.'

Try to bring the child's movements under your verbal control and then transfer this verbal control to the child. Continue to practise after the child gives the correct response and revise from time to time. Attend to letter formation only if it is essential, and only focus on one of the confusable group at any one time.

Attend to common faults

Sometimes the child adopts a strange starting position when forming a letter. Direct attention to this only if it seems to be important. Be firm about essentials (whatever your most important teaching points are) and ignore other minor problems. You cannot afford to teach what is non-essential at this point in the child's progress.

Letter names

You may direct the child's attention to movement or to visual shape. But use letter names if you want to refer to letters. They seem to act as a shorthand kind of label representing many different experiences with letters.

An important point

A lot of letter learning is done incidentally by children in classrooms as they learn to read stories and write simple messages but special help with letter learning is needed for children in Reading Recovery. It should always be a part of early intervention lessons but should take little time. The child cannot afford to waste time on letter-learning activities or games when he could be reading well-chosen books.

Careful judgement is needed to give the child enough opportunities to gain control of letter identification. (Further discussion on the child's own alphabet book is in section 5.)

How do we foster fast visual recognition?

Speedy access to visual information in print is of the greatest importance in literacy learning. As you begin to engage learners with the earliest literacy tasks their fast visual perception of forms is building up *a network of links of what is seen to what is heard*, that is, the sounds of language. Teaching at this early stage provides the foundation for later progress.

The learning of any visual percept — letter, cluster of letters, or words — might occur in a sequence like this (but not necessarily so!).

- Attend to any aspect or feature in the print at first.
- Bring the child's attention to other detail.
- Sharpen attention and awareness.
- Shape his response to a more decisive one.
- Speed up the response.
- Fade out the conscious attention given to decisions made.

If you are puzzled by the child's behaviour, think about some of these things.

- Intervene to prevent wandering attention.

- Make sure the learner is visually attending to what he needs to attend to. Check this. Telling is not enough.

- Control the task. Organise things so that the correct response does occur. What you tell the child should make it obvious what you want him to do.

- Intervene to prevent the occurrence of an old unwanted response. Do not give an old bad habit any chance to recur when you are trying to eliminate it.

- When the child has begun to attend to a new letter or word, vary the places in which it occurs. The child needs to be able to 'carry' the learning to somewhere else on another occasion.

- Teacher talk is not very helpful for guiding visual learning. Limit instructions to simple imperatives and/or use minimal verbal prompts such as

'Where is the first letter?'

'Where do we start?'

'Do this!'

'Cover the end!'

Synchronise your words with what the child is doing.

Rayner is a well-known researcher and critic of research on how we adults move our eyes across print. In 2004 he and his co-author, Juhasz, wrote:

'… there are very little data examining the relationship between oral reading and eye movements' and 'Given that beginning readers spend a lot of time reading aloud … more data are needed on this issue.'[8]

An example of cross-checking

Nearly five-year-old preschooler Arthur could write his name (backwards or forwards depending where he started on the page) and knew some letters. He had good control of book language and quickly grasped the principle of one-to-one matching on simple little books that were read to and with him. Although he probably didn't recognise any of the words, Arthur was 'reading' the two-line caption book, *We like ice-cream*, with accurate fingerpoint matching when this happened: Reaching the end of a page for which the text was 'We like ice-cream in the snow', Arthur stopped, his finger under the word 'snow', the sound of the word still in his ears, and announced with interest and surprise, 'It's got an "o".'

The first link between story and print had been forged — through the sound of the 'o'.

In conclusion

Children make the print-to-language link only when they have learned how to work on the visual features of printed text.

Children learn the print-to-sound link more easily when they try to work with words and messages constructed from their own speech.

Children show that they understand that 'letters make words' when they have worked in both reading and writing and begin to make analogies, saying 'this is like that'.

The aim is to have a child recognise letters rapidly without needing props, or prompts. He needs to end up with a fast recognition response. Be careful to arrange your teaching so that it leads to this.

---

5 What is 'reading' during these early lessons?

The titles for each following subsection a)–f) call your attention to how little the child knows about reading during early lessons. Yet he is already making different processes work together.

a) I read and write messages and stories (drawing on *my* oral language)

b) I know a few letters (*my* alphabet)

c) I know some words (*my* words)

d) I can take words apart

e) In the first weeks of intervention:
   What does it mean to 'know' a letter?
   What does it mean to 'know' a word?

f) What does it mean to 'read' a text in the first weeks of an intervention?

a) I read and write messages and stories

Four or five times in a lesson the learner has to pull together all the bits and pieces he knows to read simple stories carefully chosen by the teacher, and to write simple messages that he has composed with her help. Text reading and writing demands that disparate kinds of knowledge are pulled together. In the beginning this is a challenge.

5

Both Kevin and Collin are trying to pull disparate things together at an early stage of the lesson series. These brief accounts should tempt you to go to the original reports by Carol Lyons. They illustrate how intertwined saying and doing, or looking and doing are. An observant teacher knows how and when to help the child achieve the necessary coordinations. Carol is also pointing up the emotion involved at moments of difficulty, the exasperation and self-assertion.

T:	Kevin, help me clap your name. *(she says his name and makes two claps)*
K:	I don't want to clap. I want to hit the desk. *(he makes one pound on the desk)*
T:	*(taking Kevin's hands in her own)* Let me show you how to clap your name. *(they clap 'Kevin' several times)* There are two claps.
K:	*(withdrawing his hands from the teacher)* Let me do it alone. Kevin *(one clap)*
T:	How many times did you clap?
K:	Two.

The teacher persisted and by the end of the episode Kevin successfully clapped and said 'bas-ket-ball'! Learning the coordination of sound and movement had begun.

Collin read seven pages of a Level 1 book with a repetitive sentence pattern 'The XXXs go down.' On the last page of text 'The farmers go down' was followed on the next line by 'to town.' Collin read 'to eat their supper with the people.'

T: Did that match, Collin?

C: *(in an angry voice)* Matching! Matching! You're always talking about matching. I don't know if it matched!

(T took the opportunity to teach him about this.)

C: I get it, but my ending to the book was better.

Further reading:
Read more about these boys in *Teaching Struggling Readers*, pp. 101, 103, by Carol Lyons.

During these first weeks of lessons the teacher will choose books that draw upon what the child knows, that challenge him in one or two new areas, and that invite him to retell a part of the story. One or two questions will elicit a partial retelling. This will highlight understanding (comprehension) as an expected outcome.

When you have seen a child struggling to point to words in a new book while trying to match his spoken words to printed words across a line of text, it is obvious that some different things are being pulled together. Here is a reconstruction of what might be happening, as the five-year-old might view it.

- I used to scan a page of print like I scan the world. I began anywhere and moved anywhere.
- Then I learned to go left to right across one line of print using my finger to guide my eyes.
- I find places where I get a clear view (space) of what comes next.
- A strange thing happens. Every time I see 'go' and I say 'go' the print looks the same.
- But every time I see 'get' and I say 'go' my teacher says 'No! Try that again.'
- So what I am saying has something to do with the look of those 'squiggles' that come after the clear view. And 'get' and 'go' start the same and sound the same, don't they?

Many different kinds of new learning are probably interactive in early literacy learning. As each new feature of the code is noticed the child is enabled to notice more things in that code. Although the first pieces of a jigsaw puzzle take time to assemble, the more complete the puzzle the quicker you can place the last pieces. It makes sense to assume that learning the concept of word in text could facilitate the acquisition of phonemic awareness.[9] Finding the separate words on the page of print may consolidate and confirm what the child is learning about letter-sound relationships. Moving the finger left to right through a word can be easily matched with saying the word from beginning to end.

Children can learn to read on texts. And when things work well together the brain seems to know when it is making a good response and how to get to even better responses in the future.

b)   I know a few letters (*my* alphabet)

Use one or two minutes of the letter identification segment of the lesson

- to extend the child's range of control over letters,
- to work towards perfect performance on the whole set,
- to increase fast responding to all letters.

As the child begins to recognise more letters faster, spend half the time on breaking words into letters, and left-to-right assembly of words out of letters (see pp. 40 and 42). Some letters are easier to learn than others.

> *Further reading:*
> See p. 89 in *An Observation Survey of Early Literacy Achievement* (2005) for lists of easy and hard-to-learn letters. Teachers could discuss what they think are the reasons for some of the difficulties.

My alphabet book sums up what I know

To the young child making slow progress the whole alphabet is overwhelming. We need to show him how well he is dealing with this task, and that it is manageable. So we make him his own book and put into it only the letters he has mastered.[10]

The teacher might be asking him questions about these symbols that he does not really understand. She can choose *one or two* of these questions.

- *What is its name?*
- *What sound does it make?*
- *What is a word that starts with that letter?*
- *What is a word that starts with that sound?*
- *Is that a little letter or a big one?*
- *Is that a capital letter or a small one?*
- *What is another letter that looks like that?*

She must not go through that list! That would surely confuse the child. The child needs to have at least one way of identifying or distinguishing a particular letter from all the other 'squiggles' on the page.

A small handmade book with room to enter one letter per page allows us to solve three or four problems. First, a teacher must get past the idea that there are 26 letters to learn in English. We are thinking about learning all the different visual forms that occur in the alphabet and for children learning English there are commonly 54 letter forms used in the early reading books. (These are tested in Letter Identification in *An Observation Survey of Early Literacy Achievement.*)

It is a bonus for the learner that some of the lower case and upper case letters have exactly the same form so that reduces the size of the set to be learned.

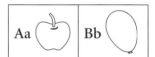

It is still a large set of visual learning. Differentiate 54 symbols one from the other. What does visual learning mean in this context? It is learning to use the eyes to distinguish each and every letter form so that you never confuse any of them.

Suppose the child demonstrated on testing that he had control over, say, eight letters. Working with the child during his first lessons the teacher would enter into this book only those known letters. She is knowledgeable and enters the letters in their alphabetic order leaving enough blank pages so that later on she can enter the letters that have yet to be learned. Use one key picture that this child already identifies with that letter (his choice). Preferably it should not be the teacher's choice of picture, and a published alphabet book almost never matches the experience base of each child. We should be working with the child's memory store, not with the teacher's favourites.

Use the form of the letter that the child already knows. One clear letter to a page (capital and/or lower case), one picture or drawing, and room for another form of the letter to be added later if necessary. *This is not the place to accumulate known vocabulary or to indulge in word study*. Avoid clutter. New letters are added over several weeks, and slowly the correct alphabet sequence builds up. This helps learning in several ways.

- The child knows everything that is entered into this record. It was learned *before it was entered*. He sees the growth of his own control over that seemingly unending set of letters as the book fills up.

- The child has a feel for the size of the task, how far he has gone, what he knows for certain. As the empty pages for the letters not yet known are flipped over, this tells him that he can use what he knows and for the present there are challenges that can be overlooked. The task is manageable.

- The alphabet book is also a record that reminds the teacher of what this child controls. It is about letter knowledge, but it allows the teacher to observe how well the child works with many complex things like:
  — Is he sure of the letter form?   (Visual form)
  — Does he know the letter name?   (Name)
  — Can he name the object?   (Object)
  — Can he tell you the first sound of the object's name?

To observe the child's control the teacher should be aware of which question she is asking.

In early literacy intervention teachers will encounter some children who do need detailed attention to letter identification. There will be other opportunities to pay attention to letter forms in reading. And there will be daily practice of letter forms in writing.

Do not underestimate the need to tidy up this control over the letters of the alphabet for the group of children who already know a lot of letters. It is common for teachers to assume the remaining letters will be easily learned. That assumption must be checked because it is often false.

The alphabet book is a record: *it is the book of those letters that the child knows something about*. Written languages use a limited set of visual symbols to print the spoken language, and in an alphabetic language a visual symbol represents one or more sounds in the spoken language. The child learner comes to grips gradually with the alphabet during the beginning reader stage, a few letters at a time.

For children who know many letters the teacher can tell the child that magical number of letters which he can recognise quickly, say 30–35, and enter into the alphabet book only those that need some attention. I do suggest that the pages for the 'known' letters be included, left blank or have a small letter entered. It helps to clinch the concept of the alphabet as a limited set arranged in an unchanging order. It also allows for dealing with any quirky alphabetic issues that do not reveal themselves until later in the lessons.

The personal handmade alphabet book used in Reading Recovery should contain only the letters that the beginner can recognise by the letter's form, or by naming it, or by one of the phonemes it represents. Any one of those ways of knowing is a good beginning. Teachers record a letter after a child has shown some knowledge of it. (The alphabet book is not a place to record the letters he doesn't know.)

Published series of 'letter books' (a book for each letter) can be very confusing for slow learners. They contain pictures of objects the children cannot name, more items than are easily remembered, and often they depend on letter-sound links that do not apply across dialects and countries. What we need for our learners is one or two clear exemplars that this particular child can immediately call to mind.

There are links between the visual symbols and the sounds we speak but languages differ in how regular and consistent those links are, and English is one of the least regular. Far too often early literacy teaching misrepresents letter-sound relationships to children. Teachers tell children that two things sound the same when they do not, and then those teachers have also to explain that some symbols can make two quite different sounds. Children accumulate experience with printed language and their brains come to 'know' some of the regularities they have encountered at an unconscious level. If a teacher tells them that X sounds like Y when they cannot hear the similarity the children become very confused.

How you pronounce any particular English word depends on the dialect you speak and the accent you commonly use.

Teachers in training could well discuss with their colleagues examples like the one shown.

> One teacher asked me to include 'ch', 'th', 'wh' in my alphabet test. She called them blends but then she corrected herself. She omitted 'sh'. She also claimed that 'th' and 'wh' each represent one sound. (Say 'then' and 'thick' and 'where' and 'who'.)

We need to think of the child as a language user, who is used to hearing language, and not yet a language speller (like the teacher) who has years of experience with looking at the orthography of English. She is likely to confuse him because she is such an expert language speller.

The teacher will choose to select a letter for attention for a variety of reasons. When most of the letters are not known the choice will be guided by what might be easy to tackle next; evidence of difficulty will arise during lessons; remembering may have to be coached; and occasionally a child cannot pronounce a sound that then needs practice.

The alphabet book is merely a record of what is known with spaces for what is 'yet to be learned'. That gives the child a sense of the size of the task and a feeling of control over his own progress. It also provides a location to return to when a troublesome letter, still being confused, turns up. For Reading Recovery children their own alphabet books have proven to be more useful than published books for all those reasons.

The child's working alphabet book might become redundant by halfway through a lesson series.

A beautifully illustrated published alphabet book might create interesting interactions between a teacher and child or parent and child *once the learner has control over all the symbols used to print language.* It might be very interesting to the child after he has completed his Reading Recovery lessons. Nodelman provides an interesting analysis of how confusing alphabet books can be for learners.[11]

Further reading:
An Observation Survey (2005), chapters 2, 4, 6; *Becoming Literate*, chapter 5; *Change Over Time*, pp. 55–68.

Discoveries do not occur in alphabetical order

The most recent studies I have read on alphabetic learning send a clear message. Alphabetic instruction is important.[12] Alphabetic instruction without phonemic awareness training is not as effective as alphabetic instruction and phonemic awareness instruction. Reading Recovery children get daily practice of these links in their writing, and in particular in the Hearing and Recording Sounds part of the lesson (see pp. 69–80).

We think that learning letters is easy. It is quite easy to learn to sing the alphabet in a song but visual recognition of many letters builds up slowly in young children. From alphabet books, or magnetic letters, or blocks, and from simple things they ask us to write down for them to copy, children come to know a few letters. Most children separate out one or two 'easy to see' or 'easy to write' letters from their experiences, and then discover a few more from their scribbling, find them on labels around the house, on important belongings and food packages, and on mail that arrives from important people, like grandparents. *Those discoveries do not occur in alphabetical order. Alphabets are a way of organising letters that adult readers use.*

What contribution does knowing the letter names make?

- It is very helpful to have a way of talking about these small units of print in either reading or writing.

- The entire alphabet as a whole is not very useful for the young child. It merely provides the child and the teacher with a record or inventory of the reference points to which he can anchor his current efforts.

- The book provides the detail of the journey taken and a map of the length of journey yet to be taken.

Neither letter names nor letter sounds need to dominate. They are useful alternate labels for the symbols.

Teachers need to know ...

Sometimes in the middle of a complex teaching interaction the teacher offers the child poor guidance. Unwittingly she makes the task harder to understand. She makes a bold statement that contradicts something the child has experienced differently.

To reduce the risk of this occurring the teacher must bear in mind several features of English. There are 26 letters and 38–45 phonemes (depending on the analysis and linguistic theory you consult).

- The 26 letters have 'lower case' or 'upper case forms'. Some have the same form in both cases, but others have two different forms.

- Consonants in English seem to be fairly regular in the sounds they represent but we say them differently depending upon what follows or precedes them or which dialect we speak.

- When it comes to vowels in English we overuse a few letters to represent many phonemes.

c)   I know some words (*my* words)

At this time the child is also learning his first reading words. He knows so few words that we need to think of the words he can read plus the words he can write as the pool of all his knowledge about words. A glimmer of recognition in either reading or writing is the vague beginning, out of which further knowledge of the word can emerge through many contacts in different settings.

Even though beginning readers and writers have small vocabularies of known words, any letter work or word work they are asked to do should arise from the texts they are working on, and not from the teacher's extensive knowledge of the English dictionary. If something is to be recognised again then it should pop up often in different contexts.

For the child who has a limited repertoire for literacy work it is not helpful if this is his experience in one lesson:

- new things pop up in the letter identification work,
- further new things crop up in writing,
- there is some kind of surprise in the cut-up story,
- and more new things are introduced in the new book.

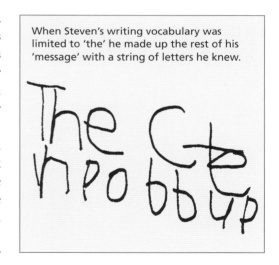

When Steven's writing vocabulary was limited to 'the' he made up the rest of his 'message' with a string of letters he knew.

5

Expand the meagre knowledge of words

The teacher must create opportunities to link new features, letters and words that occur in any activities but not overdo it. There should be echoes from one part of the lesson to another part. The learner can discover some of these links for himself. The child's brain is excited to find what it already knows in a different setting. Fortunately language allows this to happen all the time. Words pop up again and again. What does not help very much is the introduction by the teacher of unusual words dragged up by the teacher's brain that the child may not encounter again for a long time.

New words will be acquired through reading books, and others will come from the daily writing. Either route can be useful. The learner will come to notice more and more of the visual features of print he is reading and writing.

Children work on words in several ways during a lesson.

- From working with the child in reading text the teacher decides which word (or words) she would now like this child to focus his attention on.

- Make it clear when you want the child to attend to a word (a particular pattern of letters) and when he should attend to a single letter. Use the two terms carefully. Point precisely to a letter OR across a word from left to right.

- One way of remembering a word in all its detail is to be able to write it. This requires one to have learned a little program (like a computer program) that produces the word from beginning to end, with all its parts in the right order.

Some of the things that may help a child learn to read and write a new word are these.

- Assemble magnetic letters from left to right to make a word as the child watches. Have the child stand on your left while you break the whole word into individual letters, move them out to the left in letter order, first to last. If you think the child could mimic you, have him remake it (left to right), prompting him and commenting as necessary. Doing it more than once may be a good idea.
  Learning what to do is paramount. Do not complicate the task by asking him to say, to name, or to sound it at this time.

- Write the word in big print as the child watches you.

- Ask the child to trace the word with his finger, saying the word slowly as he traces it. The goal is the left-to-right scanning, not the sounding out.

- Use a paintbrush and water to make a disappearing word on a blackboard.

- Use wet chalk to make a magical 'appearing' word on a blackboard.
- Ask the child to construct or write a word that he is still learning several times so that he becomes fluent at this.

Use the particular words this child has worked on in other activities. Just do not make him fed-up with any of them! Keep in mind the need to extend two vocabularies (reading and writing) at any time in the lesson. A useful initial vocabulary can be selected from a list as shown.

> Child's name, I, like, see, is, the, in, am, to, come, my, we, and, at, here, on, up, look, go, this, it, me

However, 'come', 'look', 'like', 'here' and 'this' provide a better introduction to how words work in English than two-letter words like 'to', 'is', 'at', 'on', 'up', 'it' and 'me.' In some ways, two-letter words are hard, exceptional, and they do not contribute much to dealing with the sequencing or clustering of letters in the language.

Teachers often find lists of, say, 100 commonly used words from children's writing, listed by frequency. Some list only 'regular' spellings (that is, ones that follow a common pattern) and others include words that might be exceptional in some way. Teachers should keep the 'regular' and 'not regular' distinction in mind when they are working to accelerate individual children but should avoid talking to the children about 'rules'. Brains constantly search for consistency but they build up that consistency from meeting up with a particular feature again and again.

Two vocabularies should help the child: one used to write his stories and the other used to read his first books. Keep in mind all the words that any one child controls at this early stage. Known words are a rich source of information of several kinds for the novice reader and writer, so avoid your own pet words and work from the child's own knowledge base, and from the books he is reading. Reading Recovery teachers have found it useful to build up their own reading and writing vocabulary charts for individual children, to be referred to, and added to during lessons (Appendix, pp. 190 and 192).

Another idea for later in a lesson series is to build up a box of word cards indexed by letters of the alphabet. Such a collection of partly known words has several uses. This might be used with a child moving into higher levels of book reading with some children.

- It provides a child-sized concept of what he is trying to master (just as the alphabet book does for letters).
- It helps him to remember a word, that is, it is a retrieval device.
- It reminds the teacher of earlier work the child has done. Either well-known words or words that prove unmanageable can be (discreetly) withdrawn from the collection.

These matters are discussed in more detail in sections 11, 12 and 13.

5

d)   I can take words apart

When the teacher starts to work on 'breaking words apart' she must watch her own behaviour closely. She must invariably make her models from left to right, building up the string of letters needed. If the child catches on to her demonstrations she will not need to talk about this emphasis on letter order.

When the child can work well with letter identification, knowing, say, 15–20 letters including lower and upper case, supplement the letter work for the day with some quick work on words in isolation. Choose words from familiar reading or the second reading from yesterday's book, or yesterday's writing. Select words made up almost entirely of letters the child already knows.

1   Build a carefully chosen word deliberately from left to right, letter by letter, at eye level directly in front of the child. Then talk about *breaking up the word into letters.*

> Say '*If we were going to write this word we would have to make it letter by letter.*' Use known words at first to make it easy. You are teaching *how to do this.*

This is not an activity intended to have him memorise a new word.

Initially children do not understand the relationship of letters to words. They find it difficult to decide what is a letter and what is a word. We must be careful not to increase the child's difficulties.

- Drilling does not help.
- Talking about this distinction almost always creates confusion.
- Most children begin to clarify this for themselves.
- Learning to think about breaking words into separate letters helps (p. 40).

In the first year of learning to read the child is establishing the habit of working left to right through a word. In a sense his eyes are also learning to recognise the identity of each letter *when it is approached from the left side.* (A slight turn and these letters could have a different identity for the beginner: b, d, p, q, e, a, k, y, t, f.) Teachers can help but sorting out these concepts will take time.

- In your own demonstrations of words on the magnetic board, break the letters out of the intact word on the right and move them one by one over to the left.

- Have the child on your left. Construct words at the magnetic board letter by letter first to last and then read the word (sometimes using a left-to-right sweep with your finger).

- When you get the child to build a copy of your word pass him the magnetic letters for that word one by one in correct sequence. Then ask him '*What word have **you** made?*'

In a very short time the child should have a consistent left-to-right approach to letters in words he sees. Then from time to time check on the concepts of 'a letter' and a 'word'. Is he holding on firmly to the distinction? On a three- or four-letter word ask questions like this depending on the child's competence.

> *How many letters are there in that (short) word?*
> *Show me one letter.*
> *Show me one word.*
> *Show me a short word.*
> *Show me a long word.*

This is just checking! Progress is gradual: slip-ups are to be expected. Lapses may occur occasionally. Sometimes they even occur on the final Concepts About Print test. Lapses can reactivate old confusions so take time to deal with them early.

Two things are important.

(1)   Be consistent youself and always work from left to right. The left-to-right habit will become established quite easily (without talking about it) and will be reinforced in every text reading and writing situation. Do not force the issue, but make sure every child perfects it within a few weeks.

(2)   Letters make up words. Children may be slow to consolidate this idea. This is not about teaching words or counting letters. It is possible to know many letters, and many words, without being clear how letters go together to construct a word. Teachers must allow for the fact that from time to time there may be a child who does not understand this relationship until late in the lesson series. As writing improves, this distinction becomes clearer.

2   When you judge that this is just 'too easy', and the child is ready, you can shift to another kind of break, assembling a word quickly, and then adding on a final inflection like plural 's' or verb ending like 'ing'. The possessive 's' and the 'ed' endings introduce some confusions. Use with care.

- Choose a word of one syllable plus an inflection from a previous text context, perhaps 'looking' or 'going'.

- Assemble it quickly, left to right. (By now it should not need to be a demonstration.) Ask the child to watch carefully as you run your finger left to right under it. Say

  > *What's the first letter in 'look'?*
  > *Can you hear the last part of 'looking'?*
  > *We can take the first part away (to the left).*

- Demonstrate, moving 'look' to the left and then bringing the inflection over to it and reading it for the child. Have the child do this and read it as a whole and as two parts.

- Repeat this for a day or two with the same word, or for a fast learner with another known and common word like 'go'. Then have him try it alone on another word he knows.
- Make a note to 'refresh' the experiences from time to time. Find further examples in his writing or reading, today and for the next few days.

Now he is probably ready to do this on a new word, one he is currently learning to recognise.

3   Consolidate steps 1 and 2. Don't move to the third step too soon. Moving left to right across a word should be becoming a preferred way to do this work. A next step would be to demonstrate breaking *a known word of one syllable* (with no inflection) into two parts ('hand', 'wish', 'with', 'book').

The teacher should use a standard procedure in her demonstrations: *I recommend that she consistently use the onset and rime break although she would not be teaching or encouraging the child to copy this.* Choose the beginning part (called the onset, made up of one, two, or three consonants) and the ending part (called the rime, a cluster of sounds found in several words that have the same sound pattern, as in a rhyme that is spelled the same way).[13] Onsets and rimes are two kinds of letter clusters.

- Ask the child to watch. Build the word 'went' and very deliberately, pull the 'w' towards the left leaving the 'ent' on the right. Move the 'ent' across to complete the word and then ask the child to break the word into two parts. *The child may make the break anywhere as long as he gets two parts.* Often, however, he will mimic the teacher. Do not bother him with your concepts of onset and rime until much later after he has become very comfortable with breaking into two parts.

You have already taught him to break the word up into single letters. *Now, in contrast, he is breaking words into just two parts.* Let him find some way of taking that word apart (in either reading or writing). Be flexible! At this point we only need the child *to learn the general principle, that words can be broken in more than one way.* Ask the child to

- use the hand and eye together on the manipulation task. This is important.
- assemble the intact word first. All the letters are supplied by the teacher in the correct sequence.

Attend to one type of break in any lesson!
    Steps 1, 2, and 3 above have helped the child to break words apart,

- to do this letter by letter,
- to take off and put back an inflection,
- to break a single-syllable word into two parts,
- and to respect sequence, from left to right.

You may have talked about the number of letters in earlier lessons to stress the letter-word distinction. At this stage the child's attention should be on parts and wholes. The number of letters should not be mentioned.

If the teacher consistently uses one kind of break (like the onset and rime break) this will become vaguely familiar to the child. At a later time in his lesson series when taking words apart in reading text or in writing messages, or when he is ready to get to new words by analogy with known words (see p. 143) you may re-introduce the onset and rime concept.

4 Make a note of examples from other parts of the lesson of the child's current work in reading or writing which lend themselves to this work on breaking. Spend a little time on them here.

5 Take occasional opportunities to break a word apart in other lesson activities. Leave the child free to break the word anywhere, but make sure that his eyes move left to right across the words.

Although children can hear syllable breaks and final inflections (as in 'shopping' and 'played') it is probably too early for the child to use those sound signals to guide his word-solving in reading, despite what you taught in step 3. Drawing too much attention to the end of words breaks the left-to-right habit being fostered in this early period. It encourages the eyes to jump about in random ways. Avoid this until you recognise that the child is reading well. As a competent reader or writer the child will have to respect sequence to handle multisyllabic words like 'crocodile' or 'caterpillar'.

6 As the child progresses through these steps the teacher will be aware that both the visual forms of the letters and the phonemes they can represent are becoming more familiar to the child. Sometimes he lets you know that he 'hears' the letter and sometimes it is obvious that he 'sees' the letter. Use letter names or sounds following the child's lead as to which he finds easy. Gradually help him to switch easily from letter name to letter sound so he develops two alternate routes to the written language code.

Examples of breaking words out of text

Daily the teacher cuts the child's writing into words, breaking words out of text. Breaking text into words is obvious to the child in writing, especially when you insist on spaces between words.

Examples also occur in reading books where the printer has 'broken out' the words in the text layout. Take any opportunities that arise to comment on print in his books when the publisher has broken words out of continuous text. An extreme example is

> Green
>> eggs
>>> and
>>>> ham!

It is not the main purpose of these early activities to teach new words. While the child is extending his reading and writing vocabularies he is also becoming more aware of how words can be broken out of speech, and sounds (and letters) can be broken out of words. Later the child will be learning how to work with new words on the run as he is reading texts.

e)   In the first weeks of intervention: What does it mean to 'know' a letter? What does it mean to 'know' a word?

Here is a framework which teachers find useful. It assumes that for children having difficulty with aspects of literacy learning it usually takes several encounters to learn a new word or letter. It is rare for what psychologists call 'one-trial learning' to occur. (I know you have probably been surprised when it does occur, but most of the time it does not.) We can think of a new response coming into a child's repertoire of literacy behaviours as being

- new
- only just known
- successfully problem-solved
- easily produced but easily thrown
- well-known and recognised in most contexts
- known in many variant forms.

> *Further reading:*
> This is referred to in *Change Over Time in Children's Literacy Development,* p. 123.

When a child reads a simple storybook he may give an accurate reading of the text, but his knowing of the words may be only at the first three or four levels of that list. We cannot assume that a correctly read word is known in all its detail.

A teacher may need to ask herself from time to time 'Where is this word in the learning hierarchy? Can I do anything that will shift it towards "known, and in many variant forms"?' This is unplotted territory. After a while, because of how a child works with words you begin to judge quite well which words are known and which words are still in the process of becoming known.

Sometimes what you think is old and established learning can be disturbed by some new competing learning and for a short time confusion rather than knowing is observed. The observant teacher tries to work out what new experience has upset the old established responding.

Encourage flexibility

Encourage flexibility in thinking about letters and letter groups in words. Engage in as much word building with magnetic letters as is needed to foster the later visual analysis of new words in text. The manipulation of letters, the breaking of words into letters, and the construction of words in writing are important for Reading Recovery children. Work to ensure that what is learned in one place is transportable to another place.

A teacher should work carefully through these early achievements if the child has had very little experience with literacy. If the child seems to be able to work easily and accurately at higher levels at the beginning of his programme the teacher should spend two or three lessons checking out these early accomplishments thoroughly before proceeding to work on higher level concepts and strategic activities. Assume nothing about this foundational learning. Check it out before you lift your demands.

f) What does it mean to 'read' a text in the first weeks of an intervention?

At this early stage the child is 'reading the context' keeping in mind the teacher's comments and her introduction, and what he knows about books, and the few letters and words he knows, and guided by the appearance of the book and the pictures. He is relying heavily on his oral language.

This girl looked for the things she knew, and composed her utterances to suit the contexts she could work with. She attended left to right across lines of print locating the few letters and words she knew. There is much in the text that she cannot yet give her attention to. Returning to this as a familiar text several times she will be able to 'read' more of the detail in the print next time. She became a very competent six-year-old reader.

We used to think that children picked up some of their early knowledge of letters and words from the environmental print around them. A recent large and careful research study[14] came to the opposite conclusion: when children were tested for knowing about features of print and phonemes their scores on these predicted how good they would be at noticing environmental print! It seems like each factor influences the other.

> This girl was trying to read the phrase 'look after'.
> The story was about Mother buying a hat, so 'look at' and 'hats' could have been expected in the text. Unprompted the reader worked aloud, sorting through her possible choices.
>
> It wouldn't be 'at', it's too long.
>
> It wouldn't be 'hats'.
>
> It wouldn't be 'are'. *(getting closer to the letter sequence)* It's too long.
>
> Lacking a solution she continued with the story.

2   Learning to write words and messages

Reading and writing are two different ways of learning about the same thing — the written code used to record the oral language. It is like having two hands. What knowledge you have about writing can be used during reading, and vice versa.[15] Children give us hints about the common ground they notice between reading and writing.

Most literacy instruction theories pay little attention to the fact that the child is learning to write words, messages and stories at the same time as he is learning to read. The reciprocity of early reading and early writing is grossly undervalued.

Writing, like reading, involves paying close attention to the learning of letter features and symbols, and to clusters of letters that are likely to occur together. It involves searching with the eyes for visual forms and patterns in left-to-right sequence and linking new input with what you already know about the language you speak. Recent studies in Spanish and in English concluded that 'children's ability to deal with oral segmentation tasks is linked to their knowledge of the writing system'.[16]

Writing also involves the young writer in listening to his own speech to find out which sounds he needs to write, and then finding the letter forms with which to record those sounds.[17] (It involves learning about the sequence of phonological information coming to his ear.) The sounds in a word form a pattern that has a beginning and end.

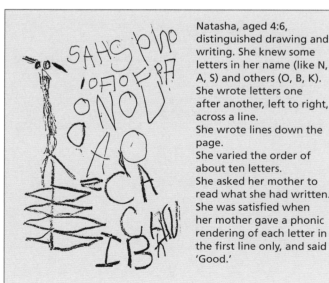

Natasha, aged 4:6, distinguished drawing and writing. She knew some letters in her name (like N, A, S) and others (O, B, K). She wrote letters one after another, left to right, across a line.
She wrote lines down the page.
She varied the order of about ten letters.
She asked her mother to read what she had written. She was satisfied when her mother gave a phonic rendering of each letter in the first line only, and said 'Good.'

Study the attempts of two preschoolers to write down their messages. Untutored, Natasha and Sally-Ann are learning some basic things about the written code and they have not started school yet.

Natasha and Sally-Ann are preparing themselves to be readers. They are beginning to have some ideas about the marks of a code which might carry a message.

Teachers look for signals that the child is making progress in reading but often forget to look for signals of progress in early writing. They should be able to comment on progress in both reading and writing throughout the lesson series.

Sally-Ann was younger, aged 3:6, and a precocious writer.
She drew a story about a girl taking her tortoise for a walk.
Then she wrote the story around the picture.
She knew many letters, many more than the letters in her name.
She underlined her lines.
She went down the page.
She varied her line length.
She told her family the whole story.

At the time of early literacy learning writing helps the young reader to analyse some of the detail in print. Consider carefully what the learner is attending to.

- Writing fosters a slow analysis of print, from left to right.
- Writing highlights letter forms.
- Writing left to right coaches the eyes to scan letters in a word from left to right.
- Writing forces the learner to attend to different levels of analysis (features and letters) and to the importance of letter sequence.
- Writing requires the eye and hand to coordinate awareness and actions.
- Writing puts the learner under pressure to group letters so they can get the message down quickly.
- Writing consistently but subtly seduces the learner to switch between the different levels of letters, clusters, words, phrases and messages.

Catherine knew some letters in her name and had a vague notion of length when she wrote this.

Catherine

Attitudes to writing may have been set up at home or in the classroom, and negative experiences may have made children reluctant to write because of an emphasis on correctness. Teachers need to be sensitive to this possibility.

T:	Patty, let me show you how to write the first letter of your name.
Patty:	I don't want to know how to write my name. *(The teacher makes more encouraging remarks.)*
Patty:	My name has too many lines. It's too hard to make them. I tried once.

Child 1:	I ain't even messed up yet.
Child 2:	Me neither.
Child 1:	I seen you erase.
Child 3:	I never mess up.
Child 2:	Me neither.
Child 4:	Me neither.

Further reading:
Carol Lyons (2003) wrote about Patty in *Teaching Struggling Readers* and the second example is from Ann Haas Dyson's Research currents: Who controls classroom writing contexts? *Language Arts*, 1984, 61, 6, p. 622.

In the child's first lessons

From 'Roaming around the known' the teacher must estimate how vague or detailed the child's knowledge of writing is. The examples of children's attempts to write their names indicate how limited that knowledge may be.

However, many children can have extensive knowledge of letter names and letter sounds and yet make little progress with learning to read.

Theresa was at school for nearly a year before she could write her name.

5:0   5:6   6:0

Gordon, Sharon and Carmen completed three-piece jigsaw puzzles of their names written in letter couplets. None of them was attending to left-to-right order.

Go / rd / on   Sh / ar / on   Ca / rm / en

6 Learning to compose and write messages

Introduction

Many of the operations needed in early reading are practised in another form in early writing. The teacher's role is to get the child to compose and write his own stories. Writing is as much about composing as it is about spelling. It is about building a known body of words, a writing vocabulary. It is also about constructing words from their parts. It is about shifting from simple sentences at first to complex sentences later, and about using a variety of ways to structure sentences, and packing more interest into the message.

When we speak or when we listen to speech we are constructing and composing. When we write down a phrase, message or story we are constructing and composing. When we read what someone else has written we are constructing and composing. These three activities draw upon language knowledge in similar ways. So, children who have learned to be storytellers, whether their stories are originals or not, have an advantage. Being able to 'tell a story' is probably a giant leap forward for prospective readers. Other children will have to learn to do this.

When the child composes the 'message' that he will write during his lesson it is not a matter of copying words or stories. It is about

- going from ideas in the head
- to spoken words
- to printed messages
- and finding out that you can reconstruct those messages.

In the first lessons of a Reading Recovery intervention the teacher will have exploited the letters and words the child can already write. The number of letters he knows should be expanded as quickly as letter learning will allow (see pp. 23–32).

Activities like 1) breaking up words made by the teacher with magnetic letters, and 2) Hearing and Recording of Sounds in Words, support early writing. These are concurrent activities (that is, they all occur in every lesson) but they are described in different sections of this book.

The child can talk. He has been composing messages orally for three or four years. Now teacher and child, together, get some short messages written down. Message writing here is a shared activity between child and teacher. Either may write words in the message, with the teacher choosing which words the child will work on and which words she will contribute because she judges that they are too challenging for the child at this time. The teacher is governing the difficulty level of the task by making those judgements. The teacher writes more at the beginning and less as the child takes over more of the task. *The learner is expected to write all that he can independently.*

Further reading:
See the profile of a successful writer, Appendix, p. 212.

Teachers ask 'What are quick ways to extend a child's control of oral language during Reading Recovery lessons?' *There are no quick ways to extend language* but the best available opportunity for the Reading Recovery teacher lies in the conversations she has with the child in and around his lessons. The authors of the books she chooses for the child provide other opportunities for extending language. We know something has changed in the child's language when we hear him construct part of a sentence in a new way.

If we keep a note of the longest sentence we have heard him use, we can update it when a longer one comes along. Length of utterance is a reliable indicator of growth in early oral language skills.

The teacher can use some of the words that she has to write into the child's story to demonstrate word construction, emphasising an important teaching point. This should not be overdone: it is easy to destroy the cooperative tone of the activity. Even when the teacher says 'Watch me write that word for you' she might also enlist the child's participation saying something like 'We need an "e" here. Could you make one, here?'

Calling these simple sentences that the children write 'stories' may seem to teachers to be pretentious. The messages that the lowest achievers tend to produce in the short time allocated during a Reading Recovery lesson are brief. Some children struggle to compose orally even a short message. Yet during the course of a series of lessons a child learns to bring together

- the ideas
- the message (which must be his own)
- the search for ways to record it
- the monitoring of the message production
- and the reading of what he has recorded.

When the child is at the end of a series of early intervention lessons he will have fluent control of these practical aspects of story production and will be ready to blossom into producing stories of greater length and quality back in his classroom activities.

The Reading Recovery teacher and child work together so closely on the writing that their interactions model what the child needs to do. A correct record is obtained that can be used for reading and rereading.

Notice in the quote which follows (from Rodgers, 2000) how much work on word analysis and letter-sound relationships occurs in a simple writing task. The example shows *how the teacher works with* what the child already knows.

1 What seems to be a casual conversation between child and adult … is actually an excellent example of a highly skilled adult moving a child through his zone of proximal development. It was the role of the teacher to point up discrepancies to the student. It identified how the teacher does that: through her questioning, telling, directing, demonstrating, praising and confirming moves. (pp. 79, 89)

The teacher and child had talked in preparation for writing, and this interaction followed. This illustrates what 'teaching' can look like in an individual teaching situation.

T: Okay. Let's write about your lost toys.

C: 'I lost some of my toys from last year' (writes 'I', gives the first sound of 'lost' searching for the letter she needs). l-l-l.

T: All right, we've got a word to work on. (She draws four boxes on the work page.) We're going to say …

C: l-o-s-t (pointing in sequence to each box in turn)

T: Good. You're already saying the word slowly. (She makes a jumble of four magnetic letters.)

C: l-o-s-t (finds and places the magnetic letters correctly)

T: My goodness! That's great! Write it in your story. Put the letters close together in the story.

C: lost (She is gathering up the story so far. The teacher reminds her of the next word.)

T: 'some'. Do you know 'come'? You've read that a lot.

C: (writes) c u m

T: (opens a book they had read recently) If we write 'come' like this, how would you write 'some'?

C: (writes 'some', then 'of' and 'my')

T: I didn't know you knew how to write 'of'. Good. Now let's write 'toy'.

C: With silent 's'.

T: No, we hear the 's' in 'toys'. (The teacher helps her write 'from'.) You wrote 'lost' and 'last' is almost exactly like 'lost'.

C: Just put 'a' instead of 'o'.

T: Yes!!! (They finish the writing task working on 'year'.) Are you putting the space in your writing in class?

C: Yes.

T: Good! We have to do in your class writing what you do in here.

Further reading:
Rodgers, E.M. (2000). Language matters: When is a scaffold really a scaffold? *National Reading Conference Yearbook*, 49, pp. 78–90.

That kind of interchange is described in two other research reports from Reading Recovery sources.

2 Teachers make deliberate teaching decisions that increase accessibility to the task while supporting the child's performance.

Further reading:
Clay, M. and Cazden, C. (1990). A Vygotskian interpretation of Reading Recovery. In L. Moll (ed.*)*, *Vygotsky and Education* (pp. 206–22), New York: Cambridge University Press.

---

3 There is no relaxation of the challenges posed and the teacher is constantly moving to what can be considered as the outer limits of the zone of proximal development.

Further reading:
Hobsbaum, A., Peters, S. and Sylva, K.(1996), Scaffolding in Reading Recovery. *Oxford Review of Education*, 22, pp. 17–35.

And here is a quote from research in classrooms.

> We found a close relationship between children's levels of writing and their levels of oral segmentation (of language) and concluded that their knowledge of our writing system enables them to write at a higher level and to segment words phonemically.[18]

Contrast the changes from simple to complex sentences in the following two lists. I invented a list of examples we often see (on the left) and a Reading Recovery tutor provided the second group from a child's records.

Lesson 1	I love my family.	I love my family.
Lesson 15	I played outside with Jo.	I was outside with Jo and I did a trick.
Lesson 32	Grandpa took us to the fire station.	When Grandpa took us to the fire station we had a ride on the fire truck.
Lesson 65	I got a bee sting on my foot.	Three days ago I got a bee sting on my foot when I was playing outside.

During the writing slot of the lesson teachers can prompt the child to search his reading knowledge by saying *'I think you could write that word. You read it yesterday'*, showing the child his earlier work if necessary. Or she might say *'You wrote it in this other story'*, taking him back to a text he wrote and having him read it. Children have to know that reading and writing can contribute to each other during early literacy.

> *Further reading:*
> For more discussion refer to Clay, *What Did I Write?*; *Writing Begins At Home*; *An Observation Survey* (2005), pp. 18–21; *By Different Paths to Common Outcomes,* chapter 2, pp. 13–36, chapter 10, pp. 146–51; and *Change Over Time*, pp. 17–24, 25–28, 28–30, 31–35.

Reading Recovery procedures

Use a working page and a 'message' page

Reading Recovery teachers use unlined exercise books (the size of commercial letter paper) turned sideways for these written messages. There is a working space for teacher and child to use on the top page as they discuss, problem-solve, and construct together. The child writes the message on the bottom page.

In classrooms children are often invited to draw a picture to stimulate the composing. To save time in a Reading Recovery lesson, this activity must be omitted after 'Roaming around the known' in the first two weeks. Provide bright felt pens for the child to write with to motivate the writing. Other opportunities to produce messages occur at whiteboards, blackboards, and with magnetic letters.

Working space for teaching and trials
Child's story

Unlined exercise book turned sideways

On the top page the child may try out a word that he thinks he knows. An analysis of hearing the sequence of sounds in a word may be carried out using boxes recommended by the Russian researcher Elkonin (see section 7). Sometimes the child will be asked to construct the word three or four times on the practice page (see pp. 57 and 58). The teacher can demonstrate the construction of letters or words that the child may copy into his story. This working page provides a record of many teacher-child interactions that occur. It should be full of evidence of the variety of words teacher and child have explored during writing.

The child composes a story

The child is invited to record a message or tell a story *following the procedure outlined below*. Early in a series of lessons this will be a sentence but later he may compose two or three sentences, writing one before composing the final form of another. The message can be about anything that interests the child, something he has done, a message to someone, something going on in his classroom. The two important emphases are that he composes the message, which means he puts the message into a structured sentence or two, and that he feels some ownership of it.[19]

Procedure for eliciting a story

Start up a conversation, guided by all you know about this child. Talk about something that you feel sure he would be interested in. This should not be an interrogation. In a genuine but short conversation help reluctant children to compose something. The topic might come from a variety of sources:

- from a classroom theme or event,
- from something that captures his attention,
- from something you have brought along to spark his interest,
- from a discussion of one of his books,
- or from some other source.

Give some thought prior to the lesson to how you will get this particular child to compose a message.

At first the teacher creates the conversation.

- She asks genuine questions,
- elaborates on the child's ideas a little,
- and makes only minimal change to the child's ideas or use of words.

Then, at an appropriate point, the teacher asks the child to formulate the message to be written.

- '*What could you write about that?*'
  Encourage him to tell you the message he would write.

- As you respond to his effort stay with his message, but encourage him to expand on his statement, say a little more or tell what happened then.

6

Ms B. went into Bobby's classroom to walk him down to his Reading Recovery lesson and noticed the classroom science activity. When they came to the writing part of his lesson the conversation went like this.

Ms B.: I saw you were doing some research upstairs.
Bobby: About barracudas.
Ms B.: What did you learn?
Bobby: Some barracudas are six feet long!
Ms B.: That would be a great sentence to write!

Surprisingly Bobby had no trouble writing the big word but needed help with each of the other words. Ms B. took him from 'come' to 'some', and from 'see' to 'feet'.

Courtney Cazden (2004)

T: You told me a lot of things. What part do you want to write about today?
C: The part where I came tumbling down and I rolled.
T: Okay. Tell me one more time.
C: *(suspecting something)* This is not going to be a long sentence at all!
T: You don't think so?
C: I rolled over and hit my face and scraped my arm.

The child's spoken grammar allows him to say
'They all chuckeded him out of bed',
or 'Them together ride the bike',
or 'The mans are boxing on.'

'I saw boxing on TV' is a 'safe' and formal composition. How can you convince him to write as he speaks? Ask yourself where he learned this formal kind of statement. From his books? From his teacher? Or peers in the classroom?

The child only gives a caption 'Tall tree'. Fine, that's a place to start. The challenge is to have him expand this himself.

- One alteration from the teacher may be enough to throw the child so that he cannot recall what he composed. The process of composing is at a delicate stage of formation and is thrown by interference of this kind. Alter the sentence he gives you as little as possible.
- This is not a time to correct grammar. Use the correct grammar in your conversation to provide the appropriate model for him to hear. If you alter the child's sentence he is very likely to become confused and may not remember the alteration. Note down whatever bothers you so that you remember to work the alternative phrase into your conversation now and again. Be brief and clear and try not to confuse the young composer at this point.
- After the child has become an eager writer the teacher may suggest how a sentence might have some more ideas, or be changed in structure, just a little. If the child cannot go with your suggestions, back off. He is the composer, and the goal is for him to want to write tomorrow.

Teachers should take time to scribble down the child's composed message or story for their own reference.

By the end of a lesson series the child's construction of messages should show an increase in syntactic complexity and some skilful packaging of ideas.

Early in the lesson series the teacher may want the child to repeat the sentence to be sure that he remembers it. But if this request sounds like a rejection of what he said, he may alter it. There are some delicate issues around composing! The goal is for the child to have a clear memory of the sentence he composed, so that he can monitor his writing production against the remembered sentence. At first he cannot be flexible. Hopefully during his lesson series he will become more skilful, and his writing will become more like that of his high-achieving classmates.

In the later lessons children might compose two or three sentences, write more, write faster, with less help, and construct more interesting messages. Notice any attempts by the child to elaborate or increase the complexity of what he composes and greet them with enthusiasm.

Towards the end of the lesson series children will usually be composing on the run, probably writing one sentence, then composing another and writing it, and so on, much the way they would work in the classroom. At this stage the teacher will have to record each sentence as it is produced.

Before writing

From time to time the teacher could invite the child to reread one or more of his previous written messages. This will be familiar text and written in 'correct form'. It indicates the value placed on writing and the messages in writing. The teacher can revisit an old achievement, or a good turn of phrase, or a more complex structure.

As the child writes

In the early lessons the teacher will introduce the child to what the task will be and support the student's writing in the following ways.

- The child writes what he can independently (from merely dotting the 'i' or crossing the 't' to attempting 'hippopotamus'). Encourage the child to write anything he can, alone, from the first lessons. Urge him to try the words you think he might know on the work page. Praise him for his efforts. When you ask the child to write a word on the work page before he puts it in his message you are giving him time to check on himself, and you are giving yourself an opportunity to interact if you need to.

- The teacher writes into the story what she judges to be too hard for the child to attempt at this stage of his learning. Perhaps she shares the task (we could call this co-construction), or she demonstrates by writing the word in a deliberate way on the work page for the child to copy before he writes it into his story.

- The teacher selects from the child's composed message each day two or three words that offer a challenge to this child at this time *for learning how to hear and record the sounds in words.* (See section 7 for these procedures.)

- The teacher may select other words from the child's composed message *because they are not suitable for analysing in sound boxes* (words like 'they' and 'why') but this child uses them often — they are high-frequency words in his usage. Using the work page, the teacher helps the child to remember such words.

- The teacher will ask a child to repeat the writing of a new word (or a troublesome word) on the working page again and again and again in different places once she has reason to believe that he could do this correctly.

Extend the child's writing vocabulary

In 'Roaming around the known' the teacher will have worked with the child's personal pool of knowledge and the words he knows how to write. She will have created opportunities for him to produce fluently what he can already write so that he feels comfortable with this body of knowledge. That is the foundation upon which she will begin to expand his writing vocabulary. The teacher uses the working page in a variety of other ways to enlarge the child's writing vocabulary. These are co-construction activities with many types of teaching interactions occurring.

The writing vocabulary consists of all the words the child knows how to write and consistently records correctly.

Make the task easy for *this child*.

- Think carefully about the letters in the words he is trying to write. Which letters does this child produce easily and quickly? Introduce words that have letters he knows how to write. A new word containing two 'not yet known' letters is going to triple the difficulty of that new word. Ensure he knows a lot about the letters in the words you select for attention.

- It is a good idea not to teach words that look very similar close together in time. When a child only knows a few words it is easier to learn words that look very different.

- Letters in a word have to be written in the correct order. Therefore longer words increase the challenge, but two-letter words are not necessarily easy and do not teach much about English orthography.

- Be aware of when the word you choose to work on has potential for getting to other words (because it fits into some common pattern) and when it is a useful word but exceptional in its spelling.

- Keep thinking of the complexity of the task for this child at this time.

When the child is writing his story, stop him at a word you would like him to add to his writing vocabulary. You suspect that this would be a good learning task for him. The word might be

- a word he unexpectedly wrote (and is not yet known),
- or was nearly correct when the teacher asked him to write it on the work page,
- or was a word used during hearing and recording sounds in words
- or was already on the work page.

Explain to the child that this is a word you will help him to learn so that he will be able to use it whenever he wants to. Start by writing the word clearly on the work page.

Early in the lesson series he may need to copy your word. But copying the teacher's model is not a preferred way to help the child because it does not make the learner think about the construction of the word to be learned.

You can help him to construct the word correctly, to look at it carefully, and to write it a few times on various parts of the work page. Encourage him not to copy as soon as he is able to 'recall' it correctly.

Sometimes providing the child with a correct copy can be useful. It allows the teacher to interrupt an unwanted habit and prevent the repetition of an old error. And it allows the teacher to urge the child to speed up the production. We want the child to learn how to solve problems but also to habituate the fast production of the correct solution! There is a delicate balance to be struck between allowing the child the opportunity to (slowly) solve the problem and prompting for speedy production.

How the teacher interacts with the writing should change as the child moves through the lesson series.

- In the early lessons the teacher's contribution is high. She creates opportunities for the child to write what he can and for her to introduce something new. For example, when the child comes to write a new word the teacher can help him to attend to and isolate at least the initial sound and predict what he would expect to see at the beginning. She may get him to write the first letter and then she may write the rest of the word 'in demonstration mode' for him. That is, she may choose to write it quickly, or she may invite him to watch her carefully.

- The child should gradually take over the problem-solving of new words, and the teacher then reminds, prompts, and facilitates the production.

- How the teacher uses the Elkonin boxes will change across the lessons. (See section 7.) Through this activity the child is introduced to regular and irregular features of English. At first the teacher uses the work page with 'boxes' daily to develop phonemic awareness. Later she will use the boxes when she wants to stress some aspect of the new word — hearing a difficult sound, or introducing a spelling convention. Towards the end of a lesson series a similar analysis may be done without Elkonin boxes.

- The teacher's role shifts to monitoring the child's performance, anticipating any problem-solving difficulties, and teaching more by talking than by demonstration.

- Towards the end of the lesson series the child should be trying to solve words in a variety of ways by himself, supported by the teacher, because the child will have to 'go it alone' back in his classroom.

Ways of solving words for writing

A Reading Recovery series of lessons lasts from 12 to about 20 weeks and during this time many changes occur in children's control over writing. *Each change in the child's control calls for an adjustment in what the teacher does.*

Some of the ways of getting to words are these.

1   Over time the child accumulates a 'writing vocabulary'. He gains control over words he uses frequently, and the writing of those known words shifts from laborious scribing to fluent production. Meanwhile, new words will be constructed slowly.

2   One essential way to get to new words in English is by trying to hear the sounds in spoken words (see section 7). Sometimes when the child wants to write a new word he tries to analyse it.

- He can hear sounds but cannot write them.
- He can record some dominant consonants.
- He can hear and record first and last consonants.
- He can hear and record some vowels.
- He gets most of the consonant framework.
- He gradually becomes able to hear and record the sounds in sequence. This cannot be hurried, but it is important that it occurs quite early.

However, hearing and recording sounds in words will not always give the child the right solution, and he learns that too.

3   Sometimes it is helpful to ask the child to try to construct a new word because it is like another word he knows. Invite him to bring something he knows to the construction of the new word. He may

- see the relationship of a word he wants to write with something he has already written. For example he wants to write 'it' and the teacher points out he has already written 'is', or he adds inflections without seeming to have to work on them (-s, -ing, -er).
- suggest a word like the one he wants to write (even if the teacher has to gently edit any 'wrong' associations for him).
- initiate the use of several things he knows about letters and words to 'solve' the new word.

Note that he has to know the 'known' word very, very well to be able to use it to get to another word.

4   *The teacher acts as the authority when she demonstrates particular features of printed English (the orthography). No child can be expected to work these out for himself.* Gradually he will come to use them appropriately. These would be things like

- adding inflections without having to do a 'sound analysis',
- using silent letters, particularly a final silent 'e', and 'k' as a first letter in some words,
- doubling final consonants in some words when adding inflections,
- dropping the 'e' in some words when adding inflections,
- analysing hard-to-hear consonants in clusters (like tr, sw and spr)
- or using common vowel combinations (like oa, oo, ai, ow, ur) or spelling patterns (ight, tion) that occur in his reading books,
- or spelling a short word with an unusual spelling like 'who' or 'why'. It is ridiculous to try to analyse those words in boxes.

Shifts occur over time in the way the child uses 'the writing space' and the size and legibility of print.

Remember to direct children to what they know in reading to help them with their writing.

It is not possible to describe the infinite range of ways in which a teacher might work with individual children but the changes described above provide a reminder to teachers of how and when they might change the emphases in their teaching.

Consistent with a major principle of Reading Recovery the emphasis is on children's strengths and what they can do. The observant teacher knows when to provide 'input' with things the child could not be expected to work out, and when to prompt or hold back and require the child to engage in problem-solving on his own. *Usually the gain is not that the child gets a particular word right but that he has strengthened the range of ways of solving new words he will use in the future.*

These would be helpful questions to use as the child prepares to write a new word:

> *What could you try?*
> *How do you think it would start?*
> *What do you know that might help?*
> *Do you know another word that sounds like that?*
> *Do you know a word that starts like that?*

A helpful question to use after success in word-solving is:

> *How did you know it was written like that?*

There is a lot to be learned about writing down a language. When you teach the child how to attend to new features on his own, or how to engage in a new type of analysis on his own, then that 'knowing how to do it' can be applied to hundreds of new instances.

> Word walls and dictionaries are not a simple solution to adding words to one's writing vocabulary. The child usually needs help to formulate his problem and then to find the information he needs, as this example illustrates.
> This child's appeal to the teacher is understandable:
> 'I can't find "avocado" in the dictionary, but I've got it in my head.'

6

Rereading the completed story

Get the child to reread the story once or twice. At first he will need to point word by word, and the teacher may need to reread his story with him. Before long the completed story is something the child can read independently, monitoring the reading against his inner knowledge of what he intended to write. Since it was his story he should be able to phrase it fluently.

The teacher might choose to have the child reread a story he had written earlier in his lesson series for several different reasons. One of these could be to ask the child 'Does that help you to remember X (something specific)? What else do you remember? Oh! So you could have put that bit in your story, couldn't you.' This is an invitation to write richer stories.[20]

Martin spoke a local dialect of English. He was working on his 53rd lesson when he composed this message: 'I want some silver teeth.' He pronounced it something like this: 'I wan' sum siver teef.'

'Want' and 'some' had been in books he had read and he had used them in his stories on other days so I chose to use letter-boxes for these words.

I pronounced 'want' and drew four boxes. Martin said the word and put 'w' in the first box. I quickly told him the next letter was 'a' as he was repeating the long 'o' sound. Then he put in the 'n' and said that was all he could hear. I said we sometimes said 'want' so he put in a 't'. As he looked at what he had written he said, 'That's the wrong word. I don't want "want", I want "won".' I explained that this is how the word looks in his books, and even though he says 'won' they are the same word. Some words are like that. Did he remember that we talked about 'de' and 'the'?

Then I drew four boxes for 'some' as he was working on spelling boxes. He wrote 's', and I wrote 'o'. He wrote 'm' and said, 'That's all I hear.' I agreed but asked, 'What letter do you think you might see at the end?' He wrote in 't'. I asked 'Why?' His response was this. 'There's a 't' on 'won' but you don't hear it either!'

Martin's quick brain had tried to form a rule; his teacher had unwittingly led him to confuse himself.

When a child's pronunciation is unhelpful

Reading Recovery has to be ready to meet all challenges. It is not unusual for the child's own pronunciation or dialect to be very different from standard English and this presents his teacher with new challenges. The child's analysis of his spoken language may be good but it does not bring him to a written statement that his teacher is looking for. Read about a Teacher Leader's account of Martin's pronunciation challenge.

Children derive words and rules about words from their experiences, and that is what Martin did. His response was utterly logical. He was working well on the language puzzles and so was his teacher.

There is no easy way around this difficulty. Usually when a child mispronounces a word in his spoken dialect the teacher's articulation will be enough to help the child to 'hear' the sound. Martin, however, had done what she had set out to teach him to do. He had done a fair analysis of his own speech. Discuss with colleagues when you would talk with a child like Martin about such a language issue, and when you might leave it alone!

Whenever the child has unclear articulation or uses a dialect that is not the standard one used in his classroom there will be many interactions like this one. Teacher and child both have a lot to learn about the cross-dialect traps!

To write known words faster

When a child has shown that he knows a word, select from these prompts.

Think carefully before you start and write it here. And here.
Look closely at it and check it.
Do it faster. Once more.

Use the whiteboard for easy production, a clear view of the word being written and the opportunity to get speeded responses. Early in the lessons you will probably want to write the word again for the child in this new setting to start the learner off correctly, but erase your model as soon as you are confident he can write it. Vary what you say as you prompt the child to repeat the production.

Try it another time. Once more.
Check it carefully
Write it faster … and even faster. Can you go faster?

Erase the word from the whiteboard after each attempt.

Consider the purpose of what you are doing. The task is not to get X number of repetitions. It is to have the child produce the word 'out of his head'. Stop when you are sure that the child has full control of this production (at least for the moment). The word must be known in every aspect.

These requests help a child to practise producing the sequence of letters needed for that word, from first to last, and to do this with a minimum of attention. It is like having learned a little programme of movements to produce that word.

- This builds fluency in constructing the word.
- It helps the child to remember the word in every detail.

There will be fluctuations in performance.[21] We are constantly urging the child to lift his performance and add new knowledge. This will challenge some old knowledge. Think of a time when you thought you understood something but the rule that you thought was good just did not work. You have to change your rule. This weakens the system temporarily until it strengthens again at a higher level of complexity.

Adding new writing vocabulary in English is a matter of finding a place for a new word amongst the many other orthographic patterns one is accumulating.

Deal with persistent errors

If a word is known and is correct each and every time it is used this will be great. At any time during the lesson series if false moves stubbornly recur the teacher will need to thoroughly and carefully retrace the learning path, not allowing an error on letter selection or order to occur. Have the child construct the word in different places with a variety of materials — with magnetic letters, with chalk, with his finger on the desk, or water and a paintbrush on a board, or with felt pen.

These activities help the child recognise and produce the same general features of the word in any context.

Interrupt a child who is writing an 'old' word incorrectly to prevent him from practising a wrong sequence or routine.

Which words would the teacher select for the child to learn to write?

The easy-to-write words that occur often in sentences provide a scaffold for the sentences, leaving the writer's attention free to work at constructing less familiar words. Choose

- words that will be used often by this child,
- words needed often in writing (though perhaps not in talking),
- words the child almost knows that need a little more practice,

- words that capture things he knows but also take him into new territory
- words that occur often in the language (but published frequency lists are very unreliable at this early stage, often derived from adults' reading material).

When the child has a useful knowledge of high-frequency words then a word might be selected because its spelling pattern could lead the writer, by analogy, to other similar words. This shifts the emphasis from phonology to orthography (the spelling patterns of the language). Teachers should not make this shift until they are sure that the child controls hearing and recording sounds in words. Establish phonemic analysis and letter-sound relationships as a primary achievement before you make this shift.

Be careful not to choose words because they fit your personal ideas about word families and phonological similarities. The words should contribute to accelerated learning for this particular child, given his current knowledge.[22]

Records of words written independently

Prepare a list of the child's known words from his initial Writing Vocabulary assessment as a guide to what you can ask the child to write independently in his early stories.

Make a record each week of the new words the child can write without your help, as the child learns them (see Appendix, p. 192).

The following format has been found useful as a record of the build-up of writing vocabulary, *used for teaching purposes*.

Weekly record of writing vocabulary

At entry	Week 1	Week 2	Week 3	Week 4	Week 5	Week 6
is	go	and	cat	in	off	of
Starkey	on	going	Nana	it	he	they
to	up		at	had	she	was
a			went	look	looked	day
the			me	big	this	Today
we			for	got		
my						
Mum						
Dad						
I						

continued

Week 7	Week 8	Week 9	Week 10	Week 11	Week 12	Week 13
then	with	have	some	made	new	them
where	get	make	gave	out	Sherilee	there
here	from	you	playing	so	are	love
	by	will	use			give
	when		school			don't
	played		zoo			Tristram
	want					

Keeping a cumulative graph of writing progress

A record of the number of known words should be kept to show progress. There is a form in the Appendix, p. 193, for plotting this graph. This could record the number of words that the teacher observes the child writing independently. Reading graphs of progress can be made for one child or for all children the teacher is currently teaching. So similar graphs records could be kept for writing vocabulary. Some Tutors or Teacher Leaders say this enables them to quickly review the progress of a teacher's children during a consultation visit.

> *Further reading:*
> *An Observation Survey of Early Literacy Achievement*, pp. 75, 109.

Use your teaching prompts thoughtfully

Teachers need to distinguish between a prompt to the reader and a prompt to a writer.

- In reading the child is looking at letters, using his eyes. He is encouraged to look and search for visual information.

- In writing, the first analysis the child must do is to search his oral message for the sounds he needs to record. So for the writer the teacher will often need prompts that focus the child on what he can 'hear' in his speech.

If you wanted the child to search his reading knowledge your prompts would stress 'seeing' and 'looking'.

You can read a word that looks like that.   Or: *Can you …*
You can read a word that starts like that.   Or: *Can you …*
You can read a word that is like that.   Or: *Can you …*

For writing select from prompts such as

Say the word aloud. Say it slowly. Is that like a word you know?
You can say another word like that.
Have you heard another word that starts that way?
Have you heard another word that sounds like that?

Errors in written stories

One way to approach writing and spelling errors is to anticipate a child's difficulty and offer help before errors occur. The child can rapidly access and repeat old error patterns if the teacher is busy attending to her records. Teachers must watch as the child writes and intervene to prevent old errors from occurring. *Repeated errors strengthen brain connections and increase the chance that the neural network will use that route again.*

Allow the child to stop when he recognises that something has gone wrong. That acknowledges his self-monitoring. If the child is too quick for you and the error is already on the page, mask the error in some way. White stick-on labels are useful. Then help the child to construct a correct attempt, perhaps using the work page.

Intercept a too hasty response. Call for the child to demonstrate control over the constructing saying

> *Try it on your work page,*
> or *Show me up here how you would start that word,*
> or *Tell me what you would write.*

Make this both an interruption and a call to have the child attend to the detail of what he is doing.

The visual analysis of words into useful letter clusters will be reinforced in writing because working with chunks gets the word down quickly. Working with chunks will also show up in the sound-to-letter analyses. The child will want to hurriedly write down the clusters he thinks he knows, resisting a teacher's attempts to get him to work letter by letter.

Typing the story for the child to reread is an option

Early in a lesson series it may be appropriate to type out whatever the child has written and have him read it. This motivates some children who like to have printed copies of their stories. Computer printout facilities may be used. Larger type fonts with generous spacing are a particular help to some children. DO NOT use capital letters to solve the type-size problem.

If you are reproducing the child's story resist the urge to edit or elaborate it. Change as little of the child's story as is consistent with good teaching. You could paste this typed version into the child's unlined exercise book for revision reading.

Later in the lesson series

The teacher's role changes as the child becomes more adept at writing his stories. The work page is used less. The child may suspect that he can write a new word without the phonemic awareness boxes (see section 7). If the teacher judges that he does not need to trial the word on the work page *she can check out what he knows orally.* Some of the following things may be appropriate.

- She may ask him for the initial sound or cluster and let him write it.

- She would expect the child to construct the word in sequence from beginning to end, or offer help to achieve this.

- She would tell him about any hard bits (often the vowels or some spelling features) before he makes a false move. A small dose of 'telling' may prevent the child practising confusions. Practising confusions is bad news in writing.

- When she is no longer writing the words into the story for the child, she could still write an unusual word somewhere for him to copy. This could remove the possibility that the child might make a series of poor moves.

What the teacher used to write down on the work page can be explained in conversation late in the lesson series. *But the teacher would not give up demonstrations altogether because they give the child quick access to new information.*

The general changes during the writing task

What has to be learned should be driven by what this child has been exposed to in his lessons so far, and not by any standard agenda or favourite scheme or sequence of learning occurring in classrooms.

When a new feature pops up unexpectedly during a lesson take it from there. If that is exposure 1, look for exposures 2 and 3.

Towards the end of a lesson series the learner:

- needs less teacher help on the new words he has to work out for himself,
- can write an increasing proportion of words independently,
- is gaining more control of the spelling combinations of English vowels from both reading and writing experiences, and
- writes increasingly long and complex sentences as if this were a challenge.

The early intervention teacher must continually lift the performance level of the child, taking his peak performance level into more facets of word and sentence construction. As more attention to early writing in classrooms raises schools' expectations of children's written language performance, Reading Recovery teachers will need to keep an eye on the writing children are expected to do in the classrooms. The Reading Recovery children need to be able to perform well back in their classes.

Activities like those described in section 10 can be introduced momentarily while the child is writing stories, if this is helpful.

It is not possible to produce a map of the changes that could or should occur in children's writing. If a child is to work within the average band of his class his writing needs to become as varied and complex as that produced by the better children in the average group in his classroom.

One fast-moving child in weeks 7, 8, 9 and 10 of a series of Reading Recovery lessons composed these messages.

Week 7   Baby Bear wanted a blue car and Father Bear likes trains.
           Mother Bear said, 'Let Baby bear pick his own toys.'

           Elkonin boxes   wanted, pick, trains
           Other trials   funny, happy

Week 8   I did not go to the market day because I was asleep.
           My Mum went to the market day.

           Elkonin boxes   asleep, market
           Other trials   was (4 times), not, because

Week 9   I went to the Christmas parade and I saw the kindy.
           I saw Mrs Keyte dressed up like a cat. I saw three Monsters.

           Elkonin boxes   parade, kindy, monsters, dressed
           Other trials   looked, played, jumped

Week 10   On Friday I went to the vet clinic. I saw a dog with a broken leg
           and he had a bandage on his leg.

           Elkonin boxes   clinic, broken, leg, dog, with
           Other trials   saw, g

How good should a child's composing be? From time to time you should write down the longest utterance you hear the child construct as he talks with you. This provides a rough indication of this child's control over the structure or grammar of his oral language; that is, what complexity you can reasonably expect of him.

It is not easy to capture what 'increasing the complexity of a sentence' means here. As a speaker of the language the teacher must become a good judge of increasing complexity in the daily composing sessions.

Observation by Reading Recovery Trainers across different countries indicates that teachers expect too little progress in writing and consequently their children are not able to work independently in writing back in their classrooms. Expectations need to be discussed. Teachers can encourage children to write more, with speed, fluency and accuracy, and this will contribute to faster progress in literacy learning.

> *Further reading:*
> See Appendix, pp. 212–13, for an example of sentences from a successful series of Reading Recovery lessons.

Final comments from three research studies

Here are summary statements from three research reports.

> There is no relaxation of the challenges posed and the teacher is constantly moving to what can be considered as the outer limits of the zone of proximal development.[23]

> Reading Recovery teachers make deliberate teaching decisions that increase accessibility to the task while supporting the child's performance and maintaining the child's accelerated learning.[24]

> What seems to be a casual conversation between child and adult in the context of reading and writing is actually an excellent example of a highly skilled adult moving a child through his zone of proximal development.[25]

7 Hearing and recording sounds in words

Introduction

Since the mid-1970s the buzz words in early literacy have been phonemic awareness. It took educators and publishers some years to shed their confusions about this term and clearly define phonemic awareness as *becoming aware of the sounds within spoken words*. We are referring to those sounds that make the smallest difference between two similar words, what linguists call the phonemes of a language. Can you *hear* the difference between two similar words, for example 'pupil' and 'people', in your own speech? Can you *hear* such differences in someone else's speech? The brain is involved in recognising phonemes coming in through the ears.

Young children have been making distinctions between the sounds of language since infancy. What research began to uncover in the 1970s was how young children learn to consciously isolate the phonemes of a language from the flow of speech. Marked changes occurred in phonemic awareness in the early years of school.

Most beginning reading programmes bring children in classrooms to the awareness of sound sequences in words effectively. And it is clear that becoming aware of phonemes is essential for becoming good at word recognition. In many different approaches to literacy instruction teachers have taught children directly to distinguish between letters and to link sounds to those letters. The successful children are able to do that. However, some children in classrooms find it extraordinarily difficult to separate out the sounds of the language they are hearing or speaking.

A seven-year-old English-language learner wrote this 'story'.

The ugly duckling was really a singlet.

The activities in this section are designed to help a child *to hear and to think about the order of sounds in spoken words. This has to do with the ears hearing sounds and transmitting messages about those sounds to the brain.* To write some new words in this writing segment of the lesson a child must analyse words into a sequence of sounds, must identify what sounds he can hear and must deal with the order or sequence in which the sounds occur. Often a beginning reader will consistently focus on the last sound or a dominant sound in the word, even when this makes it hard for him to hear the initial sounds.

Why does Reading Recovery include these activities in the reading lesson?

Authors of a recent study concluded that:

> Alphabetic instruction without PA (phonemic awareness) was not as effective as alphabetic instruction with PA ... What seems to matter are activities where phonemes are blended and segmented in speech, then connected explicitly and systematically to graphemes in print ...[26]

Writing requires the child to pay close attention to the words he has chosen to write, to hear the sounds in those words and to write down some letters that will represent those sounds. It is an activity well suited to developing phonemic awareness.

The teacher chooses from the story that the child himself has composed two or three words that are likely to strengthen the child's phonemic awareness if he pays them more attention. The writing task calls upon the child to hear the sounds in words he speaks but has not yet learned to read or spell, if he is to get his message on to the page. The teacher can offer help or she can call for independent solving by the child, and her interactions with the child can be adapted to any level of learning challenge.

For children who cannot isolate individual sounds or hear the order of sounds in words the teacher must demonstrate this analysis. She articulates the word herself, slowly but naturally, and gradually develops the same skill in her pupils. These steps are usually necessary.

- The child must attend closely.
- The child must hear the word spoken.
- The child must articulate it slowly, trying to break it into sounds but in a natural way.
- The child may look at himself making the sounds using a small mirror.

- The child is asked to demonstrate what he is hearing by pushing counters into the appropriate number of 'boxes for sounds' that the teacher has drawn.

No letters are used in the earliest stages of developing phonemic awareness. The child needs to use his ears. The task is first to develop an awareness of the sounds in words. They are hard to hear because they are embedded in a pattern of sounds.

In the intermediate stage the focus involves not only hearing the sounds but also representing them with letters. There is a shift to consider the connections between sounds and letters — linking hearing with seeing! Pathways must be built to link sounds with letters and vice versa.

At first the teacher accepts any sound the child can hear, whatever its position in the word (last, middle or first), to make it easy. Whichever phoneme is salient for the child is accepted at first. Towards the end of the intermediate stage the teacher requires the child to hear the sounds in sequence and to scan the word visually from first to last letters (from left to right).

The hearing of sounds and the seeing of letters involve two different parts of the brain learning to work together. As teachers talk to children they should ask themselves:

- Do I want the child to hear a particular sound?
- Do I want him to recall the visual form of a particular letter?
- Do I want him to attend to the position of the letter within the word (last, first, middle)?
- Does he understand I am asking him to analyse the sounds in sequence (from first to last for the ears or left to right for the eyes)?
- What is it I want him to attend to?

The final shift is made when the teacher draws a box for every letter in the word and introduces the child to any mismatch between the sounds of the language and spelling conventions. This only occurs when the child can hear most of the sounds, and can find letters to record those sounds. The goal is to have a consistent first-to-last analysis (occurring in time) and a consistent left-to-right analysis (occurring in space).

Tell the child you are going to show him something new. Now you are going to draw a box for every letter in the word. It is time to become aware of the spelling requirements of the language (the orthographic features of words), and this involves both the regularities of letter-sound relationships and the irregularities.

In Reading Recovery lessons the teacher ensures that the messages are correctly spelled. She writes some things herself and helps the child to get to correct versions. But once children can hear the phonemes well (as Michael could, see p. 77) they must shift to attending to *orthography as well as phonology.* So then the teacher asks herself:

- Is the child clear that now I am asking for spelling sequences?

Phonemic awareness must be embedded in and integrated with both word recognition and language comprehension from the beginning of literacy learning. It is not sufficient for the child to become competent with the phonemic analysis; he has to expand his view of the task. Both sounds and spellings have to be thought about.

Further reading:
Look at *An Observation Survey* (2005), pp. 111–19 and *Change Over Time,* pp. 24–25, 174–75. In *The Reading Teacher,* January 1999, Laurice Joseph reports research[27] on using 'word boxes' in classrooms using an interesting research design.

Reading Recovery procedures

All Reading Recovery children should begin at the beginning of these procedures. Some could move rapidly through to the intermediate stage, while others will take a while to understand what this task involves.

Early learning

Hearing syllables   Hearing big chunks of sound is easier than discovering single sounds so a good first step is to ask the child to clap the parts he can hear in a few two- or three- syllable words he knows well. Return to this now and again, just as a reminder.

Do not skip this step. Use it to provide an easy entry to the path you are now going to take. Choose words of one and two syllables at first, and later three or four. Repeat this activity from time to time as opportunities arise in connection with reading or writing stories. The activity will help him with the longer words he will want to write into his stories, and the multisyllabic words of higher-level reading books.

Hearing the sounds   *Use the Elkonin 'boxes' as a supporting framework for hearing the sounds.* In the first few trials the child will be learning what it is the teacher wants him to do. This includes slow articulation, listening to himself, and pushing counters into the boxes. It is critical that the child understand the task. Take time to make clear what the task involves.

Prepare for the activities that help children to hear the sounds within words.

- Make a few picture cards for simple words such as cat, bus, boy, ship, house. Use these to introduce the task.
- Prepare other cards on which you draw a square for each sound/phoneme in words of two, three and four sounds, for example:

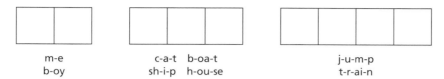

| m-e | c-a-t | b-oa-t | j-u-m-p |
| b-oy | sh-i-p | h-ou-se | t-r-ai-n |

- Have a selection of counters ready.

In the first lessons after the roaming around the known, attempt only two or three of the activities in the next two lists.

Step I   *Slow articulation and hearing sounds/phonemes*

Introduce the child to the task. Select a picture card.

- Slowly and deliberately articulate the word for the child. Let him hear the sounds separated but in a natural way.
- Ask the child to articulate the word aloud. Ask him to '*Say it slowly*'. This transfers the initiative for the activity to the child.
- Ask the child to watch your lips while you say it, and then to copy you.
- Use a mirror to help the child to become more aware of what his lips and tongue are doing.
- Use stress to emphasise any sound you want the child to notice.

You want the child to be able to say the word slowly and attend to the sounds in sequence.

Step II   *Using the boxes for hearing the sounds in words (phonemic analysis)*

The phonemic analysis cards provide a visual model within which to place the sounds that are articulated. (Choose a card with a square for each phoneme in your demonstration word, that is, a three-square card for c-a-t or for ch-o-p.) You need a square for every sound in the aural task, NOT for every letter. The transfer to an emphasis on letters comes much later.

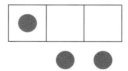

- Model the task for the child. Articulate the word very slowly and push the counters into the boxes, sound by sound.
- Now get the child to try this. Share the task with the child for as long as he finds the coordination of saying slowly and pushing counters too difficult.
  - i   Get the child to articulate slowly while you push the counters.
  - ii Alternatively articulate the word slowly for him while he moves the counters.

iii Change roles to enable the child to practise both parts.

iv Model what you want the child to do. You might guide the child's hand or work alongside him with another card.

• As soon as possible have the child complete the whole task himself.

> 'Oh, I get it!' said the child as he pushed the counters saying 'h-o-me'. He is able to write in the letters that matched the sounds in this order — h, me, and o, but in the correct position. He said, 'Hey, I did that all by myself today!'

Accept his approximations. Coordination will come with practice.

Beyond this point the child would use counters in the exceptional case: for example, when he had to split apart two sounds which he has been saying and hearing as one sound.

Intermediate steps

The teacher helps the child to establish a basic skill that he will use routinely in literacy tasks, but she is also lifting the difficulty level of the task, day by day. When the child has difficulty think about why the child found that analysis more difficult. (It may be necessary as a temporary teaching strategy to revert to an easier level of the activity.)

As the child is writing his message for the day select two (or three) words from it and at the appropriate time (being helpful to the child) draw boxes on the work page. Choose the words carefully to suit *this* child and *his* current learning level. Choose words with three or four sounds. At first the focus is on hearing the sounds. Gradually it will shift to hearing sounds (or clusters), and finding some way to record them. This activity enables the child to write words he has not yet learned. Select activities from the following list according to a particular child's needs. There must be a lot of input from the teacher, who models correct sound analysis and prompts correct letter-sound associations, but gradually passes responsibility to the child.

• Articulate the word slowly for the child, emphasising the sounds.

• Draw a box for each sound segment on the work page of the child's writing book.

• Ask 'What can you hear?' Accept a sound that the child can hear clearly and write it in for him as he watches, if necessary (for example if the child does not yet know the letter required). It is usually possible to involve the child in the writing.

• Encourage the child to say the word slowly. He used counters and boxes at the early stage but now he will learn to point to boxes, and finally he will be able to segment the word and write the letters without boxes.

• Say *'How could you write it?'* if the child gives the sound but hesitates over writing the letter(s). If the child cannot recall the letter's form help him; provide a model of the 'forgotten' letter.

- Or ask: '*Where will you put it?*' Let the child record any sound for which he knows the letter but ensure that it goes in the correct box. (This means that for a time the teacher will need to show the child where to put it.)
- Give helpful links to what he knows somewhere else — in his alphabet book, or his name, or a word he can already write, or a word in his reading.

If the child thinks he knows but is unsure, get him to do a trial letter on the work page or write the letter in the air or with his finger on the desk.
Use questions like these to help the child locate other letters.

- What else can you hear?
- What do you hear at the beginning?
- What do you hear at the end?
- What do you hear in the middle?

Accept what the child can hear in any order at first. Do not insist on a beginning-to-end approach. This will come later, as the child gains control of the task. (This is a permissible exception to the left-to-right emphasis we usually need.)

The child can record only those letters he knows how to form and the one or two he is currently learning. The teacher can act as his scribe to produce words like these,

with the child writing only those letters he knows. Alternatively, the teacher may get the child to fill in what he can by himself and then complete the word for him, perhaps teaching one new point but not explaining everything.

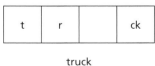
truck

monster

Gradually shift from using the question '*What can you hear?*' to the question '*What letters would you expect to see?*'

A note on consonants and vowels

Be satisfied if the child can separate out some of the consonants. Vowels at the beginning of words are easy to hear but early in the lesson series you will probably have to give the child the vowels buried within words for they are difficult for the child to hear.

Linguists who study English spelling have also warned us about 'buried consonants' like the 'n' in 'find' or 'pond', and the 'l' in 'hold' or 'milked'.

For the teacher who is not used to a linguist's analysis of the sounds of spoken English there are traps in this activity. For example, one child responding well to her own phonemic analysis of 'cousins' wrote:

Kusns

Except where the 's' should have been 'z' (if you are writing the sounds or phonemes in 'cousins') this is an accurate rendering of the sounds in the word but not one that helped the child to reach the correct spelling of the word. It was not an appropriate word for training sound-to-letter analysis early in the lessons; in fact it would not be easy to explain to any child!

The teacher must be alert to detect the difference between what analysis of sounds will move the child forward and what might confuse the child at this time. When he has more control over analysing words a group of words with irregular spelling could be appropriate for learning about a particular feature of English orthography. Here are some examples of accurate 'hearing' by children that should not be undervalued.

plac	aftr	childrn
(place)	(after)	(children)

There will be an improvement in recording sounds heard as the child identifies more letters and vice versa.

Shift to hearing and recording sounds in sequence

We call for consistent left-to-right analysis only after the child can hear most of the sounds and can find letters to record those sounds. It is critical that the child has made the transition to hearing sounds in sequence well before you want to move him to spelling boxes. Have the child identify the first sound in the word, and the remainder in sequence. This requires a shift; he had been attending to any sound he could hear, irrespective of position in the word.

Have the child fill in the letters in the boxes *in sequence, from beginning to end, from left to right* (making only an occasional concession to this requirement).

It is unlikely that the child would be using counters at this stage. For a very insecure child it could help to return to using counters temporarily when you begin to ask him to listen for the *first* sounds of the words and for the remaining sounds in the correct sequence.

Choosing the words to use in boxes

How will the teacher choose the words to use in this section of the lesson? The child composed the message to be written so the words are his words. Ask yourself two questions.

- First, where is the child in the sequence of learning about phonemes, letters, and letter-sounds in sequence across a word?
- Second, what will provide the easiest 'next learning' for this child?

Then select

- words in which it is easy to hear the sounds (not 'saw')
- words which use 'easy to see' letters he already knows (and avoid confusable situations, like 'bed' or 'dog')
- words he will need to use often (not 'picture')
- words which have simple letter-sound relationships in English (this is NOT the place to learn words like 'light' or 'knee' or 'police' or 'eight')
- words which will lead him to other words (rather than words which are exceptional in English orthography like 'was' or 'there')
- words of four or five sounds.

Despite all the above, at some time during the programme the child will be ready for the teacher to break with those restrictions. This is a matter of teacher judgement on the basis of her records and knowledge of the particular learner at a particular time in his programme, and how fast he is exploring the variations in the language.

Advanced learning: attending to spelling using boxes for letters

After the early and intermediate steps the child is usually able to

- hear and record the consonants well
- have control over writing letters
- select some vowels correctly.

7

If the teacher has noted this kind of control over analysing the sounds in words and finding a 'likely' spelling, she will decide that he is ready for the added skill of attending to spelling. (This is additional information, not alternative information!) Now the teacher draws a box for every letter.

This shift is made when the teacher judges that her pupil knows how to listen for sounds, how to find letters for recording them, and how to find the beginning sound and move through the sounds of a word in sequence. To this we add the idea that how words sound and how they are spelled is sometimes different.

We have taught the child how to segment the sounds in a word and to depend on the regularity with which sounds are recorded by letters and now we are going to tell him that there are many exceptions to this. *He now has to think about sounds (phonology) but he also has to think about spelling (orthography)* — and he learns to juggle these two things.

The teacher explains the shift to the child — a box for every *letter* he needs. This means two boxes even though two letters may not represent two sounds, as in doubled consonants.

Here are two extracts from the beginning and end of Michael's story about Puss in Boots. This was a piece of personal writing discovered by his mother. He was listening for phonemes and recording them quite well but he was overdue for some teacher feedback to overcome the severe limitations of this approach. It is time to learn more about spelling conventions.

It was Nicholas' birthday and puss in boots was invited. They played pars the parsle and had byuteefool food. Oow goody I just carnt wait for this lovely food. M m isn't this dellishas …

But luculy he escapte. But he was still lost in the forest. When sadonly he came across a wordrop. He whent in side.

The teacher should be very helpful.

- Articulate the word clearly for the child. Let him hear the sounds in sequence several times.

- Provide a box for every letter.

- Help the child to fill in the letters of the word using stress or pausing on a sound in an exaggerated way so he can focus on the sound you want him to hear.

- As soon as the child can attend to the sound, return to a natural rate and mode of articulation.

- Find similar spelling segments (with the same sounds) in known words.

moth<u>er</u>   wat<u>er</u>   monst<u>er</u>   ov<u>er</u>

- Help the child by writing for him if the word has unusual elements or ones that he is not yet ready for (especially vowels). When necessary give explicit attention to orthography.

Sometimes I have seen teachers provide children with some of the letters for vowels and ask them to select the letter they think could be right. This is probably not helpful since children may have no basis for finding any rule for it being this or that vowel, and because our pronunciation of vowels tends to vary with our accents. Give information rather than making it a guessing game.

Introducing exceptional 'sounds' and 'silent letters'

Inevitably reading books and children's writing will introduce some of the unusual features of letter-sound relationships in English. The following are reminders for teachers and not a list to be taught to children!

- 'Ch' uses two letters to represent one sound.

- 'Th' behaves like a single letter and can be pronounced in two ways. It represents two phonemes (for example 'thin' and 'then').

- 'Wh' behaves like a single letter but has three common pronunciations ('w', 'wh', and in the common words 'who' and 'whose').

- Often a consonant is doubled — 'll', 'dd', 'mm'.

- 'e' is often silent and final; 'k' and 'g' at the beginning of some words are not sounded.

- In some combinations like 'nt', 'nd' and 'ld' the two sounds are very hard to hear, even if you say them slowly. Words we often use like 'went' and 'find' fall into this group.

In early lessons the teacher should anticipate the recording problem and quickly put in the correct spelling for the child, saying something quite simple like this: 'For this sound we use two letters to make one sound.' That will work for 'ch', 'sh', 'th' (in 'this' and in 'thin') and 'wh', and the teacher should watch for recurrent opportunities to illustrate these in upcoming lessons. The same can be said of doubled consonants.

In English we do cluster consonants together, and children do have to hear the consonant sounds and record them. Therefore consonant clusters are treated in a standard way in Hearing and Recording Sounds in Words. We often use consonants in clusters like 'pr', 'bl' and 'str'. Children do have to hear each phoneme in consonant blends.

I prefer not to insist that children discover the 'hard to hear' consonants like '-nk', '-mp', '-ld' and think that teachers should provide the letters. It seems easier to 'hear' the letters after they have been identified for you and you have met up with them a few times.

Working without boxes

In the later stages of a child's Reading Recovery lessons the word boxes will be used less. By then the child will be using sound analysis as he writes new words directly in his story. He will continue to encounter new words and it will be good to refresh how to do a sound analysis from time to time. Select also from the following activities. The teacher will work with or without boxes as required.

- Articulate the sounds in sequence several times for the child.
- Encourage the child to 'say it slowly'.
- Use stress to emphasise a sound you want him to focus on.
- Use pausing on that sound or draw it out in an exaggerated way to call attention to it.

Towards the end of Reading Recovery lesson series boxes may be used occasionally to help the child to take short multisyllabic words apart. Return to any of the earlier ways of helping children to hear sounds in words.

A brief review

The main purpose of these procedures is to take the child through a steep learning curve of phonological analysis. How the teacher uses the Elkonin boxes will change across the lessons.

- First the child has to learn how to do the task.
- Then he learns how to do a phonemic analysis of words he wants to write.
- Then he learns some rules about spelling and some exceptions.

Hearing and Recording Sounds in Words is one essential way to get to new words in English by trying to hear the sounds in words. Sometimes when the child tries to analyse a new word that he wants to write

- he can hear sounds but cannot write them,
- he can record some dominant consonants,
- he can hear and record first and last consonants,
- he can hear and record some vowels,
- and he gets more of the consonant framework.

He gradually becomes able to hear and record the sounds in sequence. This cannot be hurried, but it is important that it occurs quite early.

Do not give up demonstrations altogether in later lessons just because you thought something was learned back in the early lessons. Call it up into the more complex analysis the child is now trying to do!

The task is to teach children to hear the sounds in English words. The brain is required to listen for and find the sounds and, in an instant, link these to appropriate letters. That is a helpful way to work with the code although it will not always give you the right solution. Using the Elkonin boxes, and manipulating counters, and writing letters in boxes provides the brain with opportunities to form new networks that then learn to carry out these strategic activities at speed as the child reads and writes.

The child is learning that

- sometimes you know a word, you've written it before,
- sometimes you can write a word you know and then you can make a new word with some of the same letters,
- sometimes you can analyse the sounds in new words you want to read,
- sometimes you can analyse the sounds of words you want to write and find the letters to write down those sounds,
- and sometimes you need someone to tell you how to make the word 'because that is the way we spell it in English'.

This is not a matter of merely learning letter-sound relationships. We are not repeating the task to establish a memory. There is much more to the daily exercise than merely practising hearing and recording sounds on simple words! The main purpose of the activity is to help the child to distinguish

i   easy-to-hear sounds,
ii hard-to-hear sounds,
iii and common spelling/sound patterns in English,
iv and the 'quirky' things about spelling in English.

Through this activity the child is introduced to regular and irregular features of English, gaining increasing control over most of them. 'Quirky' things about the language should not be emphasised early because it interferes with the learning of regularities and rules.

Direct the child to what he knows in reading to help him with his writing and vice versa.

Watch out for the unexpected links that children find

For the teacher who wants to teach a child sounds the generalisations she makes about letters and their sounds in English can often be just wrong. Think about the worst scenario, the letter 'y'. It provides a reminder of how careful you have to be. The letter 'y' occurs frequently in easy words — 'my', 'by', 'fly', 'baby', 'happy', 'funny'. It has at least four jobs in English orthography. It is a symbol that represents three vowels and one consonant.[28] The consonant is the first sound in 'yellow' and 'yes'. The vowel alternatives are

- the final sound in 'baby' and 'lady';

- the vowel embedded in 'gym' and 'chlorophyll';

- the final sound in 'cry', 'by' and 'try'.

And I recently saw a Reading Recovery child who was struggling to find the relationship of 'y' and 'u' having just learned to read and write 'you'. Those are complications that we should avoid rather than explain to a beginning reader!

The secret of successful instruction in hearing and recording sounds in words is to have a teacher who knows how to help a child 'hear' the sounds singly or in clusters, and how to 'see' the letter forms and recurrent patterns. The teacher guides the child to the most efficient links between letters and sounds, or clusters of letters and patterns of sound. Being able to do this will improve every aspect of learning to read and write.

> *Further reading:*
> This topic is also discussed in section 11, Linking sound sequences to letter sequences: massive practice in text reading.

8 Assembling cut-up stories[29]

Introduction

Cutting up the story (which the child composed, then wrote and then reread more than once) provides the child with opportunities to relate reading to writing, writing to speaking, and reading to speaking. The interrelationships of these three language activities become implicitly and explicitly apparent to children as they learn about

- assembling messages (one sentence or more),
- one-to-one correspondence of spoken words and written words,

- directional behaviours,
- checking behaviours,
- monitoring behaviours,
- self-correcting behaviours,
- and breaking the oral language into segments.

The cut-up story is taken home in an envelope which has the correct version written on the outside. It is a known text. The child's competence can be demonstrated to members of the family. The story that was written in the child's writing book or on the envelope provides a correct model that the child may or may not consult, as needs be.

> *Further reading:*
> *Change Over Time,* pp. 28–30, and *Becoming Literate,* chapter 12, pp. 258–87.

Reading Recovery procedures

The teacher asks the child to reread his story from his unlined book while she writes it again on a strip of light cardboard.

The story as it was written can be cut into language units that the teacher knows the child will be able to reassemble. Most teachers have the child read from the card as she cuts it up. She could use larger segments for the poorest readers for a brief period before forcing a word-by-word reconstruction. The descending order of size will be cutting the message into

- two or three phrases
- whole words
- and to emphasise a particular segment of a word such as

  i   a first letter
  ii endings like 'ing', 's', 'ed',
  iii syllables in two-syllable words like 'ba/by',
  iv the rime part of a one-syllable word like 's/and' or 'w/ent'
      (called breaking the onset from the rime), and
  v   any clusters of letters you think he knows.

If you want to cut up a word into syllables ask the child to clap the syllables of the word to show you where to cut it. Occasionally you might cut between the onset and rime in a single-syllable word; be careful not to confuse the child. This is different from a syllable break. You might exaggerate the onset (see p. 44). This might occur as an echo of work that was done in breaking up words, constructing words, or comparing words in other parts of the lesson.

Avoid doing too much cutting and too much talking about this. Just demonstrate clearly what you are doing. Teacher talk like the following is likely to confuse the child.

> *I am going to cut this so that when you're putting it together and you are saying it slowly, you can hear all the parts. Where shall I cut it so there's a part that looks familiar?*

Get the child to reassemble the cut-up story, reading aloud as he does this. This usually calls for careful self-monitoring and checking but it can be made easy or more difficult in the following ways.

- Assembly on top of the model is a matching response — easy
- Assembly below the model is a matching response — harder
- Assembly without the model is a reading response — hardest

Then if the assembled cut-up story contains errors, say 'Something's not quite right', calling for a self-monitoring response. If errors remain, get the child to reread with careful word-by-word matching to the syllable level if this was used.

Working on the cut-up story at a very early stage

- The child was asked to tell a story and could not be encouraged to put pencil to paper.
- The teacher offered to write that story in his book. She wrote it again on light cardboard.
- The child pointed to A and said he could do that one. (The teacher missed the opportunity to have him write what little he knew.)
- The teacher read the written text and modelled pointing behaviour.
- The child tried inaccurately. The teacher guided his hand. The child tried accurately.
- The teacher emphasised the word breaks by reading each word as she chopped it off.
- The child reassembled the story matching it on top of the story in his book. It became a visual matching exercise rather than a reading task. The last word, 'bus', was matched but turned around 180°. He knew 's', and 's' looks the same when inverted.

bus   snq

The cut-up story calls for the rehearsal of whatever the child is currently learning about letters, words and sentences.

How children work at a later stage

As the cut-up sentence is assembled the children often verbalise their message. They match what they are saying aloud to what they are doing as they work searching for each appropriate word, part of a word or particular letter. They keep pace with their voices as they progress with the remaking.

At some points children may help their searching by repeating the word, letter or cluster they are looking for. Sometimes they comment aloud as they search saying, for example, 'Where is it? Where is it?' Sometimes they talk about the self-corrections they are making, saying 'No, that's not it.' Final successful completion may be evaluated with a flourishing 'There!' or a grin at their success before rereading for checking. Such reactions are less likely to occur as children gain increasing competency with reading and writing.

T:	This fall I began working with Willie. We worked hard to read in phrases while rereading familiar books and the cut-up sentence. In December Willie wrote his story, and assembled the cut-up story like this.

> *We put two*
> *snowmen out in front of our house.*

After reading it, he rearranged it without prompting.

> *We put two snowmen*
> *out in front of our house.*

I asked him why he moved 'snowmen' to the top line. He said, 'It just didn't sound right when I read each line without stopping.' He had figured out the natural language breaks he needed to read his story fluently. But he had been reading *silently*.

Great potential for learning and teaching

A child has composed a message of appropriate difficulty. He has written it down as independently as possible, and the teacher has identified a particular feature like a phrase, a word or two, a syllable or rime segment or letter, or some particular feature of text to highlight.

Composing the story again, quickly, calls upon the child to put all the fragmented aspects of the literacy task together. The focus is on the assembling processes of composing and constructing rather than on the breaking down processes usually associated with writing. It says to the child 'Get your act together. Think of everything at once, and get it all sequenced as quickly as you can.' Later in the child's lesson series the efficiency with which children can do this shows degrees of fluency and flexibility and speed of decision-making, all of which are to be valued.

This is not an optional extra put into the lesson to keep the child amused. Seriously important outcomes can be expected. Watch the child carefully and you will clearly see evidence of what the child is attending to and what he is neglecting.

- Is the child monitoring this reconstruction of his own composed sentence?

- Did you see any self-correcting? Perhaps the checking and correcting could be observed before some pieces of the puzzle were actually manipulated.

- Did you notice the child change the level of his attention, from phrase to word, or word to letter level?

- Did he provide you with any new evidence of process or knowledge that you did not know he could attend to?

- By about halfway through the lesson series the child will be paying attention to alternative ways of phrasing or arranging the word order or the line breaks.

- In what parts of the story did the child work speedily, fluently and correctly? And when did the child have to slow down? Ask yourself what part of the processing needed his extra attention? It could be useful to know that!

There is a close match between the following list of what the child must do in the cut-up story and what he must do as he reads a story.

- He constructs or assembles sentences.
- He consolidates one-to-one correspondence of words spoken and words read.
- He coordinates directional behaviours.
- He practises checking and monitoring behaviours.
- As he checks and monitors he breaks oral language in various ways from phonemes to clusters to words and phrases.
- He gives attention to a word's placement among other words in the context of a phrase that no activity studying words in isolation ever does.

The text used is a familiar message, composed and owned by the learner. He worked hard to compose and record it, but the toil of having to form the letters and words has now been removed. Some of the barriers to fluency have gone. *The cut-up story provides an opportunity to orchestrate many literacy activities on familiar material, slowed up, and constructed deliberately. If this were an occasional activity it might not be so important, but in Reading Recovery lessons this happens every day.*

8

3 Reading continuous texts, whole stories and information books

We should expect diversity in how Reading Recovery children work on texts. The children we identify as the lowest-achieving 20 percent in their classrooms will be encountering difficulties, not for the *same reasons,* but for different reasons. When we design lessons to suit the strengths of a particular child and shepherd his progress despite his weaknesses we cannot expect the same things to happen in the same order for any two Reading Recovery children. It is our assumption that we need to take each of them by a different path from their classmates (and from their Reading Recovery peers) to become successful readers and writers.

It follows that there cannot be a fixed set of strategic activities, or text levels, or any test score that defines when a child's individual lessons can be discontinued.

It is essential that the child come gradually to work at reading and writing activities in ways that enable him to learn from his own attempts. This self-tutoring occurs at faster and faster rates under the control of healthy monitoring and self-correcting systems.

Some of the processing changes that occur in records of a child's text reading will be these.

- The young reader will gain control over directional movement across texts without lapses, or will know he is inclined to lapse and will be able to check his own behaviour. Having this control frees up some of his attention for other things.

- The young reader will learn one-to-one matching of spoken to written words for checking and pulling together different kinds of information.

- The young reader will become able to check on himself. This can be seen when an error is noticed but not corrected. It is also observed as the child reassembles a cut-up story. It is presumed to be occurring during correct reading.

- The young reader notices discrepancies in his own responses by cross-checking one kind of information (say visual information) with a different kind of information (such as meaning).

- When a child initiates a self-correction we can sometimes tell when the child is (or is not) using meaning and/or structure and/or visual information and has tried to achieve a match across all these. Even unsuccessful attempts to correct are indicators that the child is aware that these activities can be useful. Effective self-correcting follows from monitoring, searching, cross-checking and making all information match.

As the reader shifts his attention across the lines of print his brain is exploring many possibilities. Decisions must be made. Decisions take time and the greater the number of alternatives the more time is required to make the decision. Unlikely responses must be rejected; possible responses must be weighed up. Information that helps the reader to be decisive is what the reader needs — phonological or orthographic, or syntactic or semantic, or 'sense of story' information! It is information he has learned to use during his previous encounters with reading.

9 Reading books

Introduction

A teacher said to me 'How can we help teachers to understand what teaching looks like without too much teacher talk?' Well, this is what unnecessary talk looks like.

> I notice when you're reading that you really notice and find things that you know. When you read 'dancing there', you found 'the'. And that helps you read new words by finding parts you know. Sure does. There's 'the' and it's like 'there'. Now let's look over here.

The same teacher then moved into a 'crisp' piece of teaching.

> *Show me the word 'skating'.* (child does) *It has a part you know. Here it is in 'going'.*

That is an economy of words. Speechless demonstrations do help. Structuring the task so the child succeeds is masterful. Don't just call for memories. Ensure that the child knows how to make good decisions.

There are twin aims to be achieved in two of the three book-reading sections of a Reading Recovery lesson.

1   During familiar reading the teacher will arrange things so that the child is able to enjoy reading books that are easy and give him a sense of achievement. The child will have scope to practise a range of complex behaviours on a familiar text, and what he does sounds like 'good reading'. This orchestration is best achieved on recently read texts, seen before but

not memorised. Fluency, comprehension and speed would be good outcomes from these experiences.

Prior to the rereading teachers may sometimes encourage the child to try to solve his own problems (on the run, as it were), or caution him against some false practice, or 'adjust his mental set' for the task. During the reading they should support independence and keep out of the reading as much as possible. The teacher may identify some words she might attend to later during the remainder of the lesson. After any of the two or three familiar books, teacher and child may discuss the story (focusing on what it meant to the child).

2   Reading the new book (the last task in the lesson) provides different opportunities. It allows daily practice in attempting to read new material. The child will learn to use any strategic activity he can to read novel texts. The teacher chooses the text carefully to suit this child at this time, helps the child to recognise what he already knows, and introduces new features of printed English to him. The teacher actively supports any tentative efforts to solve new problems.

The third book-reading opportunity is the daily assessment of reading behaviours on a Running Record.

Children who have many skills and a fair grasp of letters and words may still find it hard to pull all this information *together* when they are moving across lines of continuous text. There are two sides to this challenge. On the one hand the child must sort out what to attend to on the page of print and in what order to use which pieces of information (*awareness and attention*). On the other hand he has to call up things he already knows from different parts of his brain to meet up with the new information in print in the text he is looking at (*the integration of different kinds of information*).

The opportunity to bring these two things together occurs when the child is reading books and writing texts. It receives little attention in some advocacies about how to teach children to read.

- Integration here means pulling together what you know in order to reach a decision about the language of the text, and this is needed when reading familiar continuous text (see below).

- Integration occurs in reading, in composing messages to be written, in writing, and in rereading a written message (see section 6).

- Reconstructing cut-up versions of those stories is almost entirely about integration (see section 8).

> A boy in the third week of lessons was rereading a familiar book.
>
> C: I can brush my hair.
> Text: I can brush my fur.
> C: That's a funny word for hair.
>   I'll go back and figure it out.
>   *(He finished the book, turned back to the error and corrected it.)*

> Belinda was reading a new book. She was having a battle trying to take on some new learning. She said, thoughtfully, 'My head is so full of things I can't read hardly.'

The new book (mentioned earlier) must be carefully selected to challenge the child's processing system but not to 'upset' it. In the last ten minutes of the lesson when the teacher introduces that new book, most of the neural networks the child will need to use when problem-solving text will have already been alerted, activated by preceding tasks. The teacher will have thought out where she needs to take this particular child at this particular moment of his reading progress. Using the new book she will introduce something novel to his 'primed' processing system.

Children enter Reading Recovery lessons with some expectations about how and when books are read. They may have listened to someone reading books aloud or watched people writing notes, they may already have been trying to read and write themselves in school, and they will have seen and heard their peers reading and writing in the classroom. These prior experiences will shape children's expectations about what they should try to do.

In psychological terms reading continuous text is a sequential solving process involving a network of interacting systems. Working on texts, in either reading or writing, provides opportunities to develop this network. In the early days of my own research I used to refer to this network of interacting systems as 'the patterning of complex behaviour' (Clay, 1972).

> Hannah summed up her past experience for her teacher.
>
> H: When I'm at home, I read books a different way. My mum or dad reads the book to me. Then I look at the pictures and 'read' it.
>
> T: Hannah, that was a very good way for you to read when you were little but after you come to school it's important to look at the words and read the story the way the author wrote it.

> *Further reading:*
> *An Observation Survey* (2005), pp. 14–18, *By Different Paths to Common Outcomes*, pp. 171–84, *Change Over Time*, pp. 115–21.

9

Reading Recovery procedures

Choice of a new text

Choose the new book very carefully. Choose it for a particular child with certain strengths and challenges at this time. Teachers need to have experience in using little books and to learn how to progressively select books to assist individual children to read with success.

Early intervention teachers need to have a wide range of books from which to choose. From those in general use with the age group, professionals who have extensive experience with hard-to-teach children will select the most facilitative, highly motivating books. They will learn to avoid texts that prove to be extraordinarily difficult for hard-to-teach children because they introduce unusual ways of dealing with language, print or pictures. From time to time teachers should discuss with colleagues features of books they have found unduly challenging for particular children. Book lists used with Reading Recovery children should be revised regularly.

The 'Record of Oral Language' assessment allows teachers to think about children on three levels of complexity in their construction of spoken sentences (Clay et al., 1983):

(1)   those operating on simple structures,

(2)   those working on average-for-age structures and

(3)   those who can compose complex literary structures.

Knowing which of those three levels a child typically uses in constructing his sentences is something teachers find useful in making book choices.

> *Further reading:*
> Clay et al. (1983), *Record of Oral Language and Biks and Gutches.*

A successful choice of book would be well within the child's control, using words and letters he knows or can get to with his teacher's help. One or two things in the book will require new learning. The teaching goal would be to settle these new things into the integrated networks of knowledge that this child already controls.

The choice of book will determine how much problem-solving the child will have to do. From hundreds of books now available the highly trained teacher will select one that the particular child

- will want to read,
- can relate to some personal knowledge,
- will succeed with and enjoy,
- will use to establish new competencies.

The outcome should be that the reader should be keen to move on to the next exciting exposure to new things.

The teacher must preview the book and weigh up its suitability. Is she choosing it to consolidate the child's work on a particular level, or is she seeking to take the child into a new level of text? Aim to have the child read this book fluently.

> *Further reading:*
> Examples of 'easy' books for children at level 1 and 2. These titles were selected by teachers as helpful for struggling readers: *Dressing Up* and *At School* and *Travelling* from levels 1 and 2 (Price Milburn series or PMs) and *Cat on the Mat* (Oxford University Press), at level 2.

Orientation to the story before reading

Orientation (by the child) means the aligning of oneself or one's ideas to the surroundings or circumstances.

I found this illustrated book at a warehouse sale and added it to my small collection of texts I find extremely unhelpful as beginning reading material.

A cow
A cow with a plow
A cow with a plow
sees a sow
A cow with a plow
sees a sow take a
bow.
A cow with a plow
sees a sow who
takes a bow and
says, wow!

Having carefully selected a book for a particular child the teacher reads it herself, thinking about the best ways to orient this child to this book. Make the child familiar

- with the story,
- with the plot,
- with the phrases of language that he might never have heard,
- with unusual names and new words,
- and with old words used in an unusual way.

> Introduce the child to words used in unusual ways, and conventions that might take the child by surprise like 'Come over here,' said Mother, 'and look at this.'

Take the 'bugs' out of the text before he tries to read it.

You have chosen this book for this particular child at this particular point in his lesson series.

- You might draw the child's attention to an important idea,

- or discuss the pictures to give a sense of the complete plot, with or without the ending (your judgement),

- or give the child opportunities to hear and use new words and structures that he will need to use in the reading,

- or anticipate and prepare the child for something in the story that is a new object or activity,

- or you might even read a page that could be challenging without your help.

- As an early procedure you might pronounce one or two words that occur in the text, ask the child to say the words, ask him what letter he would expect to see at the beginning, or even ask him to find the word (as you open the book at a suitable page).

- With more competent readers you might build up some anticipation about what might happen at the end, without revealing it.

9

The first reading of the new book is not a test; it needs to be a successful reading. Prepare the child for correct responding on the first encounter. Success can be expected if the child has had recent and successful encounters with the language of the book, so think about what you expect him to know and help with unfamiliar words. The teacher must plan for the child to have in his head the ideas and the language he needs to complete the reading. In the first year or two of learning to read it helps if the child knows what the story is about before he reads it.

The introduction to the new book is particularly important for the child who does not have a good control of language (for whatever reason). This is the activity in which the observant teacher can introduce into her talk any concept, or word, or phrase structure that she has not heard this child use.

> T: This story is called *Nick's Glasses*. Here are Nick's glasses and Nick woke up and he couldn't find his glasses. There's Nick and he's wondering where are my glasses? Do you see them? The people in his family asked if he looked in different places in the house. They were trying to help him find his glasses.
> C: *(shakes his head)*
> T: Look, they're on his face. But he forgot that so he said, 'Where are my glasses?'
>
> The question asks the child to consider his understanding of the story. It is a call for comprehension of the plot.

Descriptions of 'a picture walk' in the literature of early literacy do not provide a suitable substitute for the introduction described above. In Reading Recovery lessons the task must be fine-tuned by the teacher to increase the competencies of the particular child.

Introductions with minimum help

As the children begin to work on higher-level texts some will encounter language structures they do not expect. So these need to be anticipated and where possible used by the teacher in her introduction. Only the very competent can take these on the run. When the book's language is more complex than language this child uses, the teacher may help the child into the reading of it by using some of the author's words and phrases. But one hearing will not be enough to enrich the child's language so make a note of it and come back to it another day.

For a child who has made great progress and who is near the end of his supplementary early intervention you could vary the book introduction according to the child's needs. Occasionally you might say, 'I want you to look quickly at the pictures and tell me what you think the story will be about. Then you can try to read it all by yourself. I will only help if you really need my help.' However, usually a lift in book level will lead to the need for some introduction by the teacher.

> Children learn language from the books that are read to them, and later that they read for themselves. They introduce new words from their books into their conversation and play. Some overheard as children played are 'feathers and foxgloves', 'good-lack-a-day', 'if you stepped into the circle you could turn into a spell', and 'wishy-washy, wishy-washy, wishy-washy, squashy-squashy'.

The pictures may lead the child to engage the teacher in conversation about the book providing opportunities to discuss new ideas and new language.

Once the child has constructed 'a reading process', he can be challenged by novel text that has not been introduced (unseen). Because the Reading Recovery teacher is lifting the level of challenge in a book across the entire lesson series there are probably few opportunities for the child to 'preview the book on his own'. However, this may be something that his teacher expects him to do back in the classroom and in that case it would be necessary to prepare the child for that in some way before his lessons end.

The first reading of the book with help …

Prepared by the teacher's introduction the child reads the new material as independently as possible. The little books now available enable children to read a whole story and this provides the child with a whole story structure or framework within which to work on the text. That is why it is more supportive to select a short story than to ration the exposure to something like 'half the book today'. The overall aim is to provide opportunities for the child

- to read a simple text with fluency and understanding and as independently as possible,

- to problem-solve difficulties by searching the print, the picture, the language, and the story so far,

- to get help from the teacher who prompts the searching and confirms 'good' responses,
- to independently and easily read a novel text, problem-solving the hard bits, and sounding good.

In the early part of a child's programme encourage strong, definite locating behaviours. Get the child to point to each word with the index finger to achieve crisp word-by-word integration of point-say-look behaviours. Discard the finger as soon as such control has been established. Recognise that the need for pointing may vary with the text difficulty. While a momentary slip with directional behaviour is a critical and negative sign, a temporary return to pointing may be a necessary part of solving a particular problem.

Support the child with any particular features that are likely to cause him difficulty. For example, demonstrate by stress, shouting, singing or some other means that particular feature. In the next examples the word 'early' at the start of the phrase and the word 'after' rather than 'at' were expected to present the child with a problem, and 'way too big' is colloquial but not predictable.

> The daisy is asleep
> **early** in the morning.
>
> **Look after** Timothy.
>
> He's **way too big** for me.

Olivia is a simple book about a little pig who likes to go to the beach, who feels it is important to come prepared, and who sometimes likes to bask in the sun. Alice, now aged four years and one month, expressed concern when the family decided to go to the beach. She said, 'I don't think I'm prepared.' A few weeks later she was overheard to say 'I think I'll bask in the sun now.'

Teaching during the first reading

The teacher's prompts and other responses during the reading have two aims:

- to improve the processing of information on continuous texts (the orchestration of efficient reading, the pulling together of everything you know)
- to support the continued expansion of the processing system itself to cope with more features of language.

The teacher helps the child to get to information from print to facilitate the reading of the story in several different ways. She must be tentative. She can never be certain what kind of help is needed.

Teachers may use apparently good prompts at inappropriate times. For example, 'Get your mouth ready for this word' requires the child to look at the first letter and work out what sound it makes. It assumes that this child knows where to find 'the first letter' and has already learned the letter-sound relationships — an unwise assumption for the child early in his lesson series.

If that child is only anticipating the (oral) word that could come next, predicting from his own speech, then the appropriate question is about 'hearing'

9

and might be 'What sound would you expect to hear?' A follow-up question might be 'Do you think this first letter (*the teacher points to it*) could make that sound?' Those questions are helpful.

Some teachers argue that they would like to do more teaching and less prompting. *Give thoughtful attention to the level of help the child needs and decide when you are prompting for processing or when you should be supplying information that the learner does not have (teaching).*

- *Most teacher help*   Direct the child's attention specifically to a piece of information he needs to solve the problem. Tell the child what to correct, or provide new information. Vague prompting leaves the child guessing what you are referring to. Solve the problem together smartly, both participating. This is not the same as telling the child the word (but that is also a possibility).

- *Less teacher help and more child work*   Direct the child's attention to reviewing the information he has used: 'Try that again and think about … ' Allow him to find a way out of the problem. It should be clear what the child should attend to next.

  Would X make sense?
  Would X start like that?

  Indicate the type of information you want the child to attend to — the plot, or the meaning, or the language structure, or the language sounds, or the print forms.

- *Least teacher help*   This is consistent with supporting independent solving. Avoid questioning because it disrupts the story, but encourage solving. Stay close to the problem-solving of *this text* and the reading of *this story* as a whole.

Make an excellent choice of a book, ensure that the challenge matches the child's learning needs, and avoid unnecessary interruption of the flow of story-reading by making too many links to other things.

Comment positively when the child corrects himself. Make a point of reinforcing self-correction early in the lesson series. Acknowledge when a child tries to use a type of information he has previously avoided. Talk about self-correction.

  Say '*I liked the way you …*
  And did you notice … ?'

This is a useful comment. Think about why it is useful. It approves the processing that the child has already done. It allows the teacher then to redirect the child's attention to some new feature, saying, 'And did you notice …?' This way of commenting need not interrupt the story. It can fit comfortably into pauses as the pages are turned. However, use it in moderation: typically it is grossly overworked!

Another useful 'wrap-up' comment is 'How did that sound?' after a good reading.

If the first reading is not good the teacher might think about her choice of book and her introduction! There are other things to be considered. Perhaps the teacher blocked the child's problem-solving because she was not brief. Perhaps she

- talked too much — be brief and to the point,
- directed too much,
- questioned too much,
- gave too little help,
- modelled too little,
- failed to notice some new challenges in the text she chose,
- or confused the child.

> C: (reads) Mother Bird looks at … looks and looks, I mean. I'm gonna read that page over again. Mother Bird looks and looks for a worm.
> T: How did that sound?
> C: Good.
> T: That sounded a lot better. You were listening to yourself, weren't you?
> C: And guess what? This thing is easy!

Do not waste words. Commend the child for good work on processing the print, praise to boost morale, say whatever is necessary to keep the story flowing BUT eliminate all unnecessary talk. Do not overwork comments like

> *You went back and fixed it up,*
> or *I liked the way you did that.*

Teaching after the first reading

During the first reading of a new text there may be some things that the teacher wants to talk over with the child. Perhaps the child did some remarkable solving. You should comment on this. Perhaps he got close to the meaning of the text but overlooked some useful information. So after the reading the teacher could turn back to the page involved and might make comments like these.

- *Did you notice …?*
- *What could this word be …?*
- *Try this again.*

From this interaction the child should get the message that stopping and noticing is what you do when 'problem-solving'. It is allowed! And when you ask later on 'Why did you stop?' the child will not be afraid he has done something wrong.

- *With your finger show me where to start. And how do you move across the print?* (The sequence of visual search)

- *You solved the puzzle here … Do you remember? How did you do that?* (Text processing)

- *Let's take a look at what the rabbit said on this page. You said 'I think we shall go and find him.' Is that what the rabbit said? Read it again, and see if you can find the tricky word.* ('should' was read as 'shall') (Word processing)

9

A good teacher can help or approve with a gesture, and guide with clear, crisp language like

> *Do this. Don't do that.*
> *What is the first letter?*
> *I liked the way you read that, just using your eyes.*

After the first reading

- there should be only a few things to discuss if the book was chosen carefully to suit the child's current competencies;
- the teacher would *select only one or two points* and teach with an economical use of words and examples;
- and the kinds of things that she would attend to would change over time.

This is a good place to make more links to other knowledge the child has. Next day, what you did after the first reading should be easy for the child to remember during the second reading of the new book.

Rereading for fluency

This is a rescue move after things have not gone well. If the first reading is not very successful the teacher should question her choice of book or her introduction to the book.

Even at the early levels the child should 'hear' the reading going together well. The teacher may choose to focus on some phrases, saying

> *Let's put these words together.*
> *Let's put 'Here comes …' together.*

Or try to improve the phrasing with a comment like this:

> *And here Mother Bear is asking a question.*
> *How would she ask a question?*

At every book level the child should be able to 'hear' that his reading sounds like his speaking. If the first reading was interrupted by a large amount of reading work (at the early levels perhaps), the teacher might ask the child to read some of the story for a second time *in the same lesson* to get an easy flow of words, and a real feel for the story. Offer whatever help is necessary to get this. Rereading of this kind should occur rarely.

'Who points during the second reading for fluency?' asks a teacher. Perhaps the teacher points to speed up the scanning of the eyes across the print, but, on the other hand, probably pointing by child or teacher will reduce fluency. Hands are slower to move than eyes.

Contrast this example of 'teacher talk' with what I have called 'crisp language'.

'Good job. I liked the way you found lots of ways to figure out the tricky parts. Over here I noticed some really good reading work you did. You first said six legs on a bug. It made sense and it starts right for bug, but in order to fix it and say "bee" you had to look at more than the first letter. Does it end right for beeeee? Does it have what you expect on the end?'
The poor child shakes his head and says 'Yes!'

After reading *Along Comes Jake*[30]
T: Would you like to have Jake for a brother?
C: *(nodding his head)* Jake always makes a mess. That kid is so bad. Look *(turns to the last page)* — he is so funny.

Brief review of the story after the first reading

A brief conversation after the reading can achieve a variety of things. A good question can reveal a wealth of understanding.

> *What did he do that was nice?*
> *Does the pot look too small to you?*
> *How did Mum trick Greedy Cat?*

You could ask what the reader thought about the book. Good questions give the message that the whole story was the point of the reading activity and it lets the teacher know what the child has attended to and understood.

A second reading of the book next day

When a new book has been introduced and read, take a Running Record at the next session. We are looking for independent reconstruction of yesterday's experience. The teacher might read the title (to refresh the child's memory), and then invite the child to read. Observe directional behaviour and clear locating behaviour (matching speech to print), and record the behaviour for later analysis.

Check on things you have recently emphasised like making sense, or noticing errors, or monitoring carefully, or cross-checking, or using visual information. Also check things like visual searching or attempts to use features like 's', '-ed', '-ing'.

Teaching after the second reading (early in the lesson series)

Teach after the reading of the book has been completed *and teach not only on errors but also on successful solving.* Quickly check words, phrasing or language features that were teaching points for this book. Use a masking card if that helps to isolate a word swiftly.

Teaching after the second reading (later in the lesson series)

The teacher must give a major share of her teaching opportunities to shaping up fast, efficient processing of continuous text. It is possible to become trapped in the detail of learning vocabulary and the challenges of spelling English. Being able to pull several processing activities together to solve a novel problem and to do this on the run will set the child up for success back in the classroom in the weeks to come.

After reading *Quack, quack, quack*[31]

T: What do you think Dad is going to do now?

C: He's going to act like a frog and jump around. Like on TV's funniest videos.

After reading *The Hungry Giant's Soup*[32]

T: What happened to his bommy-knocker?

C (an English-language learner): … in the tub.

T: Was it in the tub?

C: No, in the fire. It burn all up. The fire cook the soup.

George showed he understood what he had read and no comprehension question was needed. In the story the children told their mother that they were not afraid of anything. When he composed his story for the day he said, 'The kids lied to their mother.'

And here is a missed opportunity to check on comprehension after a familiar reading of *Nick's Glasses*.

T: Let's finish the story.

C: 'Have you looked in the mirror?' 'Oh,' said Nick. 'Here they are.'

T: Was he surprised? I think so. Here they are. I bet he felt silly. Which books would you like to take home?

C: I like fishing. I will go with you said *(for 'and')* …

T: You're saying 'said' for a word you know. Write this word. *(points to 'and')*

C: *(writes slowly)*

T: Write it quickly. Good job. What word is that?

C: 'and'?

T: Now read the sentence.

C: I will go with you and help you.

The teacher noted that there was no confusion the next day.

9

Questions tying up the reading may invite the child to negotiate about something he did not understand. Here is an example.

In a text called *The Rescue* a fisherman on the rocks is cut off by the tide and calls for help from a family who are coming along the beach. The family, called Lee, has been introduced to the reader already but the fisherman is a new character. The text said 'He called out to the Lee family' and in a speech balloon was 'Help! Help!'

C:	*(to his teacher)* How does he know it's the Lee family?
T:	He doesn't. He just sees some people who could help him.
C:	But it says he calls to the Lee family.
T:	He just called out 'Help! Help!' The writer of the story tells us it is the Lee family.
C:	But how did he know their name?

Texts can confuse us. In a helpful but brief conversation meanings can be negotiated. This gives the message that we must understand what we have read.

The child's box of familiar books

After this second reading the book is placed in the child's box of familiar books, the ones he has read previously.

From time to time the teacher will remove some of the books from the box because they are no longer a challenge for the child. He knows them very well. She will also remove a book if she thinks the child has memorised it because the child no longer has any reason to search the print for information to guide his reading. A memorised book will not challenge him to carry out 'reading work'. The time is better spent on texts that help him integrate (pull together) the things that he knows. It requires a careful weighing up to make a decision between keeping a book for the enjoyment or the fluency practice it allows, or discarding it because the child can 'read it' without reading it.

Familiar reading

Accumulate a box of familiar books and reread two or three at the beginning of a lesson. A familiar book is not a memorised book. It is a book that still challenges the child to do some reading work, engaging with print, and picking up new information. Although a child reads a book with a high level of accuracy there may be many features of the text that have not yet come to his notice. The practice of rereading familiar books encourages confidence and fluency, and provides practice in bringing reading behaviours together (orchestration), but it also allows the reader to discover new things about print during the rereading.

Control over the text allows attention to shift to features of the text or the story not previously attended to.

Home and school practice

Send easy books home for independent practice. *A child who is on the way to independence needs to read often from many different books selected to be easy for him to 'go it alone'. It is the quantity of successful reading that builds the assured independence of the competent reader.*

If a child's home language is different from the language of instruction in school we work a little differently but we get to the same outcomes in the recommended times. Schools may sometimes need to ensure in some way that someone listens to the Reading Recovery child read his take-home book, even providing for this to happen at school.

Almost inevitably ...

Teachers must prepare their children for the transition from the supplementary help they get in Reading Recovery, back to the classroom activities only. It is almost inevitable that curricula and the classroom practices planned by teachers will ask children to engage in practices for which the Reading Recovery teacher has not had time to prepare them. So, in the last four weeks of a child's supplementary programme some effort must be made to prepare the child to perform independently in the tasks of his particular classroom. The variety of possibilities across different education systems is too great to capture in this manual. These adaptations must receive attention in the final weeks of his lesson series.

Children completing a Reading Recovery lesson series will not yet have completed the construction of a self-extending system. They are well on the way but they need to continue to be successful readers and writers in their classrooms able to access their teacher's help with oral reading for another 12 to 18 months.

Some organisational points

Arrange for massive opportunity for each child in Reading Recovery to read enchantingly interesting texts fluently, at just the right difficulty level. Plan for how this can happen more often. Vary the type of text to foster flexibility so the child is not thrown when the classroom teacher introduces an information text for science. Strengthen the child's processing on new texts, and briefly question and discuss what he has read to you.

More to come

Four of the next five sections of these procedures are also about reading continuous texts, and only one is about the study of words in isolation.

10

10 Finding and using the information in the print: developing the brain's activities on texts

Introduction

This chapter discusses some things that are important when one is reading continuous texts. Many theories of reading are theories of reading words in isolation. Most young children engage with books at the level of the story, not with isolated words. Children like to read short stories and they learn a great deal about print and texts as they do this. The comments in this introduction apply mostly to how the brain is involved with the reading of continuous texts.

On new texts children must engage in extensive problem-solving. They solve their problems by using their theories of the world and their theories of how to work with written language. They become aware of different kinds of information in print and they learn to check the options the print suggests to them. They search for an option that is a good 'fit', and they make judgements and decisions. During beginning reading young children give us overt signals about what they are attending to and what links they are making. Their behaviours provide signals that help teachers to decide how best to lift their performance levels. Over time reading becomes a very fast and silent process and then we get little evidence of what the neural networks are doing. For a short time the child's signals provide teachers with opportunities to be very helpful.

By the start of this century scientists who were studying vision were telling us that it was not a one-way street from the eye's retina to the brain. Information comes into the brain through the senses, and the brain rapidly activates what it believes is relevant knowledge stored from prior experiences.

> For each connection that carries information from the eyes (to the brain) there are at least 10 connections coming in the opposite direction from the brain to the eyes. It seems that the information leaving our retina is not complete enough to create a full and rich interpretation of the world. Our imagination then allows us to fill the gaps and convert the distorted image from the eyes into the complete and vibrant world we see.[33]

Ask yourself two questions when you hear a child substitute a word he knows for a word in the book.

> What visual information do you think he attended to?
> What information came from prior experiences stored in his brain?

Those two questions are most helpful when analysing children's reading behaviours on text. 'Our visual experience is a mixture of information coming in from the eyes and prior associations. That is how we interpret what we see and give the world significance,'[34] wrote Susan Greenfield in her book, *Brain Story*. Past experience contributes to what we see and understand. However, vision can also lead us to invent, ignore or distort the incoming perception.

When learners monitor themselves and self-correct on parts of a new text this provides some evidence of when messages from the outside and messages from the inside are coming together. When we follow children's progress over time and record carefully the evidence is very powerful. We are able to record what we see them do and track some of the changes in their problem-solving as their reading improves.

The monitoring and problem-solving that young readers can learn to do seems to involve more complex brain activity than the word-solving tricks that are often taught in literacy instruction. (For example, sounding out a word, phoneme by phoneme, or skipping a word and reading on to the end of the sentence, rarely occur in the records of successful young readers unless these activities have been relentlessly drilled in the classroom. Brains give some attention to both those activities but not in the simple way that is prescribed in many instruction manuals.) The brain's activities are complex. Practices like recommending 25 repetitions of a word to establish learning do not fit well with how the brain acts to get to a solution. Simple explanations are not enough.

Reading Recovery children have lessons directed to making them constructive — to actively process information, to find and relate information from different sources, to bring it together, construct a decision, and monitor the effectiveness of that decision. The child should feel that he is a reader, not just a 'rememberer'!

Good readers

Classroom reading instruction focuses a great deal on items of knowledge — words, letters, sounds. Children practise these items in busy activities while the teacher 'hears' a few children read texts individually. The contrast is between teaching items, and teaching children how to produce messages couched in language structures. Consider the mingling of strategic activities in the problem-solving of Clare, a young competent reader.

Most children respond to most teaching in active ways. They search for links between the items, they begin to thread the items together, putting letters into words, words into sentences, and they make new discoveries. They operate on print as Piaget's children operated on problems, searching for relationships, and they find some order in the complexity of print. Their active minds are making discoveries and they even direct their minds to things that their teachers' programmes do not stress. *For such children the teaching sequences described below are unnecessary. Evaluations of instruction of many kinds show that many children can learn to read well in different classroom programmes.*

> This is a record made by an observant teacher. Clare was thinking aloud while reading to herself.
>
> C: *(reading aloud)* … the f-fish … fresh.
> Now what could be fresh?
> *(She looked at the illustration, searching and returned to the print. She sounded out some more of the letters.)*
> gr … ee … green leaves.
> *(She combined her findings and reran the phrase.)* … the fresh green leaves.
>
> Casual observers might praise her left-to-right sounding out of words. Talking to herself as she read she demonstrated that her text-solving behaviours were more sophisticated than that.

10

Poor readers

Children who fail to progress in reading do not have that kind of success. The brain work that they have tried to carry out has not brought order to the complexity. Instruction has confused them more often than it helped them. As a result, they often become passive, waiting for the teacher to 'put the learning into their heads'.

Reading Recovery teachers have to change passive poor readers into readers who search actively for information in print that can help them. Two things help.

> They try out possible responses,
> and they learn how to verify their decisions.

I have referred to this in some of my writing as 'reading work'.[35] (That refers to many electrical impulses racing around the brain looking for a best-fit solution: it does not mean that you wait for the child to do a lot of huffing and puffing and stumbling over the words.) Reading work clocks up more experience for the neural network. It allows the partially familiar to become familiar and the new to become partially familiar in ever-changing sequences.[36]

Brain functions

New knowledge about the brain is emerging every day. Being highly selective I will use some quotes from a Dana Foundation video made in 1996.[37]

> We know that the brain goes on developing and that its formation is impacted by learning and remembering … the brain retains the capacity to form and break circuits throughout life. In a sense we are all carrying around different brains. Each experience drives the brain to make some connections and break other ones.

> Language involves lots of brain parts working together as a symphony and some learning is (about) how to feed new minor parts into the ongoing symphony.

> The moment of truth is in the moment of input: how you attend, how much you care, how you encode, what you do with it, and how you organise it. You relate what you see and hear to things you already understand. How well you access it depends on how well you stored it in the first place. How do you (the learner) become more savvy about your way of remembering things? Put things in the same place. Have a good system. [I am repeating the excellent quote which appears at the front of this book.]

Squire was speaking about brain functioning in general in everyday life. However, you could read this as if he were speaking of learning to read and write. Interpreting the quotes in that way would make for a good discussion among teachers! It is false to assume that a central processing system for literacy already exists in the brain when the child begins literacy learning. While learning the items we are teaching, the child is building a processing network that will deal with literacy tasks. He has to learn the letters and the words, and their relationships to sound, but he also has to build and expand the intricate interacting systems in the brain that must work together at great speed as he reads text.

A self-extending system

It has helped early intervention teachers to think of children as building a network or system for working on print that becomes smart enough to extend itself.

As children work on simple texts they solve complex problems and become able to read slightly more difficult texts. Teachers and school systems have for more than a century provided a gradient of difficulty in texts and tasks intended to gradually lift the children's problem-solving. This seems to be just what is needed if the children are to construct a self-extending system (an effective neural network) for reading. If you successfully solve the problems of a simple task then this prepares you to tackle a more complex problem at a higher level. Slowly, through success, the system builds a greater capacity to solve the new challenges and get to the precise reference of new words used by the author.

At some time between beginning reading and what an average nine- to ten-year-old can do, teachers describe children as reading to learn rather than learning to read. This end point is reached quickly and early by some children who put the right activities together, but it is reached far too slowly and far too inefficiently for far too many children.

As adults when we work on a problem we engage in a conscious search for solutions. In reading we sometimes consciously search for a word or a meaning or a correction but most of the time our active search is a fast reaction in our brain that appears to be automatic and is rarely conscious. I use the words

strategic activities

to describe this fast brainwork. The term refers to electrical impulses that race around the neural networks as we read, *without us consciously directing them*.[38]

In earlier writing I used the word 'strategies' rather than strategic activities, but I found teachers became too certain that these were specific skills they could teach. I believe that what the brain actually does is far more elusive, fast and ephemeral than that. I think it is most helpful to think of the learner (who is successfully solving reading problems) as building a neural network for working on written language *and that network learns to extend itself*.

Teachers can help this happen but what they call 'instruction' does not extend the neural network! It is the successful strategic activity called up by the learner that creates the self-extending system.

> *Further reading:*
> Table 1, pp. 84–85, in *Change Over Time* suggests these changes are complex.
> *An Observation Survey* (2005), pp. 126–31.

Every week I recorded the reading and writing behaviours of 100 children who were learning in a formal literacy programme, and between their fifth and sixth birthdays, I defined the reading of continuous texts as 'a message-getting, problem-solving activity which increases in power and flexibility the more it is practised'. We can hardly call this 'self-extending' in the early days of learning to read. In fact most readers will take three or more years to reach the point where they can extend their own reading competencies with little help except from the author of the books they read.

As a reader you will from time to time encounter, momentarily, a small reading difficulty. Become an observer of what your brain does to solve the problem. Try to separate out what you did consciously from what happened that you did not seem to control, the implicit solving that the brain does. If what you did involved visual perception you will find it difficult to observe.

> *Further reading:*
> Consult *Becoming Literate,* pp. 156–75, 317–45, *Change Over Time,*
> pp. 84–85, 91–103, 122–24, 226–27, and *An Observation Survey* (2005),
> pp. 33–35. Lyons, C. (2003), *Teaching Struggling Readers*, pp. 70–71, and
> Schwartz, R.M. (1997), Self-monitoring in beginning reading, *The Reading
> Teacher,* 51, 1, pp. 40–48.

Reading Recovery procedures: strategic activities used on texts

A young child can acquire and practise these important strategic activities by reading continuous texts, storybooks, the messages he has composed and written, and information texts. Beyond what the teacher introduces, children will begin to work out for themselves which kinds of strategic activities are helpful on texts when they try to read their first books.

A false report about Reading Recovery instruction claimed that children were expected to memorise the texts of their first books in order to match what they had learned by heart with what they saw on the page.[39] This was never recommended and is not a valid conclusion. Such a memorising strategy would be antagonistic to what the successful reader has to do. The ongoing problem-solving of the reader on continuous text has nothing in common with memorising the text first. Memorising is not a place to begin because it gives the novice reader an incorrect impression of what it is he has to learn to do.

At an early stage of his lesson series the child begins to draw on his knowledge of language, his knowledge of the world, and his knowledge of how to work with books to discover the connections between the pictures and the print in a simple text.

In the first week or so of a lesson series a child may invent a possible text for the first page to get started. Just as mothers respond to a three-year-old's language like this:

Child: I builded a castle.
Mother: So you did. You built a castle.
Child: Yes. I built a castle.

so the teacher is likely to accept the invented sentence of the beginning reader but to respond with a measured reading of the actual text. Children are quite accustomed to picking up some added input. The teacher has modelled the sentence on that page, and she knows that most, but not all, of the subsequent pages use the same sentence pattern. What, she wonders, will the child do when the sentence pattern changes? She deliberately exposes him to that situation and observes what he does. Children quickly become aware that changes in the text mean you had better start searching and it is the reader's job to find some kind of information that will guide him to solve the problem.

Children who are getting classroom exposure to storybooks or who have had rich preschool experiences with books will already know about searching and linking things in a book to make sense of the story. *Others will need to learn this after they come to school.* This awareness commonly emerges from hearing stories read and discussed in the classroom and at home.

The earliest specific behaviours needed to read texts have been discussed in sections 1–4 of these procedures. Through them the child learns to direct his eyes to attend to print in helpful ways. *Crucial information in reading enters the brain through the eyes.* One question helps us focus on the complex early reading challenges: Is the child searching the print on the page in a helpful sequence of moves?

The following list recapitulates the earliest stages of literacy learning that precedes the important middle phase of a lesson series.

1   *Directional movement*

Ideas for encouraging appropriate directional behaviours were described in 'Learning about direction' (see section 1). This is as serious as driving on the correct side of the road. Many hazards are a consequence of not picking up information in the correct order, from the left to the right direction in English. There is nothing natural about this: it is arbitrary. It seems so simple to us that it is difficult for us to respect its importance. Natural pick-up by the brain of information from the real world out there involves flexibility, taking in information from anywhere in any order or position.

Many things we do with the best of intentions actually threaten systematic left-to-right survey. Either we drag children's attention to what we currently think is important, or we let them start with what they notice and work from there. We know very little about what the child's brain is attending to. Careful observation can at least give us records of precisely what a young child does as he points to print.

10

2   Finding the words: one-to-one matching

This was discussed in detail in 'Locating what to attend to in print' (section 2). Here are some ways to encourage this as the child reads books.

> *Read it with your finger.*
> *Did that match?*
> *Were there enough words?*
> *Did you run out of words?*

You could accompany the child's pointing with your own pointer and fail to move on when he makes an error that you think he could self-correct.

If the child gives a fast response from his fluent language, and is not using his eyes, use two pieces of card or two fingers to frame each word.

3   Locating known words or letters in continuous text

On his first books the child is picking out only a few things that he recognises in print. The other details just form the background. Begin to encourage the child to locate particular words while reading in continuous text. Focus on words that he has seen or heard at home, in his community, in his classroom or in his Reading Recovery lessons.

- Prompt the child to make use of something you know he knows. This may be any type of information in print. The aim is to have the child initiate 'reading work', that is, searching, finding, and deciding. You might say:

> *It looks like the first letter in your name.*
> *That sounds like the beginning of Jake.*
> *We made that word on the board this morning.*
> *Look at this writing. You wrote that word.*

  Welcome any contribution the child can make to solving the problem. (Gently guide him to attend to the left end of the word. Without that guidance why would he start there?)

- Tell the child the word (suppose it is 'went'), but make the child do some checking by asking a question.

> *What do you think?*
> *Would that make sense?*
> *Would 'went' fit there?*
> *Do you think it looks like 'went'?*

After the child has read a whole story with errors on one or two words that you expected him to know, turn back and encourage him to locate those items in the text. When he responds you might point to a letter and ask

> *Can you hear this letter?*

You might read back an error sentence to him and ask

> *You said … Was that right?*

You might reread the page or sentence with fluent phrasing, up to the known-word-read-wrongly and stop, or, if you need to give more help, articulate the first sound of the problem word.

Locating what you know is a precursor of the independent searching he will engage in later. At this time what you are asking for is more like 'Find the hidden object in a page of scribble.'

4   Locating an unknown word

Repeat any or all of the options used above when you shift the child's attention to words that are new to him.

> *Prompt the child to use something that you know he knows.*
> *Tell the child the word as he looks at it closely.*

Prompt to emphasise looking and say

> *You said ... Was that right?*

Read up to the problem word fluently and stop, expecting him to finish the reading. Or read fluently and articulate the first letter of the problem word. Or point to the first letter and ask

> *Can you hear this letter?*

Encourage a left-to-right movement (finger and eyes) across the word.

5   Prompt towards ways to remember words

Encourage the child to become active about 'knowing something next time he sees it'. This will be more productive than saying 'Remember that.' For words you have worked on select from invitations like these.

> *You need to know that word tomorrow.*
> *Have you got it in your head?*
> *Let's go to the board and you write the first letter.*
> *Use your eyes and think about it.*

First steps to strategic activity

Do not establish a pattern where the child waits for the teacher to do the work. The child must learn to take the initiative, make some links, and work at a difficulty. That is the general principle that needs to be established in the first lessons.

Different children will begin to initiate solving in different lesson activities, depending upon what is easy for each of them.

It is very important that the child understands what you are saying when you prompt him. One Reading Recovery student had the courage to ask his teacher 'What do you mean by "meaning"?' Other children do not understand 'Does that make sense?' and it is easier to ask them 'What do you think about that?'

10

Checking on oneself or self-monitoring

The successful reader who is making no errors is monitoring his reading at all times. Effective monitoring is a highly skilled process constructed over many years of reading. It begins early but must be continually adapted to encompass new challenges in texts. (Do you find it easy to read your computer or cellphone manual?)

- To encourage self-monitoring in the very early stages ask the child to go back to one-to-one pointing:

  Say '*Point to each one.*'
  or '*Use a pointer and make them match.*'

- Direct the child's attention to meaning:

  Say '*Look at the picture.*'
  or '*Remember that they went to the shop and ...*'

- You might allow the child to continue to the end of the sentence before you deal with the error.

  Say '*I liked the way you did that. Now ...*'
  or '*Where is the hard bit?*'

- If the child gives signs of uncertainty — hesitation, frowning, a little shake of the head — even though he takes no action:

  Say '*Was that OK?*'
  or '*Why did you stop?*'
  or '*What did you notice?*'

Questions like these tell the child that you want him to monitor his own reading. The response to be learned is checking on oneself. *It is important at this stage that the child come to check on his own behaviour*, more important than that he be required to use all the sources of information.

- Don't forget to reinforce the child for his self-monitoring attempts whether they are successful or not.

  Say '*You tried to work that out. That was good ...*'

- Encourage recognition of some letter sequences. Let the child predict the word he expects it to be based on *his* speech. Then cover the problem word and ask for something you know he knows about that word. One of these questions might be useful:

  Say '*What do you expect to see at the beginning?*'
     '*... at the end?*'
     '*... after the "M"?*'

  Then, as you uncover the word:

  Say '*Check it. Run your finger under it.*'

'Pull it altogether.'
*'Does it look right **and** sound right?'*
'So it has to make sense and it has to sound right.'

Summarise what happened. Draw it all together.

• Ask the child *'Were you right?'* after both correct and incorrect words.

• Sometimes ask *'How did you know?'* after the correct words.

• As the child becomes more skilled do less teaching and prompting and modelling; all you need to say is *'Try that again.'*

• Make sure that your voice carries two messages. You require him to search because you know he can, and you are confident he can solve the problem.

Provide new input whenever it is required. Some teachers give children too little input. You are the one with all the knowledge about the code.

Cross-checking on information

Cross-checking is a tentative behaviour. It is not possible to be specific about it. One has a hunch that it is happening after observing the child. We must ask ourselves 'Is this child checking one kind of information against another?'

Cross-checking is most obvious when a child is not satisfied with a response for some reason. The child may make another attempt, or look back, or think again, or complain that a necessary letter is missing. The child is probably using two sources of information, checking one against the other. He uses meaning but complains that the letters he expected are not there. Or he uses visual information from letters but says that it doesn't make sense.

Cross-checking will occur when

> Carol Lyons has given us a good example of cross-checking. David was reading 'If I were an elephant, I would lift a tractor.' He read correctly but substituted 'truck'. Then he checked the end of the last word and said, 'No "k".' Then he reread and substituted 'trailer', ran his finger under the word and said 'No!' Then he tried again successfully.

10

• he can get movement and language occurring together in a coordinated way, and knows when he has run out of words.

• he checks language prediction by looking at some letters.

• he can hear the sounds in a word he speaks and checks whether the expected letters are there.

• a wrong response is followed by another attempt at the word (searching).

• a wrong response is followed by repeating the sentence, phrase or word, indicating he is aware of a mismatch, and trying to get some additional information (repeating).

• a wrong response is followed by a verbal comment about the mismatch, for example 'No! That's not right!'

> *Further reading:*
> Lyons, C. (2003). *Teaching Struggling Readers*, p. 53.

The teacher must observe what kinds of information the child is using. When the child can monitor his own reading and can search for and use structure or message or sounds or letters, begin to encourage him to check one kind of information against another. The teacher can

- say '*Check it.*'
- (after slow articulation) say '*Does that make sense?*'
- say '*Does the word you said look like the word on the page?*'
- point up discrepancies: '*It could be … but look at …*'
- encourage the child to think, saying, '*What could it be?*' or '*What else could it be?*'
- insert possible words so that the child can confirm the response using some letter knowledge
- say '*Check it! Does it look right and sound right to you?*'

<table>
<tr><td>

Text: There's a mouse in my pocket.

C: There's a mouse in my pocket, … coat.
T: *(invites him to check on letter-sound relationships)* Which is it? What do you think?
C: Coat.
T: Point to it. Show it to me. Does it start like coat?
C: *(shakes his head)*
T: What would you expect to see if it was coat? *(teacher covers the word)*
C: 'c'.
T: What have we got there?
C: Pocket.
T: You're right. It just says 'in my pocket'.

</td><td>

Here is a transcript of a teacher-child interaction.
The teacher would only ask these questions to inform herself. Giving these answers does not improve learning. It may even confuse the child! But the teacher's attention probably encourages cross-checking behaviour.

T: What was the new word you read?
C: Bicycle.
T: How did you know it was bicycle?
C: It was a bike. *(semantics)*
T: What did you expect to see?
C: A 'b'? *(letter-sound relationships)*
T: What else?
C: A little word, but it wasn't. *(size)*
T: So, what did you do?
C: I thought of bicycle. *(back to semantics)*
T: *(Reinforcing the checking)* Good, I liked the way you worked at that all by yourself.

</td></tr>
</table>

Cross-checking describes simple behaviours. The child learns that one kind of information can be compared with another kind. A simple act of cross-checking will be superseded before long by self-correction when the child demonstrates that he can make several kinds of information agree in the solution. Before this happens a teacher can notice that the child is clearly trying to check one feature with another.

When a teacher pays attention to cross-checking the child is more likely to engage in it. Her attention to it shows the child that she values the checking behaviours.

Sometimes when children are working at higher levels of text they may revert to simple cross-checking when their more complex processing system fails to solve the problem.

Searching for information of any type

To develop the child's abilities to search for all types of information use the following set of questions in flexible ways. *In your first attempts* to call new features of print to the child's attention use the child's present behaviour in your first examples.

- Prompt for sentence structure (syntax):
  Say '*You said … Can we say it that way?*'

- Prompt for the message (semantics), asking yourself 'What meaning from prior experience can the child bring to understanding this message?'[40]
  Say '*You said … Does that make sense?*'

- Prompt for letter information (graphic information):
  Say '*Does it look right?*'

- Or more generally:
  Say '*What's wrong with this?*'
  (Repeat what the child said.)

As children gain greater control and encounter new words the teacher would ask the child to

> *Try that again and think what would make sense.*
> *Try that again and think what would sound right.*

And eventually, when the child is checking in several ways,

> *Try that again and think what would make sense, and sound right, and look like that.*

Helpful ways to encourage the use of visual information [41]

The visual analysis of words in text can be encouraged by the teacher's questions as the child reads text.

- After success in word solving:

  Say '*How did you know it said "was"?*'

- When the child stops at a new word:

  Say '*Look for something that would help you.*'
  or '*What can you see that might help?*'
  or '*Do you know a word that looks like that?*'
  or '*Do you know a word that starts with those letters?*'
  or '*Look carefully and think what you know that might help.*'

10

The teacher is prompting the reader to pay visual attention to certain features or to the fact that he can use something he knows to help him solve his problem.

But suppose the child has a bias towards using mainly letters and letter features. If so the teacher's prompts will be directed towards the message and the language structure.

- She may need to orient the child to the picture as a source of meaning.

- She may need to introduce new vocabulary.

- Sometimes it is necessary for a child to gain control over a particular language structure first (saying it aloud) before he returns to using the visual information.

Four types of information in print

According to the theory of reading behind these recovery procedures there are many sources of information in texts. In Reading Recovery lessons teachers pay particular attention to four kinds of information that young readers must learn to look for. Different kinds of information may be checked, one against another, to confirm a response.

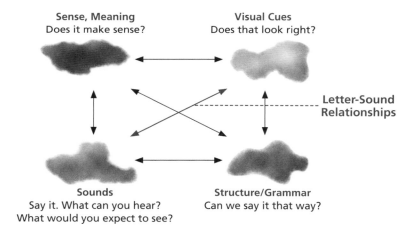

This square is a grossly simplistic diagram and *it is not a model of what amazing links the brain is making*. The diagram is drawn to help the teacher think about some unseen strategic activities that the reader might have used.

Note that letter-sound and sound-to-letter links are represented by the two-way arrow from the sound box to the visual box.

It is quite easy to provide examples of children using information from three of those sources; the use of structure is not so easy to capture.

Following are two clear examples of children considering 'structure'. The example on the right shows a teacher giving a child permission to search for information that he can use in problem-solving. This teacher is making some aspects of the searching more obvious to the child.

In this beginning reading book the last word of every second line was replaced by a picture of a bucket. The text was:

Father Bear's blackberries went into this

Mother Bear's blackberries went into this

Baby Bear's blackberries went into this

Each time the child ended the line at 'this'. The teacher said, 'You can say "bucket" here if you like.' The child read the page again inserting bucket three times. Then he looked at the teacher and said, 'But you can say it this way, too' and he reread the sentences ending at 'this'. It is as if he had checked his grammar and found both kinds of sentences permissible in English. Clearly he was making judgements about sentence structures.

T: You almost got that page right. There was something wrong with this line. See if you can find what was wrong.
C: *(silently rereads, checking)* I said 'Lizard' but it's 'Lizard's'.
T: How did you know?
C: 'Cause it's got an 's'.
T: Is there any other way we could know?
C: *(rereads in whisper)* It's funny to say 'Lizard dinner'! It has to be 'Lizard's dinner' like 'Peter's dinner', doesn't it?
T: *(reinforcing the searching)* Yes. That was good. You found two ways to check on that tricky new word.

The outcome achievement is not that the child was 'corrected' and got the rendering 'right', but rather that the child will attend to monitoring because the teacher attended to it.

Self-correction

When a teacher encourages a child to monitor his reading or to search for more information she is encouraging self-correction. However, children do begin to correct themselves very early, on their first books, often without any prompting. The child who monitors his own reading, and searches for more help in the text, and cross-checks at least two types of information, will be self-correcting some of his own errors.

- Comment positively on self-corrections:

  Say *'I liked the way you found out what was wrong all by yourself.'*

- Allow time for self-correction. The child must take the initiative. Children must have opportunities for independent self-correction.

- To make a confident reader even more independent of the teacher don't do anything when he makes an error or stops. Don't give him any clues. Place the responsibility on the child.

  Say *'You made a mistake on that page/in that sentence. Can you find it?'*

10

The 'pebble in the pond' effect

New learning can create a disturbance in an old response pattern that had seemed to be learned. If learning were just a matter of adding bits of knowledge to our memory banks this would not happen. When a response is controlled by a pattern of movements (and a network of brain reactions) it is not surprising that the established pattern could be disturbed by adding a new component to the pattern. It takes a little time to rearrange the old learning. And at times when two old ways of working seem to combine into one, the entire process might become a little uncertain for a time.

Verbalising the process

Check on some words that were accurately read:

> *How did you know?*
> *Were you right?*

The teacher's prime goal here could be to get the processing under way so that the child can teach himself new words! As a task becomes more familiar a young child will often be able to comment on what he can do. The question

> *How did you know it was …?*

invites the child to examine his own behaviour after he has successfully carried out some operation in his reading.

   This should not be a common practice. Asking the child to tell you what he is thinking or how he is problem-solving is *a demand that interferes with reading* and should be used sparingly. It is legitimate when the teacher needs more information to help her understand what is happening. But it can readily become an impediment to developing fast, fluent reading.

   The ultimate need is for fast, automatic responses to words and phrases, and if you ask the child to talk about how he is thinking or acting this slows up the in-the-head solving. It interferes with the fast responding that is essential for fluent reading.

The reader must build towards a self-extending system

Teachers aim to produce independent readers whose reading and writing improve whenever they read and write. Each statement below could be applied to either reading or writing.

   Children become more independent:

- if early behaviours are appropriate, secure, fast and habituated.
- if children learn to *monitor* their own reading and writing.
- if they *search* for several kinds of information in word sequences, in longer stretches of meaning, and in letter sequences.
- if they *discover* new things for themselves.
- if they *check* that one kind of information fits with other available information.
- if they *repeat* themselves as if to confirm what they have read or written.
- if they *correct* themselves, taking the initiative for making all the information they find fit the word they decide upon.
- if they *solve* new words through their own strategic activity.

By some intricate process of connecting up and integrating the elaborate networks of several strategic activities children increase their speed of processing.

Beyond these simple operations

As the child reaches out to more complex texts and writes longer and more involved stories these operations must be used with increasing speed and fluency:

- on longer stretches of meaning
- on increasingly complex syntax
- on less predictable texts
- on new vocabulary.

The competent reader drives forward through an interesting text making speedy responses. Using what he has learned already he solves new challenges on the run and extends his own competencies.

The teacher's prompts and questions are critical

What is the teacher's purpose in the questions she uses when she prompts? Her prompts have many different purposes.

Sometimes the teacher invites the child to think about meaning:

Where do you think the bear lives? (target word: cave)

At other times the prompt may be to check something:

Perhaps it was sleeping in the …

Another kind of leading question may point the reader towards letter-sound or sound-letter relationships that he already knows like:

What sounds can you see in that word?
Get your mouth ready for the first sound.
Say it slowly like you do when you write.

Yet another prompt may be intended to encourage the child to solve the word by analogy using a word he already knows. This is sometimes difficult, and 'cave' is an example of such difficulty. (The obvious high-frequency pattern is 'have' which is a match in spelling but not in sounds.) Some difficulties with teaching children to search for analogies are discussed in section 13.

If the child has a bias towards the use of language information, the teacher's prompts will need to be directed to a strong locating response, or to print detail:

Try that again with your finger.

She may get the child to confirm a prompt by attending to initial and final letters firstly in the spoken word and then in the written word.

The words the teacher uses when prompting are important. Is she asking for monitoring of what the child has done, or is she asking the child to search for more information? And is she calling for the child to work on his own,

10

independently, or is she directing him to a particular type of information (meaning, structure or print-based visual information)? The box that follows summarises an article for teachers by Schwartz (2005).

A teacher prompting for independent monitoring might say
> *Were you right?*

But for independent searching further she might say
> *What can you try?*

A teacher prompting for monitoring meaning might say
> *Does that make sense?*

But for searching further she might say
> *Try that again and think what would make sense.*

A teacher prompting for monitoring structure might say
> *Can we say it that way?*

But a teacher prompting for further searching might say
> *Try that again and think what might sound right.*

A teacher prompting for monitoring visual information might say
> *Does that look right?*

But a teacher prompting for further visual search might say
> *Try that again and get ready to say the first sound.*[42]

An advantage of the one-to-one teaching situation

There is a particular opportunity for revision and reworking in the one-to-one teaching situation. Child and teacher talk about reading and writing as it occurs. There is opportunity for the child to initiate dialogue about his response as he works and for the teacher to help in many different ways. However, Reading Recovery sets the highest value on independent responding, and this must involve the risks of being wrong. Children should gain some measure of independence on their tasks at each book level, even novice readers.

The goal of teaching is to assist the child to construct effective networks in his brain for linking up all the strategic activity that will be needed to work on texts, not merely to accumulate items of knowledge. It is necessary to develop self-correcting by allowing room for self-correcting to be initiated by the child. A teacher who allowed only for correct responding would not be allowing the child to learn self-correcting behaviours.

Any theoretical position that includes self-monitoring and self-correcting as significant behaviours in reading or in writing implies the existence of near misses, approximations, responses not corrected and sometimes corrected responses. The important thing about the self-corrections is that the child initiates them because he sees that something is wrong and calls up his own resources for working on a solution. This is one kind of critical literacy!

Occasionally we will ask a child 'How did you know?' just to check on what it is he is doing to problem-solve his difficulties. Be careful not to do too much of this. That analysis is not something that a good reader does.

A psychologist can describe many psychological processes that we use as we read and write such as:

- using visual processes
- using motor processes
- controlling over direction
- using letters to make up words
- using words to make up messages
- coding our speech into print
- forming habits
- using expectations about what can happen
- deciding what is the same, similar or different
- monitoring how everything is 'coming together'
- searching for additional information
- integrating the acceptable input.

To state this briefly, the child is processing information about the code, picking it up from the page, working on it, putting it together with other things he knows, and making a decision.

Reading Recovery procedures have been questioned because they appear to require correct responding from children. What they provide is a misty window on the perceptual and cognitive working of the brains of young readers and writers who are tussling with the complexity of messages. Teachers are trying to interact appropriately with that processing.

Further reading:
Changing Futures: The influence of Reading Recovery in the United States by Schmitt et al. has a chapter on one-to-one teaching.

10

A bridge to be built

Much of this section has been about making the child constructive. This constructive activity must be tentative and flexible, open to change; for the child's understanding of the written code will change almost daily in the first two years of school. Teachers can help children who are reading to construct solutions using visual, structural, semantic, story information and real-world information. They must search for response alternatives, switching tack, evaluating choices and monitoring the integration of all these things.

Two emphases in this section have been constructing and integrating (pulling together). Those two concepts are found in the constructive-integration theory of how competent adults read and understand text. There is a large literature of theory and research about this, derived from many years of investigation around the theories of Kintsch.[43, 44]

I think that the theory that is developing in early intervention research (and in particular, in Reading Recovery) may one day be aligned with the processes being described by researchers like Kintsch who study mature readers. Experienced Reading Recovery professionals will pick up many echoes of the work they do on the effective processing of young children in the following description from a paper by Arocha and Patel.[45] (The terms are carefully defined in the report and this text has been slightly modified.) Those researchers studied adult readers and concluded that:

> each cycle of construction-integration roughly corresponds to the processing of a clause or a sentence … The construction process is composed of several sub-processes:
>
> - getting information from the text about concepts and propositions;
> - elaborating these concepts and propositions by finding related concepts in one's mental knowledge base;
> - inferring additional concepts;
> - and assigning strength values to relevant propositions while discarding irrelevant propositions.[46]

Reading Recovery professionals will recognise that they capture in their records of children's reading, observations of primitive and as yet unreliable 'processes in formation' that might provide evidence to test such a theory of processing.

That is why the subtitle of this section is 'A bridge to be built'. The good news is that the research on text processing of older readers provides us with a better sense of the direction along which our theory building might move in the future.

On the other hand that quote from Arocha and Patel makes me think that being able to tell a story or retell a story is probably a giant leap forward for prospective beginning readers!

Almost …

While teaching Katie I had really stressed three things she should do while reading: make sure it makes sense, that it sounds right, and that it looks right. One day I asked her to tell me the three things she needed to remember when reading.

She replied, 'I need to be sure it looks right, sounds right, and thinks right!'

---

11 Linking sound sequences to letter sequences: massive practice in text reading

Introduction

This section does not contain any specific teaching procedures. It is an exploration of one of the benefits of massive involvement in text reading. It builds our knowledge of what to expect. It explains in part why we can read so fast. The reader builds up massive experience with letter sequences.

Teachers talk about letter-sound relationships. Some teachers might say 'This child does not know his sounds.' What they mean is that he cannot look at a letter and tell the teacher what sound it might represent.

- Part of this learning is that the symbol (or form of the letter) must be recognised by the brain as something the eyes have seen before.

- Another part of this learning is that although a visual symbol or pattern is recognised (I have seen this before!) it is hard for the brain to isolate the specific sound or phoneme from a pattern or cluster of sounds (that is, it is not heard clearly).

- It could be that the child says 'I know that letter; it is in Sally's name' making a reference to the look of the 'S'. He also knows the wall frieze picture of a snake has something to do with the sound 's-s-s'. But there may be no two-way pathway in the brain yet that links the 's' he is looking at with the /s/ he can hear.

So three quick questions would be:

1 *Is the child aware of the visual form and its features?*
2 *Can the child hear the sound in the spoken word?*
3 *Has the child linked these two things?*

The Reading Recovery lesson is designed

- to work with what the eyes recognise in visual forms (letters) and in visual patterns of letters (clusters and words),

- and to work with what the ears can isolate in speech patterns (hearing words within utterances and phonemes within words, and clusters of phonemes in words).

The learner has to link a visual form with a phoneme (sound) in order to 'learn' a letter-sound relationship. The hardest-to-teach children struggle to distinguish letter forms that they see, one from another, and to distinguish sounds that they hear, one from another, and to link the two. When the links have been made they have to be used at high speed. Information coming in from the eyes (when reading) meets up with oral language information that was learned through the ears. In literacy learning brains become fluent and fast at sending information in both directions as we read and write.

When every letter of the alphabet, both lower or upper case, is recognised as distinct from every other, and one or more common letter-sound relationships are known for each symbol, then the learner's brain sends single-letter messages backwards and forwards across the neural network in millisecond flashes.

Only a few languages (codes) have consistent one-letter one-sound relationships.[47] In English the consonants are fairly consistent and regular but the vowels are not. In most languages there will be some letters that can

11

represent more than one sound; in English there are many exceptions to the single relationship rule.

It does not take young readers of English long to 'know' in some way that

- two letters can make one sound — 'ch', 'sh', 'll', 'dd';

- or that one letter (for example 'a') can carry a heavy load of alternative sound associations ('a' represents a different sound when it stands alone, is read in 'hat' and 'hate', or 'saw' and 'was', or 'bath').

Sounds often change when they occur in the company of other sounds to make it easier for us to pronounce them at speed as we speak. It might be the preceding or the following sound that forces a slight change in pronunciation. Think also about how much the vowels change in multisyllabic words like 'nation' and 'national'. *Knowing things like that should make teachers very cautious about asking young children 'What sound does this letter make?'*

Children who need help in an early intervention programme typically show greater variability than the children who succeed in classrooms. So Reading Recovery teachers can expect to encounter unusual difficulties of many kinds among the children they teach when they are learning to distinguish the letter forms they see, and the sounds in words they speak.

How words are constructed

All the words in an English dictionary can be constructed by varying the number and order of 26 letters. Some preschool children begin to play with this idea. They use the few letters they know to make up imaginary spellings of words. They will tell you what their made-up words say (see the example of dolls' names on p. 22).

The beginning reader comes to control vital concepts concerning how the oral code he speaks can be recorded as a visual code in his reading book.

- There is a required order to the letters in a word.
  (Learning to recognise and write 'my name' helps here.)

- 'The first letter' is determined by its left-end position.

- The letters link 'in some vague way' to the way we speak.

- Although we are barely aware of it our brains compute (for any language) something about the probabilities with which letters might follow in a sequence or pattern of letters, and which letters would almost never follow.

Through classroom activities and early intervention lessons a child is introduced to different ways of

- constructing a new word out of letters when he is writing
- or working out a new word never heard or seen before in his reading book.[48]

What is a letter? What is a word?

Some children are puzzled by the relationship of letters to words (and these children fail items 21 and 22 in my *Concepts About Print* book). That relationship becomes more obvious to the child as he constructs words in writing and breaks up words at the magnetic board. Teacher talk during writing might help the child to understand the letter-sound relationship, but teacher talk can also confuse children.

Reading Recovery includes a deliberate manipulative break-up of words using magnetic letters early in the lesson series to allow the teacher to observe the child's progress, and to work on any confusions about how words work.

By constructing words in writing and problem-solving words while reading the child comes to expect words to fall into patterns of letters. The learner's brain takes aboard regularity easily if it experiences it day after day. Yet the reader and writer of English will have to be ready for lots of irregularity. He will discover things that seem to contradict each other.

The child builds a vocabulary of words he can read, and a vocabulary of words he can write. (These two vocabularies do not necessarily contain the same words. It is interesting to discuss why this could happen.) The Reading Recovery teacher should know the contents of both vocabularies. The child learns to work with words, their parts, and their variants. This contributes to a general awareness of how to work with words (see Appendix, pp. 214–16, for John's story) and to the understanding that words are made up of certain letters in a fixed order.

Reading and writing both represent oral language written down. They are as close as two hands, the left hand assisting the right hand and both able to work together.

- The child must learn to work actively at constructing words in writing and analysing the make-up of words while reading.

- *The teacher must make clear to the child that what he already knows in writing can be of use to him in reading and vice versa.* Encourage the learner to use what he knows from both reading and writing to understand how words work. This will build up two-way pathways.

If you make the child construct lists …

In much literacy teaching it looks as if we were trying to get the child to produce long lists of rhyming words so that he can say to himself '*If I can write "at" then I can write other words like "at": "cat", "bat", "hat", "mat", "pat", "rat".*' That party trick is not something you need to do often in real life. What the child does need to do is to say:

> *If I know 'hat' I might be able to get to 'sat'.*
> *Is that how it goes? 'Fat' is like 'hat' too.*

11

The second option is more useful for solving new words in reading or recording new words in writing. Children do not benefit directly from making long word-family lists. The child has to know how to cut and paste to solve new words or write new words.

Sound sequences and letter sequences

Whenever a child reads a piece of text aloud he is coordinating sound sequences with letter sequences. Thousands and thousands of these opportunities are built up in classroom activities. Every correct reading or writing of a word is yet another successful coordination of sound sequence with letter sequence. Think of a high-frequency word like 'and'. How many successful encounters does it take to 'know' the word?

The skilled reader achieves an exact coordination between what his eyes are attending to and what he is saying. (More precisely that should read 'what his eyes have just been attending to and what he is now saying', because his eyes will have moved along the line to pick up the next set of visual information.)

There are many sources of information in text that can help the reader to 'read' a new word at the first encounter. However, sometimes the child will need to do some extensive solving work at the word level to discover what the new word is. There are of course two distinct kinds of new words:

- those you have used or heard other people use for which you have some kind of 'sound' image in your brain,

- and those different and difficult words that you have never heard before. In the latter case you have to learn the sound pattern, and the visual pattern, and what it refers to.

If the beginning reader has had few incentives or limited opportunities to talk to people in his preschool years then many of the words he encounters in his reading books could fall into that second group. Teachers must be alert to the newness of the vocabulary items and of the newness of the grammatical structures in which they occur.

In earlier sections ideas were introduced for helping Reading Recovery children to make

- an analysis of sounds in spoken words (auditory)
- an analysis of signs in written words (visual).

Reading Recovery teachers find children who can do the sounds but not the signs, and vice versa. They also find children who can respond to sounds and signs in separate activities but who do not seem to link one with the other very easily. The children know many things about hearing, seeing and making letters but can become confused about how to use what they know.

This is NOT a simple problem of what theorists, researchers and teachers call 'phonics'. This is a difficult task of coordinating two complex sets of operations:

- sound sequence analysis
- and visual letter sequence analysis.

Reading Recovery professionals know from their work with hearing and recording sounds in words (see section 7) that some children find hearing the sound sequence in words particularly hard. *They should make the same assumption about seeing the components in the visual pattern of squiggles that make up a word in print.* In addition to that, for some children breaking the word up from left to right has not yet become important.

The three activities suggested below have proved useful for developing flexibility.

> Text: My mother likes me.
> C: *(reading)* My Mother
>   cooks me.
>   *(He says to the teacher)* I
>   don't know that word.
> T   Yes, you do. Write it.
> C: *(writes li— and says)* Oh!
>   'likes.'

- Analyse the sounds of a word you need to write. These will be words he has spoken or heard, composed for writing his messages. This learning is addressed in Hearing and Recording Sounds in Words.

- Then begin to attend to the order of sounds within words while you are reading them.

- Eventually link the analysis of letters and letter clusters in a word you scan from left to right, to the word you are hearing 'in your head' (from beginning to end).

The challenges will change as the child becomes more competent. The brain is very clever at building up a sense of what can happen and what cannot. It is like my computer. Sometimes I hit the key for a drop-down menu and it gives me only one alternative. That is because for the last ten times I used this menu I always went to that one instruction. (This idea raises a caution: consider what is happening when you allow the child's first response to be an error or a confusion, and then let him repeat it 20 times over the next few weeks!)

To produce brains that activate several alternatives *we need to provide learning opportunities that develop a large menu to choose from.* We do not want the brain to specialise in learning one response for each symbol. Why? Because English is not like that. It is more important that the beginning reader adopt a different stance: 'It might be this, or it could be that.'

In the first years of literacy learning the learner builds up a tacit knowledge that letters are likely to occur in certain sequences in English. They also understand quite well that a letter or a cluster may represent one or two sounds. That knowledge is acquired by reading quantities of print that does not distort the naturally occurring frequencies of the English language. (In many early reading books in the past these frequencies have been manipulated in a number of ways.)

11

The children who need early intervention lessons need extra help to make these links. At first they are not as good as other children at judging what is likely to happen in language. Fortunately, once their teacher has helped them become more successful on a small early vocabulary they begin to contribute their own examples to the limited number of examples that teachers have time to work with.

In the lesson records of what children say and do you will capture evidence of children's own attempts to solve these problems. They begin to make better estimates of what a word might be. They are not just guessing. *They are computing the likelihood of the features that they recognise belonging to the word they have predicted.*

In many classrooms around the world while teachers have been teaching 'phonics' children have probably been learning something even more useful. They have been constructing the complex associations between sound sequences and letter sequences that enable us to become fluent readers of three categories of words in English:

1   those with sound sequences that can be predicted from the letters ('jump', 'left', 'went')

2   those with alternate letter-sound correspondences, because there may be two or more ways of saying the same spelling pattern (for example, the child might say 'Is it "ow" in "owl", or "ow" in "slow"?')

3   those that are better described as orthographic or spelling sequences than sound sequences ('the', 'these', 'they').

There are some tricky words of this kind which children might not need to read during their series of Reading Recovery lessons, words in which the letter sequences are misleading if one tries to relate them to sounds ('know', 'write', 'break', 'cough'). By the end of the intervention children should know that they might encounter tricky words and that they need to ask someone about them.

We glibly say 'Their learning accelerates.' Their brains are working out things you have not yet taught them! When the child can move easily from sounds to letters or from letters to sounds (single sounds or clustered sounds) it is easy for the teacher to prompt him. Knowing what the child controls she can say,

- *Does that sound right to you?*
- *Check to see if what you read looks right.*
- *Check it! Does it look right and sound right?*

In other words she is saying 'Coordinate these two things, you clever little person.'

We help children to be able to do that every time they read texts or write a message. There are no specific Reading Recovery procedures for fostering this. Opportunities to go well beyond the production of a single letter-sound relationship and to use chunks or clusters or patterns of letters occur across the whole Reading Recovery lesson.

Teachers must be quick-witted and linguistically sensitive when they select items for the child to work on. When one teacher chose to work on 'big', 'dig', 'pig' she did not leave the child much hope of finding another example among 'fig', 'gig' or 'wig'. The child suggested, hopefully, 'mig?'

However, another teacher more thoughtfully chose 'and', 'hand', 'sand' and the child went to 'stand' successfully, and might have got to 'band'. Prompt towards words you think the child will be familiar with.

Use the known vocabulary of the child's reading books and his own writing for any study of words, letter-sound relationships, and sound/letter clusters. It is the nature of language (and how the brain uses language) that if you help the child to move easily around his secure knowledge he will become able to venture beyond his known repertoire and link novel experiences to the body of knowledge that he 'owns'.

We have known for a long time that learning to write about 40 rather different words provides the child with enough 'generative power' to build a much larger writing vocabulary. It is possible to think of ways in which new reading vocabulary can be generated from the variety of words the child already controls. (For further discussion see section 13.)

12 Taking words apart while reading

Introduction

Teachers told me that they found it difficult to see how taking words apart in isolation at the magnetic board was related to what might happen while reading a book or while writing a message.

In the 1993 version of the procedures no more than one or two minutes were scheduled for 'Making words in isolation' (although teachers made it last very much longer than that!). In this book of revised teaching procedures look for clarification of taking words apart in several places:

- after familiar book reading (but only if necessary)
- when the child is breaking up words at the magnetic board
- when the child is taking words apart in isolation or in writing
- during the preparatory work on the new book
- and after the reading of the new book.

Most theorists assume that the brain is working on several levels as we read and write. If required you can deliberately give your attention to any level in this hierarchy:

> to a feature of a letter,
> or to the letter level,
> or to the cluster or letter sequence level,
> or to the word level,
> or to the phrase level,
> or to the sentence level,
> or to the gist of the passage.

Theorists often focus on one or two of those levels rather than all of them when explaining what 'reading' is.

In Reading Recovery most word work occurs on continuous text, using the particular child's known vocabulary as the reference point. When the learner has massive opportunities to read and write continuous texts successfully he will be operating effectively on all the levels listed above.

Effective processing on all levels also occurs when the child is *writing* down the messages that he composed orally. He learns to do an efficient sound-to-letter analysis as he writes. Every word he writes is recorded letter by letter in his message. For writing then, the child constructs a language sequence when he tells you something, he physically constructs it as writing, he reconstructs the message at the word level as a puzzle, and then reconstructs it very fluently as he rereads the cut-up story.

When the child is *reading* he does something similar. Now he is trying to reconstruct the author's text. The 'constructing' he does in both reading and writing involves letters and the ways in which they 'stand for' sounds and form spelling patterns, but it also involves constructing phrases, sentences and whole passages of language. The word 'construct' is used frequently in a Reading Recovery explanation of what the child is learning to pull together.

In the earlier section on 'breaking words apart' (pp. 19–20, 42–45) there is a sequence of learning that teachers should keep in mind. It could help a teacher to follow the child's progress as he learns to take words apart while reading.

1 Breaking words apart was easy learning, because the child was given the constructed word and had only to break it up.

2 The learner who is very familiar with 'breaking words apart' *in more than one way* is very likely to show this competence during reading and will 'take words apart in reading'.

3 Studying 'words in isolation', comparing and contrasting similarities and differences, *is a final stage of control over the hierarchy of skills, not a first step.*

Most schemes for teaching word analysis begin with the assumption that the teacher needs an instructional sequence. Those schemes describe a curriculum arrived at by some logical order of things, derived from an adult view of the task. Some adults have analysed features of the language in detail and have decided on a delivery scheme — a sequence of instruction. It is rare for the writers of the curriculum to have done a complementary analysis of *what tasks and sequences facilitate the ways in which five- and six-year-olds learn.* For example, learning the alphabet from 'a' to 'z' is not the most facilitating order in which to present the letter-learning task. Things like 'need to use' or 'the frequency of occurrence' might provide more logical sequences. Yet an all too common practice is to refer to this body of instruction as teaching 'a letter a week starting with "a" and ending with "z"'. (How convenient — 52 letters and 52 weeks! But ...)

In Reading Recovery procedures we have assumed that the goal of tutoring the low achievers is to achieve *the most rapid acceleration possible for the child.* And the child must move faster than his classroom peers in order to catch up with them. This 'catching up' requires attention to several things.

- The child's skills should determine the sequence. Prescriptions waste time if they take the child through steps he has already mastered.

- The word segments attended to should be those used by good readers at this level of learning to read and not contrived texts that produce strange sentences dictated by an analysis of descriptive linguistics.

- The sequence should be determined by psychological rather than logical factors.

Following these assumptions and referring to research on early reading it has been found that:

- initial letters can usually be the starting points for a child's detailed analysis of words, although final letters do capture a child's attention (the spaces between words make the first and last letters easier to see),

- inflections added to words are easy to recognise,

- an early achievement must be to work left to right across a word,

- consonants are quite easy to deal with, although sometimes hard when clustered,

- it is easy to discriminate 'the' from 'hippopotamus' and not necessarily easy to discriminate 'the' from 'her',

- even easy-to-hear vowels are somewhat difficult,

- and there are some very hard-to-hear consonants and some rather hard vowel patterns to be learned.

12

That list is not a teaching sequence. For a particular child my description may not hold true. So my list should not guide the expectations of a particular teacher. On the average something like that occurs.

Accomplished readers probably read in chunks (even when they are noticing every letter). When it seems to work they move out of a letter-by-letter gear for analysis of words and attach sounds to a group of letters (rather than each letter). As the good reader gets better and faster at what he can do he is probably attending to a group of letters within words. *A left-to-right scanning through a word is critical in reading because letter order matters.* When writing the learner is forced to work letter by letter.

The aim is to have the child bring what he knows to bear on his attempts to read. In the short time span of a lesson series in Reading Recovery we cannot teach any formal analysis of English orthography and its sound equivalents. However,

- *we teach letters,*
- *we develop phonemic awareness daily in writing,*
- *we attend to the sounds of individual letters (especially when they are hard-to-hear sounds),*
- *we encourage flexible use of letter-sound relationships*
- *and we celebrate the use of sequences of letters as chunks.*

We cannot afford to waste precious moments teaching the child things he already knows and can work with.

Think about this example of a competent child in his first year at school, picking his way through the analysis of words, just because it's interesting! John's progress was exceptional. When he entered school he was part of a research study and was given, among other assessments, a readiness test.[49] He scored almost as low as a child could get (at the low end of the lowest quartile), and he came from a home that was not particularly interested in schooling. It is only possible to guess why, subsequently, he made such good progress. Nine months after entry to school John became fascinated by the code. He was interested in words and their possibilities and was actively comparing aloud what he saw with what he remembered, noting features and categorising words, commenting on what did and did not fit together. His was not a prescriptive sequence derived from what adults know.

The class teacher did not teach John to do any of these things but perhaps an older sibling did! He understood that the same spelling sequence could have two sound patterns, he understood contractions, and proper name conventions. He was a successful reader and a successful analyser of words. Regularities and rule-bound features alongside alternatives and exceptions did not bother him. He was aware of much more than letter-sound relationships! He was five years and nine months old, and he had made his way into the top reading group. I recommend the discussion of John's early progress to teacher training groups.

Look!
If you cover up 'painting' you get 'paint'.
If you cover up 'shed' you get 'she'.
If you cover 'o' in 'No' you don't get anything.
'I've' is like 'drive' but it's 'have'.
That looks like 'Will' but it's 'William'.

> *Further reading:*
> Read more about John in the Appendix, pp. 214–16.

Only a few children like John are able to make it quite clear what they are attending to. Teachers must be careful observers. The child may be attending to only one letter, or only one feature of a letter like the cross on the 't' and his teacher may mistakenly think he is paying attention to the whole word, or a cluster of letters.

The teacher will usually select words for 'taking apart' from the child's reading books or written messages, bearing in mind that she is aiming to expand on the repertoire he has already stored among 'his known letters' and 'his known words'. If she is helping him with something quite new then she must participate in the 'taking apart' in some way supplementing what he can bring to the solving.

Reading Recovery procedures

Take words apart only when necessary

Word work must become integral to reading and writing continuous texts. It provides the reader of all ages with ways of accessing new vocabulary.

The suggestions in this section might be used at any time in any lesson, and throughout the series of lessons.

- Teach a relevant distinction when it is important for a particular child to make that distinction (and not as a matter of routine).
- Keep a note of it and arrange for it to recur!
- Look for several opportunities to revisit the word in familiar reading in the next few days.
- Keep it on a refresh list to be revisited when appropriate.
- Link today's analysis into tomorrow's word work (or vice versa if this seems reasonable and appropriate).
- As an optional extra create a brief 'words in isolation' time later in the lesson series and use it occasionally for rehearsal and making links.
- Think about how *this* child is settling the new word into the thesaurus of words he knows, visually, phonologically, and linguistically.

Draw attention to first letters

Demonstrate clearly when you are drawing attention to the first letter of a word. Remember, the novice reader does not really understand where the first letter is in a page of print until his directional and one-to-one pointing behaviours are faultless. In fact there is a first letter on the page, at the beginning of every sentence, and every word. Names with capital letters and first words in a sentence

12

stand out clearly to you but not necessarily to the child who knows only 15–20 letters!

- Compare some capital/lower case pairs quite early if it helps.

    Going / going   Is / is   And / and   Here / here

- Pair some familiar words that begin with the same sound: Molly, mother; Harry, here.
- Recognise when you are asking the child to go from seeing the first letter to saying the first sound.
- Recognise how complex it is when you ask the child to anticipate the next (spoken) word, and anticipate the first sound, and look for the first letter. The teacher might also say

    What could you check? or *How could I check that?*

- Move on to drawing attention to going beyond the initial letter(s) to distinguish confusing words:

    and / am   this / the   Andrew / Ann

When he is problem-solving it may help to take the child back to something he has worked on successfully recently in writing or while working with magnetic letters, if that provides a clear, easy, memorable example.

Final letters, signs, and inflections

Draw attention to final letters. Just at the beginning you can use the colour of magnetic letters if that helps to catch his attention. On the other hand be cautious. You can interrupt the learning of systematic left-to-right scanning of words.

- The final 's' in plurals ('trees'), possessives ('lizard's'), verbs ('jumps') is a linguistic feature used very often.
- The absence of 's' is also a good checkpoint.
- Final letters in pairs of short similar words like 'it', 'in'; 'his', 'him'; 'but', 'bun', 'bus' allows you to point out how that final letter changes the word.
- Attend to punctuation like full stops and questions, and (later on) exclamations and direct speech. The pauses are welcome because they give the reader breathing space.

Think about what is happening in writing at this time

The child has to discover the significant features in a word that will allow him to distinguish it from other possible words in his experience. The work he does while writing his story for the day can help him to discover significant features that he will come to use in his reading.

When a child can write a word letter by letter, slowly but correctly, give him more opportunities to do it again, do it quickly, and do it in another place. Use the writing work page. Teachers forget to build up this speed of response. The emphasis here is on

- paying close attention to scanning all the details of words,
- respecting letter order,
- working on the pattern of details quickly,
- and recognising those details as a pattern in different contexts.

Prepare for sometimes hearing chunks of information: hearing the breaks between groups of letters or words

As opportunities arise with multisyllabic words ask the child to clap the syllables in two- and three-syllable words:

go / ing	jum / bo / jet	par / ty	land / ed
laugh / ing	mo / ther	Pe / ter	sand / wich / es

This will prepare the child for later work on visual clusters of letters.

Finding help within the word

What parts of words do children find it easy to work with? We usually think of letters as being the bits out of which words are built but in speech there are several kinds of natural breaks in words. Perhaps the child, who already speaks the language, can get help from these natural breaks in spoken language. These include

- a syllable break
- an inflection break
- prefix or suffix breaks.

The onset and rime break (between the initial consonant(s) and the rest of a single-syllable word) is not signalled by a pause as in

> When the first grade reader came to the word 'landed' in a story, he appealed to his teacher for help as he did not know the word.
>
> T: What do you already know about that word?
>
> C: 'And', oh, 'land', no, 'landed'.
>
> The following day he was reading a different book. He encountered the word 'sandwiches'.
>
> C: There it is again! 'S-and-wiches!'
>
> He had learned an important generative principle — that he can use what he knows about known words and known word parts to solve new words.

tr-ain   s-ent   sp-ent   cr-ash   spr-ing

and that makes it harder to learn.

One way to think of the final cluster in these words is that it makes up the rhyme in poetry and nursery jingles and songs, but the linguist's term is 'rime'. It is quite easy for speakers of English to divide a word at the onset and rime break.

We should keep all these types of breaks in mind as we prompt children to take words apart in some useful ways.

Competent readers (above text levels 20–25) use many different ways of breaking to solve new words (Kaye, 2002). That is the outcome we must aim for.

12

Taking words apart while reading continuous text

The goal of all forms of word analysis for the reader is to be able to take words apart, on the run, while reading

- unexpected known words,
- partially familiar words still being learned
- and new, unknown words.

This section focuses on some things that will help the reader to do these things without slowing the reading down too much.

All word work is easier if the teacher supplies all the material (letters, written words) that is needed for the solving.

When you want the reader to think about adding, or subtracting, or substituting letters when he is problem-solving in reading you may need to quickly point to or write the word on which he is focusing.

An example of fostering the use of letter clusters

The child reads the word 'joking' and stops.

T: *(prompting)* What does it start with?
C: J.
T: Can you say more than that?
C: Jo. k — joke.
T: Is the end of 'joke' right?
C: ing — joking.
T: Yes. You found two parts to that word, 'jok' and 'ing'. We could look at other words like that — taking, jumping. *(Wisely she doesn't and they continue the reading.)* Let's go on with the story.

Helpful ways to prompt attention to visual features

The visual analysis of words in text can be encouraged by the teacher's questions as the child reads text.

- After success in word solving.

  Say *'How did you know it said "was"?'*

  The child does not need to know the answer, but the teacher probably does.

- When the child stops at a new word, prompt him to 'look'.

  Say *'Do you know a word that **starts** with those letters?'*

  Or *'**Look** for something that would help you.'*

  Or *'What can you **see** that might help?'*

  Or *'Do you know a word that **looks** like that?'*

  Or *'What can you **hear** that might help?'*

The teacher is prompting the reader to look for known features and to search for what he already knows.

A scale of help while reading: move down the list from least help to most help

- Let the child solve the word.
- Prompt to the word beginning (initial letter, onset, cluster) or to the ending (inflection or rime or to any known part).
- The child divides the word with his finger on print or uses a card to mask it in some way.

- The teacher articulates the part clearly (a hearing prompt) and the child locates the part.
- The teacher divides the word in print with finger or masking card.
- The teacher constructs part of the word making it larger in some 'grand manner'. (Use gestures, a whiteboard or magnetic letters.)

However, a teacher usually makes more than one move when helping a child.

Taking words apart after reading books

A little work on taking words apart may follow the reading of a book.

Adding   It seems to be easy for the child if you ask him to add something to a known word. Adding inflections to the end of words he knows might teach the child the important concept that words are built up by adding letters.

book / books	look / looks / looking / looked
go / going	play / plays / playing / played

Adding letters in front is probably harder.

is / his	and / sand
am / Sam	way / away

Subtracting   Taking letters away from a word in a deliberate way is part of 'breaking words' discussed earlier. Teach the child how to delete or subtract word parts on words he already knows. It is quite easy if you know the word.

Substituting initial consonants   Thinking about substitutions at the front end of the word is not as easy as thinking about the rhymed ending. It is hard if there are two or three consonants in the onset. Approach this carefully as you help a child read his book. Start with a one-consonant onset like 'see' before moving to a two-consonant onset like 'tree'.

see	way	duck
tree	play	truck

Using a word you know to solve a new word

The next sections deal with using the child's ability to relate something he knows to something new. This will be unhelpful if it does not *start with what the child knows*. Teachers need to think hard about a child's substitutions in order to work out what the child is attending to.

- Often the child is jumping to false conclusions, grouping together things that do not in fact belong together.
- Sometimes the child is forming a habit of looking for particular details, and in fact this will turn out to be a problem later when he is reading more extended texts. For example, if the child, early in his programme, is saying 'is' for 'said' or 'as' for 'this' it could be that he is attending to the 's' without regard to other letters present or the order of letters.

12

Later in his programme a child may give

do not / down
no / now
me / came
out / shout

and it seems as if he could be looking for little words in big words, ignoring many important things about the order of letters in words.

It is risky to try to teach children to use analogy unless you are watching carefully. Look for evidence of what they are actually attending to, and what they are concluding from your demonstrations. Watch carefully how they themselves analyse or construct, before you intervene with 'teaching'.

Easy words

These are the words that the child learned in the first few weeks of his lesson series and uses confidently.

Text: He's way too big for me.
         (That is unexpected language.)
C: He's would too big for me.
T: You know a word that looks like that.
         (She pulls out magnetic letters for 'play'.)
         If I put a 'w' what does it become?
C: Way. He's way too big for me.

Here is an example of a longer interaction.[50]
T: You said, 'I will to my friend, the car driver.'
         Does this word look like will?
C: No.
T: What letters would you expect to see if the word was 'will'?
C: W, L.
T: What letters do you see?
C: W, A, V, E.
T: Look at the picture. What is the boy doing? What is the car driver doing?
C: They are waving to each other.
T: What do you think that word could be?
C: Wave.
T: Does the word look right?
C: The letters make 'wave'.
T: I like the way you figured that out.

Words of medium difficulty

You should start with known words that contain a useful cluster of letters. The child should already have shown some sense of letter clusters. It does not matter if this is not a unit that a linguist would recognise like onset, rime, syllable or inflection. A child might sometimes use a cluster that has no linguistic validity. Subsequent experience with the English language should sort this out.

Tasks can be used with two known words that rhyme using the same spelling patterns in the rhyme. A competent child might comment on the similarity of 'come' and 'some' or 'pink' and 'think'.

Working out new words using a partial analogy (maybe from two known words)

As children become more competent at reading you sometimes see them doing this for themselves. They use two words they know to get to a new word. For example, the 'st' from 'stop' and the 'ay' from 'play' can be used to get to 'stay'.

Children need little explanation of the task, just demonstration. It is as if they are already doing something a bit like this in their heads. So, using two words the child already knows,

the teacher quickly writes 'stop' and the child reads it;
the teachers writes 'play'   and the child reads it;
the teacher writes 'stay'   and the child reads it.

Use the onset of the first word and rime of the second word to make the third word. If the teacher is introducing the child to this idea she chooses two words the child knows well to get to a third word. The teacher has given the child all the information he needs to work with (that is, he does not have to call up anything on his own). Competent readers often work this way.

Harder word analysis

It is harder for the child to work with consonants and rhymes when more letters are involved, and also when the spelling pattern does not have a direct letter-sound correspondence. These are traditionally called the spelling pattern word families. They are usually words that do not follow the most common rules of letter-sound relationships; and they can be grouped together but are exceptional rather than regular.

all	mother	light
tall	brother	night

Some things to avoid

Avoid words that children are unlikely to encounter.   The task is to learn on everyday word-solving. Examples of how to do these things are best taken from words the child clearly does know.

Avoid hard tasks.   For example, it is hard to interchange two first letters to make two new words. A task like this would be *unhelpful and unnecessary* but I have seen a teacher use it as a 'game'.

way	sent	(swap initial letters)	say	went

The different tasks outlined above

- can all be made easy by having the teacher supply all the letters or words the child needs to work with,

- and they can be increased in difficulty by having the child supply some or all of the letters or words.

If the teacher takes too big a step in 'taking words apart while reading' the child will end up taking a chance and will not have learned how to apply what he knows about words to the problem-solving. It is very easy to confuse Reading Recovery children.

12

Some examples of 'best practice'

Peter Johnston discusses a Reading Recovery interaction in his book for teachers called *Choice Words*.

> First the teacher did not tell the student anything. Second, the teacher systematically socialized the student's attention to different warrants (evidence and authority) for knowledge and the importance of noticing any conflicts among perceptions and information sources. Third,

although the figuring out was collaborative with the teacher playing the primary role, her final comment, 'I like the way you figured that out,' attributed the accomplishment entirely to the student. This final step offers the student a retrospective narrative about the event in which she stars as the successful protagonist, a collaborative fantasy that makes it possible for the child to become more than herself.

And this was his evaluation:

> Talk is a central tool of their trade. With it teachers mediate children's activity and experience, and help them make sense of learning, literacy, life and themselves.

The teacher has to scaffold a child's learning so that the child can problem-solve with increasing independence on tasks that increase in difficulty. The teacher supports the child's solving of problems.

Further reading:

Rodgers, E. (2000). Language Matters: When is a scaffold really a scaffold? National Reading Conference Yearbook, 49, p. 89.

Johnston, P.H. (2004). *Choice Words: How our language affects children's learning*. Portland, Maine: Stenhouse Publishing.

Cautions

When I read transcripts of Reading Recovery interactions, I notice that teachers often do too much 'supporting'. If the child does not know or is confused, by all means provide support of the kind the teacher gave in the 'wave' example on p. 134. Make sure your point has been taken. Reinforce the achievement briefly. Hopefully the child has learned a little more about how to solve a problem. Do not extend the interrogation unnecessarily.

Make your interactions brief and to the point! Do not use up valuable text-reading time for word analysis and repetitive practice. Just interact to get the problem solved. If the child solved the problem then the child's brain already knows it solved it! Avoid unnecessary disruption of the teaching.

Engage in only as much 'taking words apart while reading' as is needed to foster helpful visual analyses of words in continuous texts. *Talk about words the child knows, or is working on; not only the 'new' words.* Do not bring in words that have no bearing on this child's current needs for reading this text or texts like this.

Do not do it because it might help in the future; only because it is needed at this time in his learning. And preferably find your comparisons in the texts currently being read.

Very occasionally the teacher might construct a comparison word quickly as a demonstration for the child, but not if that activity makes it hard for the child to remember the story so far. Preferably this work would be planned for in another section of the lesson.

Recent research (Kaye, 2002) has shown that during the Grade 2 year in Texas schools a sample of average and above readers used an amazing range of flexible and diverse ways of problem-solving texts. Almost anything you could think of was tried. Good readers did not limit themselves to a narrow range of ways to solve challenges in their reading. Kaye found that her children did not sound words letter by letter, but rather cluster by cluster. Sounding out phonemes was not a strategic activity that good readers spontaneously used to become better readers. Apparently their complex neurological networks operate on word-solving in diverse ways that almost defy description. And they were excellent readers.

Encourage flexibility in thinking about letters and letter groups within words.

Keep this in mind

Children discover regularities. In their speech they make the irregular regular, as in 'breaked' and 'eated', and 'broked' and 'ated'. We hear plural errors like 'mans', 'foots', 'tooths' and 'mouses'. In English there is an obligatory 's' ending on the third person singular verb ('I come,' 'you come' but 'she comes') but three common verbs do *not* take the obligatory 's' — 'have', 'do' and 'to be'. You can hear children applying the general rule to all three exceptions:

> *He just haves a cold.*
> *She doos what her mother tells her.*
> *No, she bes bad, then she bes good, okay?*

We hear young children struggling with comparatives and superlatives, saying 'specialer' and 'powerfullest', and perhaps you have had to pause over the construction of an odd superlative. The behaviour appears to be governed by an implicit learning of some rules.

Children's speech errors make engaging anecdotes in poetry, novels, television features, and websites for parents. But we may have a lot more to learn about such errors. Steven Pinker discussed how children's errors may help us to untangle one of the thickest knots in the science of nature and nurture.

> When a child says it *bleeded* and it *singed*, the fingerprints of learning are all over the sentence. Every bit of every word has been learned, including the past-tense suffix —ed. The very existence of the error comes from a process of learning that is as yet incomplete: the mastery of the irregular forms *bled* and *sang*.

Further reading:
Pinker, S. (2000). *Words and Rules*, chapter 7, 'Kids say the darndest things', pp. 210–34.

12

His argument is not about how to get the child to inflect words correctly. His theoretical argument is more important than that. He claims that human brains, including preschoolers' brains, work in two ways with language.

1   One way is to work on patterns. When you hear or see an irregular word capture it and store it with similar patterns (p. 135). That is, for special instances of irregularity the brain creates special categories.

2   The second way to work on language is to store the regular examples together and simply make a rule to cover that regularity. There is great economy in this. The speaker can apply the new rule to a wide range of words or sentences and then find a place for the new rule in his evolving grammatical system. The speaker can use the rule when a new example turns up and does not have to remember all the individual items.

Pinker suggests that the brain constructs regular forms from rules, and uses memory for the irregular forms. Irregular forms are relics of linguistic history. They were originally generated by rules but the rules died long ago.

The human brain might be thought of as fiendishly generating rules and probabilities in counter-espionage against all those educators who are busily driving towards segregated component skills for three separated curriculum subjects: speaking, reading and writing. It is probably fortunate that the human brain integrates our fractionated teaching. You do not have to direct little brains to handle the regularities of language, just point up the recurrence of 'an old friend'.

If the child is being schooled in a second language think of the host of make-up opportunities he needs to create the rule-governed base to language that the mother-tongue child already has. What is causing the limitations of that child's progress? Does he learn slowly or is he being deprived every day of sufficient appropriate opportunities to learn those regular rules?

13 More about attending to words in isolation*

Introduction

The early intervention teacher's task is not to analyse the language in order to present it to the child. Her task is to analyse the child's learning in order to know how to shape his encounters with the language. The child should learn about constructing words and taking words apart in many places in his lessons. The aim of this work with words in isolation is to have him know about how words work and be able to use this awareness while reading texts and while writing. To be able to work on words in isolation is not enough; the reader and writer must also be able to handle those words flexibly in continuous texts.

---

* Section 13 should probably be divided into subsections by Tutors and Teacher Leaders and introduced gradually to their training and retraining classes.

Becoming constructive

When the child can recognise some words and shows flexibility with breaking words apart then some of the Letter Identification time could be used for working with a few words in isolation. Words from yesterday's successful reading and writing could be used. This will help to settle what is new amongst what is old.

Involve the child in constructing a word or two drawn from familiar reading, yesterday's Running Record, or yesterday's writing section of the lesson. Watch for evidence that the child worked on a word and discovered something interesting. Things will go faster if the teacher can pick up clues from the child of what is beginning to catch his attention. If she knows she is taking the child into new territory it is best not to move too far too fast. *To construct something new* is complicated.

Once the child is ready to move beyond the 'breaking words' activities (see pp. 42–45), words can be studied in isolation at any time, anywhere — on a magnetic board or whiteboard, writing on paper, and in message writing, or on a masked page of text. *Most words studied in isolation should emerge from, or prepare for, the current work going on elsewhere in the lessons.* Teachers should keep good records of the words they have used in word work with each child. There are two forms that can be used to keep track of two vocabularies, the reading vocabulary and the writing vocabulary used for word work during lessons. (See Appendix, pp. 190 and 192.)

To achieve maximum acceleration of children's progress teachers must abandon the notion that they must first teach the child to remember words before that child will be able to read or write them. To the contrary, children will remember words because they have met them and worked on them many times.

New early intervention teachers should set aside their old practices that helped children in classrooms to learn words. Children who require early literacy interventions are unlikely to be able to follow along with many of the word-learning practices that teachers found worked well back in their classrooms.

Children's progress is limited when teachers assume responsibility for 'teaching words' before a reader encounters them. The art is to expose the child to opportunities to deal successfully with certain words so that they become familiar, and like old friends.

The brain forms its own 'rules', probably based on how often things have used the same circuits

Here is a topical example of how our brains handle links. Discuss these two messages with colleagues to uncover their complexities. I found them in my morning newspaper. Is the starting point seeing or hearing? The first message said '2 L8 4 tears' and the other said 'txt 4 lo r8s'. What does your brain do to 'read' these two messages? Did you notice any ghosts of English spellings in your head? What do '8' and '2' represent?

13

Reading Recovery procedures

Early word learning

Extended work with words in isolation may be necessary from time to time for some children, but time spent on this type of activity should be minimised. It is too detached from the way the child needs to work on continuous texts. It creates a kind of dependency that involves guessing 'what the teacher is thinking'. It emerges from a concept of storing items in memory for later use. The child's immediate task is *to discover ways to solve words in texts*.

If you need extra time to work on words in isolation squeeze in a minute or two at the magnetic board after letter work and breaking words apart have become easy.

Reading Recovery aims to help a particular child to understand:

- there are ways to break the pattern of a word into parts,
- there are ways to construct and reconstruct known words,
- and how 'breaking' helps us to find out how new words are like words he already knows.

The child does those things every day in the writing section of the lesson. Something very similar happens while he is trying to read texts. Keep that in mind. There should be links across these two activities.

To habituate left-to-right body and eye movements when working with words in isolation have the child work to your left at the magnetic board. Create your models on the right. Help the child to understand the task.

At first, when asking a child to construct a word in isolation, give him only the letters needed for the word in a jumble on the magnetic board (two-, three- or four-letter words with which the child is already familiar). A word that fascinates the child might be a good place to start. Choose simple words.

Select where in the following sequence of activities your planned interaction fits. Judge carefully from the sequence of difficulty in the following activities.

1 'Learning on words I know'

The point of this exercise is to develop the child's ability to construct known words, letter by letter, from left to right, easily. Choose two or three things from this list.

- Say the word and construct your model. Leave it there.
- Or ask him to make it and hand him the letters, first to last.
- Or ask him to mix his version up, and make it again.

The actions should be coordinated and carefully controlled.

- Say '*Look at the word*' (using the eyes).
- Or '*Run your finger under it as you say it slowly*' (coordinating left to right with beginning to end).
- Or say '*What do you hear at the beginning?*' (using the ears).

To increase the task difficulty as he becomes good at this task,

  • place the correct letters on the magnetic board, scrambled,
  • or have him find the letters from a larger group of letters,
  • or have him write the letters.

Working with known words allows the child to recall his prior experiences with how letters make up words, and how words that are taken apart, letter by letter, can be constructed again.[51] This will help him to get faster at constructing and checking.

2   To look for similarities

Comparing two words can be very useful. Where do the words come from? From his reading or writing. Only one example is given here.

> Have the child on your left. Begin with a known word, say 'go'.
> Construct the word in the workspace at the child's eye level.
> Pass him the letters one by one in order.
> Have him make a copy, below your model.
>
> > Say *'Check it with your eyes.*
> > *Move your finger under it.'*
> > Say *'Read it'* (which adds a sound component).
>
> Add a new word, 'no', to the right of your first word.
> Pass him the letters to make his copy below your model.
> Help him to scan it and read it.
> Do some comparing activities, looking and hearing.

The child should be able to construct and compare *before* you ask him to think about substitutions. Select words that he is likely to encounter in his books.

3   Learning to substitute an initial letter

Construct yesterday's two words ('go' and 'no' in this case) just above the child's workplace. He may want to refer to these models.

> At his eye level you construct another copy of 'go'.
> Demonstrate deliberately how you can take away the 'g' and put the letter 'n' in its place. Read it again.
> Leave it there.
> Pass him a 'g' and say 'Change my word back to "go".'
> Now offer him an 'n' and ask him to change it back to 'no'.
> His original models remain in view for reference.

Use this format with different and longer words he knows until changing the first letter is easy.

13

4   To compare three words in a set — changing the first letter

When the child is ready move to a harder task. Use a three-word set like 'he', 'me', 'we' or 'had', 'sad', 'Dad'. Work with the child to construct a three-word list. Either you construct the list while he watches, or do it together.

Have him read the list and leave the models for him to refer to.
Move to a clear workspace. Place 'h'. Add an 'e'.
Let him see you make the following substitutions.

I can make 'he'
and change the first letter to make 'me',
and change the first letter to make 'we'.

Jumble the letters. Pass him 'h' and 'e'.
Ask him to construct it.
Now pass him the 'm' and ask him to

   i   *change the first letter,*
   ii   *look at the new word (using his eyes),*
   iii   *and read the new word (using his ears).*

Repeat with the third example.
Work a little more on this set. Make it easy.

can	and	hop	like	run
man	hand	stop	bike	sun
ran	sand	shop		fun

This teacher tried unsuccessfully to shift a child from comparing two words to three. Talking too much, she said, 'Underneath those two words that have the same end part we can make another word. It looks the same at the end but we are going to change the first sound.' She added 'so' to the list. The child was silent.

T: Let's read them together.
C: Go, no, see.
T: *(breathes 's' and articulates 'so' very slowly)*
C and T: *(read together but child says)* Go, no, see.
T: *(removes all words and brings them back one at a time)*
C: Go, no, s.
T: *(prompts and helps her read 'so')*

The child did not get it, did she? It was not obvious to her. Perhaps 'so' was not a word she used. Analogy did not help. Discuss how she settled for 'see'.

Think ahead and prepare the child for things he might find hard. For example, if he wants to make 'glad' help him with the 'gl'. He may not know about using more than one letter. Try not to spring it on him while he is trying to work on the analogy.

At any time have him change back to the original word.

The child may be eager to produce his own example. Let him try, be helpful, make it successful, and pass him the letters in order. If his example is not a good match (perhaps after 'he,' 'me,' 'we' the child suggests 'see' or 'sea' or 'c') jump in, say 'That's good thinking but that one is a bit different' and do not use it. Don't try to explain what is wrong with his attempt. He does not need to know at this point.

A delightful example was provided by Charles who was learning how to do these switches on the 'dad', 'mad', 'sad' group. He ended up saying 'Yeah, I can do it.' And one has no doubt that he can.

Further reading:
Carol Lyons writes about Charles in *Teaching Struggling Readers*, pp. 98–99.

5   To change the onset — and retain the rime

Move away from two-letter words. Changing the onset means changing the first letter, or the cluster of first consonants, and retaining the rime or end-part of a one-syllable word. If 'back', 'pack' and 'sack' are the chosen words ask the child to hear and say the part that is the same. Quickly make that part on the board once, and say it. Pass the child an initial letter and have him place the letter while you say the word. Work through the three examples.

Gradually increase the difficulty. It is easier and less confusing

  i   to be given the letters than to find them yourself.
  ii to work on single letters for sounds before clusters.
  iii to work on initial letters and clusters before middle ones.

Too much attention to the end of words is a problem because it conflicts with the desirable left-to-right scan, but eventually it cannot be avoided.

6 *Retain the onset and change the rime*

Avoid changing final letters until you are confident that the child consistently scans left to right. Hesitancy or an occasional lapse is not a good sign. By now you should not need to prompt for left-to-right scanning through a word.

Two kinds of endings do not seem to be a problem, inflections like the plural 's' and 'ing', and the rime in words of one syllable like 'out' in 'shout' or 'at' in 'rat'.

Note any clusters of letters that this child uses in his writing. When one child noticed the 'sh' letter combination the teacher worked on this:

sh   she   shop   shout

> *Say this sound 'sh',*
> *And read this word.*
> *And this one.*

T:	*(wrote 'sh' to get the child's attention)*
C:	*(says 'sh' without prompting)*
T:	Give me a word.
C:	She.
T:	*(writes)* And this is 'shop'. And this is 'shout'.
C:	*(unprompted)* 'sh … out.' That says 'out'.

Not what the teacher was teaching but great 'word work'!

The child's response in the example, when he spontaneously broke off the 'rime' and said 'I know "out"!' provided a teaching opportunity. Build on it even if you had not planned for it.

Intermediate word learning

Get to new words by analogy with something you know

Notice, using analogy is placed late in the learning sequence. This is because it can be tricky. Suppose the teacher said, 'Do you know another word like "clever"?' and she constructed 'clever' in magnetic letters. The child could do several things.

- In his head he could analyse the sounds heard into *a sequence of phonemes* (like c-l-e-v-er).
- In his head he could analyse the visual pattern of print into *a sequence of letters* (like cl-ev-er).
- In his head he could *break off a cluster of sounds* (-ever).
- In his head he could *break off letters* (cl-).

13

- In his head he could also *pair sounds with letters* and make a judgement that 'cl' is what his teacher wants, so he suggests 'clap'.
- Or he could make a quick *search of his own oral language* and triumphantly link it to 'togever'!

The teacher was inviting the child to do something very complicated with patterns of sound and patterns of letters but she was not being specific about what he should search for.

He might start anywhere on that list of things depending on his recent memories. Yet all the teacher said was 'Do you know a word like that?'! Questions for the teacher to ask herself are:

> *What can he do?*
> *What am I trying to get him to do?*
> *How could my question have been more helpful?*

Consider this example. Suppose he knows 'can' and the teacher asks, 'What letter would we need to make "ran"?' She is actually saying:

> *Listen for a change in the sounds.*
> *What is the new sound?*
> *Find the letter (visual shape) for that sound.*
> *Put the new letter in the correct position.*

That's complicated. The teacher must be astute, giving as much or as little help as she judges this child will need right now!

Take another example. The teacher says 'Let's change "can" to "ran"' (or 'went' to 'sent', or 'look' to 'book'). Three different ways of doing this are listed — from easy to hard.

> The child might articulate the sound 'r', and let his teacher find and place the letter.
> Or he might name the substitute letter, letting her place it.
> Or he might say, locate and make the substitution himself.

Before the teacher can allow the child *to think of another word and then make the change himself*, he must be working with considerable independence. She has to prepare the ground carefully for that independence.

Reading or writing a new word by analogy from one you already know is complex. The teacher's questions should target precisely what she is asking for. When developing the child's skill the teacher must be aware that she could easily confuse him.

The suggestions above are not like the 'compare and contrast strategy' I have read about in recent research and advocacy reports. That is a teaching practice designed for older children and they are taught to talk about each move they are making, and what parts of words are being compared.

Younger children in early intervention can learn to do that kind of analysis at the perceptual level; they do not need to slow up the processing by talking about what they are doing. We do not need to 'teach' them a vocabulary of key words (which the 'compare and contrast' strategy recommends). Reading Recovery children can learn to work well with word analysis using the two vocabularies children are already constructing — one in their reading books and the other in their writing.

Advanced word learning

So what words do we choose? What makes it easy to learn?

In the first lessons after you have decided to do some systematic teaching of analysing words in isolation, choose words that the child already knows well. Then move into words you have heard in his own speech or those he is learning in his current reading or writing. (Words selected here should echo something from somewhere else in very recent lessons.)

- It is easy and useful to make comparisons of words that are known. *Learning how words work* could be done entirely on the words the child already knows. Do not hurry into new territory.

- Children with a good knowledge of the language like to play with onsets and 'rimes' and syllables and with a little practice they find them easy to hear. However, do not expect a child with limited language control to be able to 'play with words' or think of similar words. When you do have to provide a new word for such a child choose a common one.

These activities are about confident construction of words, and learning the trick of substituting an initial, middle or final sound or sound pattern. The substitutions can begin with single letters, and move to two or three letters. But there are two aspects to the substitution. It has something to do with sounding different, and something to do with looking different.

- It is not designed for memorising new words.
- It is not building a bank of vocabulary words.
- It is not the place to correct recurrent errors.
- It is not the place to teach letter-sound relationships.

The daily work in writing, especially in Hearing and Recording Sounds in Words, and taking words to fluency can be used to strengthen any of the above.

Teacher talk makes it hard to do this simple word work

13

Teachers underestimate how complex children find some of the things that teachers say. What is the child's task? Teachers must think hard about what they are asking children to do.

Useful questions for teachers to ask themselves are.

> Did you ask him to work with components he knew?
>
> Did you ask him to work on something he had never heard?
>
> Is he constructing something he has never seen?
>
> Is he constructing something he has never seen or heard?
>
> Is the starting point seeing or hearing?
>
> Is the outcome hearing or seeing?

Tutor your understanding of 'seeing and hearing' by asking yourself what things he has to do when you say:

> *Make another word that sounds like that.*
> *Make another word that looks like that.*
> *Make another word that starts like that.*
> *Make another word that ends with that pattern.*

What are you asking the child to attend to when you say the following?

> *Listen and say this word as I make it.*
> *Look at this word as I make it and say it.*
> *Think of a word for me to make.*
> *Tell me something about this new word*
> [which he may not have seen or heard before].

Appreciate how difficult it will be if you ask him to construct a new word he has not seen or heard.

Working with words in isolation depends for its success on how carefully the teacher matches the tasks to the child's growing competencies.

Teachers can easily confuse children. Give the child a wealth of experience with words he knows. Initial letters seem to be easier; rimes that occur frequently are often recalled. The teacher must choose very carefully so that sound clusters and spelling clusters match precisely (went/sent, look/book). Be ready to gloss over the oddities (like box/socks, cave/have).

What does the child find difficult?

Literacy learning is a continuing climb for four or five years, and there is always a new challenge ahead. It is useful to remember that at any stage in the child's progress the child may find it difficult

- to bring sound (already in his spoken vocabulary) to a new letter sequence,
- to construct the letter sequence (visual) for a new 'reading' word, already in his spoken vocabulary,
- to listen to an unknown word (auditory) and try to spell it (visual form).

The young reader will take advantage of the language he speaks to help him extend his writing and reading vocabularies. Eventually he will learn to add new words from his reading vocabulary to his speaking. You hear this when he mispronounces them while getting the grammar and meaning correct.

The teacher should be helpful. She is the one who knows about language and literacy; she should be supplying the learner with new information. She should be helping the child to make links between what he knows in reading and what he knows in writing. She should be fostering links between what he can hear and what he can see, what he can write and what he can read. The processes of making the links across what is known will in due course become processes that he dares to apply to new words on his own. *But the teacher must provide the child with new language he does not yet use.*

Link new words to words he knows

The novice reader is able to ask himself, 'Do I know a word that sounds like this one?' or 'Do I know a word that looks like this one?' Those questions ask for two different things. Be sure you know which one you are expecting the child to attend to.

- If he chooses a suitable analogy and solves the new word the teacher can praise him for how well he solved the problem. His brain may then have the two items stored together forming a new group.

- If he makes a wrong assumption about a word (for example he pronounces wash and mash as a rhyming pair) the teacher can say '*Well, it might have worked like that but this word says …*' giving him the correct sound sequence for the letter sequence so that this encounter does not clutter up the rules his brain is building.

Have the child think of words that are harder

The child's control is increasing so the teacher asks the child to bring more to the activity. The teacher should quickly edit the choices and prompt

- from the child's spoken vocabulary,
- from the child's recent reading or writing experience,
- from the simple,
- from the regular,
- from the same spelling,
- from the easy examples.

Most challenging

You can challenge the reader and writer who has become quite competent with even harder tasks. Stop giving him the letters or words that will get him to the new word. Ask the child to supply the analogous words 'out of his head'. By this time the teacher will have abandoned magnetic letters and will be asking the child to write the word.

13

An important shift is made when the child applies the process of breaking and constructing words to words he thinks of by himself. He provides the examples but, supporting his initiative, the teacher supplies the new information he needs and makes good judgements about what he is now ready to learn.

The child could begin to think that all words will fit into common spelling sequences. This, of course, is not how English words work so he must make discoveries about alternatives and exceptions.

Working with exceptions to common rules

The child will encounter clusters that can be pronounced in more than one way. For these exceptional groups I can tolerate the word 'families', but it is a strange word! Three or four examples belong to the same 'rime' family. Another group with the same spelling may have a different pronunciation. One spelling pattern may have alternative pronunciations. Perhaps all the letters are not sounded. A child who is already familiar with both 'come' and 'home' can appreciate that if it is not like 'come' then it might be like 'home'.

come	some	home
hear	near	bear

I rarely hear a child quarrel with the idea that there can be exceptions.

A gradient of difficulty for 'words in isolation'

As the child's competence increases the teacher moves through a sequence something like this.

Breaking words apart

- Supply the full word as a model and have the child break it.
- Break the same word in more than one way.
- Break two words in the same way (for example onset and rime).

Constructing words

- Supply the full word model or all the letters needed.
- Change the onsets and retain the rime (giving attention to first letters).
- Retain the onset and change the rime (giving attention to last letters).
- Choose the words for the children (from elsewhere in the lessons).
- The child thinks of words but the teacher selects the most appropriate.
- The teacher introduces new words suitable for this child to increase his flexibility.

Introduce some irregular or exceptional spelling rimes encountered at the child's level of reading (limit to two or three examples). Use clusters like '-ight', '-tion', 'kn-' when they appear in the reading books; and a few vowel clusters; and silent 'e' and doubled letters like 'tt' and 'dd'. Remember the problems with 'y'.

Continue to explore how words work

There is no end to the permutations of breaking up or constructing words in isolation that children will have to do as they progress through school. Once the child knows how to work on words in different ways and is showing evidence of initiating several kinds of analyses in his reading and writing there should be much less need for word work in isolation. Informal discussions should continue to arise over reading texts and especially over writing texts.

Teaching a dictionary of words is not the main purpose of early learning. There are many intricacies of the English language and not all of them need to be explored and discussed with the child at this time. Things that are new to him can be

- contrasted with what he already knows
- or paired with a couple of similar words
- or set out on their own as quite new, different, difficult, odd or exceptional but not ignored.

When the child gains control over working with pronounceable onsets and rimes, and spelling patterns that are not pronounced as they are spelled, he discovers some of the tricks of some English words that occur quite early in reading books like 'home' and 'come' and 'go' and 'to'. Children do not need a verbal explanation of the differences. Rather they need to be ready for the fact that 'this one is different'. It is as if many words fit with some kind of rule but there are exceptions. Language is like that!

> C: *(reads)* Mum got out her k — to knit a woolly jacket. That should be n-nitting. Is it?
> T: What do you think?
> C: It is.
>
> The child is encouraged to make a decision about an exception to 'sounding the left-hand letter first'.

Think about what you say

Some of the things that teachers teach are not consistent with the way English sounds. When teachers teach about making words plural they teach children to add an 's', but if you listen to the word 'cousins' you will hear two z sounds. If you listen carefully to yourself pronouncing

stopped   slammed   wanted

you will hear three different sounds or sound clusters at the end. One spelling pattern serves three quite different pronunciations!

So be careful when you tell children about the ways in which words are the same and different. Think about the sounds, and the spellings, and make sure teacher and child both know which parts are 'the same' and in what way!

Do not get carried away

Engage in 'words in isolation work' with magnetic letters as is needed to foster a careful analysis of words in text. Manipulating the letters when breaking up words, constructing words, substituting letters and checking the sound sequence carefully are important activities for Reading Recovery children. However,

13

extended discussion will interfere with fast processing on text once the child is ready to move beyond the basic 'breaking up words' activities.

'Working with words in isolation' occurs anywhere in a lesson when the teacher pays detailed attention in isolation to a few words that are moving into this child's repertoire. The activities refresh and repeat successful recent experience (perhaps from yesterday's words in reading or writing) and consolidate some links.

14 Phrasing in fast and fluent reading: find letter clusters in words and word clusters in sentences

Introduction

Think about the hierarchy of knowing words (see p. 46). Speed of reading will be slow if the words being read are relatively new. It takes time to work out what the word might be. Very familiar words are read 'in a flash'. What has happened is that when the child's eyes and brain attend to that particular pattern in print the brain sends vast amounts of information about that word gathered in past experience to meet up with the 'input' from the eyes. A quick decision is possible. The reader then has time to spend working on the not so familiar words. Easy books are easy because you do not have to put so much effort into solving the words and the messages.

That is why we level books, to allow for the build-up of fast responding to known vocabulary, with just enough opportunity to solve new words more slowly.

It is appropriate for beginning readers to read *new* material slowly and to focus on words. Studies show how reading gets faster as the beginner becomes a competent reader. It is also appropriate for the beginning reader to group words together whenever he is able to and as soon as this can happen. We do not want the child reading a word, pausing, reading another word, pausing, and so on.

But there is more to fast and fluent reading than just rapid action from a brain that recognises letters and words and patterns fast. We have to think about phrasing in reading. When the reading is phrased as in spoken language and the responding is quite fast, then there is a fair chance that the reader has grouped together the words that the author had meant to go together. This needs to happen if the reader is to understand the author's message. To be more technical, the reader has put several words into a grammatical phrase (or into a grammatical context). If the reader can do this easily then he attends to the letters, and the words, and the grammar 'on the run', and, as a result, he can give more attention to the messages. So perhaps you now see why learning to read in a language you do not speak well is particularly hard.

Expert readers know that there is nothing precise about phrasing. This is where being tentative and flexible pays off. How many words and which words are grouped together cannot be predicted. Two different groupings might give you two different messages; but they might also give you the same message. *What is certain is that when a person is reading continuous text, reading speed and reading fluency are linked to increasing improvements of reading test scores in older readers.*

Beginning readers read slowly. Beginning readers have many things to learn about literacy and a heavy load of new concepts, new ideas, and new language to take on board. Texts vary so much! There are different sources of information in print to learn about and new connections in the brain have to be made linking information through the eyes to information from the ears to what we already know about language and how the world is. The learner's active brain is rapidly cross-relating all this information and making decisions about it.

Sorting all these things takes time and beginning readers will tend to solve most of their texts one word at a time, one after the other, *if the teacher lets them do that*. Perhaps the rewards of understanding the message in reading exert a pressure to become a fast reader. It is the nature of the brain to move with urgency from early slow processing to fast processing on things the brain can recognise. That leaves space and time for slower processing on the things you do not know. *At no time in the Reading Recovery lesson series should the child be a slow reader of the things he knows.*

Another relevant phrase to discuss here is 'pace of progress'. 'Pace' has several meanings, all bearing on fluency. It is an established finding of research that speed of reading increases on the average as children move up through the school grades. Speed of naming letters, words and objects is now known to be related to reading success. Of course, it could well be that reading successfully enables the reader to become a fast reader! And perhaps trying to be a fast reader does not necessarily make you a successful reader!

We can all read faster on some texts than on others. How much the fast reader can read will depend on how much experience with words in different settings he gets and whether he reads when you, the teacher, are not teaching him. It seems likely that if the learner develops faster responses racing around the neural circuits in his brain this will make reading more effective.

But there is one other aspect of pace that I personally believe is emerging from studies of the Reading Recovery population. It makes a difference if you get a lesson every day and make a rapid progression up through the book levels — the pace with which your learning accelerates is somehow advantageous.

- If the child moves forward slowly, possibly missing lessons here and there, the end result is not as satisfactory as speedy progress through the book levels. It is as if the brain cells need to be involved tomorrow in what they explored today to consolidate some permanent change in their structure. This is a possible explanation.

14

It certainly seems likely that if new learning settles quickly into the network of things that are known the reader can turn his attention to more 'newness'. The pace of progress increases.

A recent review of research papers on fluency[52] concluded (guardedly) that fluency instruction generally seems to be effective although just why, the authors were unable to say. They suggested that how it affected reading was less to do with repetition and more to do with assistance from a teacher (like demonstrating and encouraging the reader to listen to himself). They concluded that there was more involved than automatic word recognition, and pointed to 'the prosodic features of language' like rhythm, expression, and perceptions of the boundaries of phrases in speech and texts. Fluency instruction is especially helpful for children in the late first and second year of school.

Further reading:
Refer to *Change Over Time*, pp. 51–52, 105, 122–24 and *Becoming Literate*, pp. 310, 333–36. An important research review is 'Fluency: A review of developmental and remedial practices', by M.R. Kuhn and S.A. Stahl, *Journal of Educational Psychology*, 2003, 95, 1, pp. 3–21.

Reading Recovery procedures

Appeal to oral language experience

Encourage the child to read familiar text quickly.

> Say '*Are you listening to yourself? Did it sound good?*'
> Say '*Can you read this quickly?*'
> Or '*Put these words all together so that it sounds like talking.*'
>   (Demonstrate)
> Or '*How would you say that?*'
> Or '*Make it sound like …*' (naming a favourite book)
> Or '*Make it sound like a story you would love to listen to.*'

And draw intonation to the child's attention (such as falling intonation at the end of a sentence or passage, or the rising intonation of the question). Especially with direct speech ask the child to read it as he would if he were talking to the character in the story. For example, '*I'll eat you up!*'

From time to time say to the child, '*Is that sounding good?*'

Demonstrate phrasing on the text

Your demonstrations must emphasise the phrasing but not lose the sense of the whole sentence or short page of text.

- Occasionally mask the text with a card or your thumb, exposing two or three words at a time, and ask the child to '*Read it all.*'

- Slide a card underneath each line (for a page or two if you wish to discourage word-by-word reading, finger pointing or voice pointing, and encourage phrasing).

- Slide a card from left to right over the text forcing the child to speed up so he processes a little more fluently without breaking down. This can encourage him to make his eyes work ahead of his voice.

- Insist that the child pause appropriately, especially at the end of a sentence, and at speech marks. Say '*Notice when you can pause or stop. Remember what this mark tells you!*'

- Have the child place his finger at the end of a line and say '*Read along to your finger*' or '*Read it all smoothly.*'

- Say '*Make your voice go down at the end of the sentence.*'

- Say '*Change your voice when you see these marks on the page.*'

For the child who is well into his lesson series and whose fluent reading is being encouraged, take his assembled cut-up story and, in an accepting way, rearrange it into the phrases you think he could use to achieve fluent reading and have him reread it in phrases.

This will provide a demonstration of what phrasing is about, on something he can and does read fluently. As he gets closer to the end of his lesson series, rearranging the parts of the sentence may be something the child can do for himself. (See Willie, p. 84.)

> | T: | Zoe, you read more like this. |
> | | 'Burton needs a bath.' |
> | | Put the words together. |
> | | Two or three words together at a time. |
> | C: | Here is *(pause)* the bathtub. |
> | T: | That's right. |
> | C: | Here is the soap. |

Select texts to facilitate fluent reading

- In the early part of the lesson series use known texts, or texts with rhythmic repetition or repeated chorus bits, or snatches of songs and poems because they carry the reader forward. For fun and fluency a few texts like that would be good in his later lessons too.

- Choose repetitive texts that can be read with exaggerated expression like *The Greedy Cat* or *Number One*.

- Read a story to the child, demonstrating fluent reading. Reread it with the child, leaving him to add the end of the sentence, fluently! This can provide support from the feel and the sound of the patterns of words and the rhythmic breaks or pauses.

- Write down a repetitive sentence or phrase from a specially selected story (like *Greedy Cat*). Have the child 'read it quickly' and return to it for several days.

> At the end of the lesson Phoenix read *Wet Grass* in a slow monotone, not attending to punctuation. The teacher had a plan. She explained speech marks and full stops, demonstrated phrasing, and gave Phoenix advice on how to read up to his finger. Phoenix responded almost instantly. During the teacher's discussion time he retired to the corner and started reading aloud using the skills he had just been taught. He was excited and read independently with new-found enthusiasm. He went back to school and told his class teacher that the person yesterday taught him how to read.

14

Fast work with letter, cluster and word recognition

Particularly in the early part of a lesson series encourage the child to engage in fast recognition in reading and fast construction of print sequences in writing, when working with things he knows about. Then try to bring new learning to the level of fast responding as quickly as possible.

In addition to these things

Fluent reading will be encouraged if the teacher

- attends to the role of oral language,
- questions so that thinking and meaning must be used,
- increases opportunities to get fast access to the visual information in print,
- arranges for plenty of practice in orchestrating complex processing on easy or instructional text levels.

Successful experience over a period of time supports fluent reading. The child is able to move up through a gradient of difficulty in texts that are superbly chosen for him to increase the complexity he can control through small steps in successful reading (see section 9, pp. 87–89).

Fluent reading has quite as much to do with rapid looking as it has to do with language.

Avoid slow reading

Word learning is a subset of reading behaviours, but some teaching leads children to think that 'reading' means 'word reading'. If the books you have to read are hard and learning is stretched across a long period of time then slow word reading can become a habit that is very hard to discard.

Are you encouraging, supporting, or forcing slow reading? Many things that teachers do in instruction reward the learner for word reading. Drill and skill exercises are usually about word reading.

Teachers must not foster slow reading, and they will need to think about these four ways that may slow things down.

1   As the child begins to match what he says with what he sees his reading should slow down until he has coordinated speech with looking at print. Then good readers speed up again. Only good observation and good judgement by the teacher will tell her when *the child should be encouraged to speed up his responding because his one-to-one matching is secure.*

Do not accept slow, staccato, word-by-word reading. When this becomes a habit it is very hard to break. As soon as control is firmly established the teacher should begin to call for flexible use of that control. *Flexibility in this context means varying the speed of reading to suit the challenges of the text.*

2   A second way to slow down young children's reading is to make them think that reading has only to do with letters, sounds, and words. Too much attention

to these levels of language will displace, in the child's mind, the idea that there are meaningful stretches of language involved. In an early intervention, with individual instruction, letter and word work should seem to the child to be used in the service of text reading or text writing. Keep the balance of attention on language and meaning in continuous text.

3   A third way to slow up children's reading is to interrupt the reading so much with your teaching that it all sounds to the child like a string of unlinked words. The child can very easily get the impression that reading is supposed to be carried out slowly word by word, with heavy emphasis on each word, and often in a special 'reading voice'. Alternatively, *a child can learn precisely this by hearing other children who read that way and matching his own behaviour to theirs.*

4   There is a fourth way to slow down young readers. If the child talks to himself about his problem-solving — say in forming a letter, or instructing himself to look at the first letter, or to 'sound the word out' — some teachers believe that self-instruction will be helpful. Such behaviour slows down the work the reader must do, like search rapidly for information and make decisions.

Another form of this occurs when teachers try to apply what we have learned about meta-cognition. Because many successful readers are able to comment on how they do their problem-solving, (see John, Appendix, pp. 214–16), some teachers have taught children with difficulties to repeat a phrase or sentence in the hope that this will guide or support their responding. I think this should occur only rarely, and it is a prop to be discarded as soon as possible.

So as a result of many influences we can have our beginning readers spitting out the words like sausages coming from a sausage-making machine, even though we try to avoid this. What can we do about it?

Saying 'Read it fast' will not do

No one can impose fluent reading on the complex task of reading continuous text any more than you can make the beginning writer a fast writer. It takes time to develop fast control of many subparts of a complex whole so that it operates smoothly and fluently. What needs to speed up can differ for different children.

Let me try a risky analogy. Suppose you were given the job of driving a vehicle with multiple gears and you really had no idea what gear changes were possible and what short-cuts could be taken. All you knew was that you had to get this vehicle going in close to top gear. It is pretty obvious that having someone alongside you urging you to speed up is not good enough, is it?

What do teachers know about what supports fluent reading? They know

- the oral language of the child is fluent, and it is phrased as language is phrased in normal conversation.

- thinking is fast and fluent, and (untutored) the brain links ideas together and groups them in memory.

14

- seeing or recognising objects is fast and fluent in ordinary life but only after we have become familiar with objects in general and some objects in particular. Recognition becomes faster as visual familiarity increases.
- oral reading comes together well when it occurs on material that is just challenging enough.

To achieve a smooth integration of all the brain's processing activity the teacher will sometimes need to drop the difficulty level of text until things are working well together. Tasks should then be selected to allow for increase in difficulty level retaining the speed and fluency of the lower level readings. Check that oral language, meaning, visual information and text difficulty are all contributing to successful reading.

On higher level texts

So, when the child is reading orally at higher levels of text, what should it look and sound like? Become conscious of the various things the reader must do while reading continuous text. The reader must do several things at the same time:

- look for visual information across words,
- recognise known words fast and break new words in order to solve them,
- decide on what word it is,
- check whether it relates to what has gone before,
- and if not, shift to self-correction mode.

In fact many of these things occur in sequence. They occur so fast that it seems like 'all at the same time'. At first everything slows down. All readers have to learn to coordinate how and when the eyes should jump forward across lines of print. One-to-one matching, with or without pointing, involves rather slow movements; and so does moving the eyes across the words and lines at first. Those responses must become fast on groups of words that the reader knows and he *should slow up* on the few words that must be taken apart on an 'unseen' text. Being able to set aside pointing allows the speed of working to increase, because eye movement is very much faster than hand movement.

When the child's series of lessons ends and he is reading a text of appropriate level he should be able

> to solve a multisyllabic word (one that is new, not yet familiar, or unexpected) within continuous text without slowing up too much, and by working flexibly with word parts and clusters of letters from an awareness of how words work.

One of the possibilities built into a Reading Recovery intervention is that, while the child is reading a new book every day, and acquiring all those competencies that call for slow reading at first, *in the same lesson every day there is opportunity to do some familiar reading.* That allows for more fluent reading, faster responding and grouping familiar words together.

Word-by-word reading may sometimes be heard on new books but phrased reading may also be heard. By the middle of a lesson series the teacher can encourage phrased reading even on new material.

It would be useful for teachers to arrange a workshop for colleagues to discuss language structure and fluent reading.

Many things that influence fluency respond to appropriate instruction: prior learning of letter-sounds, words, phrase structures, oral vocabulary, speed of response and movement, familiarity with text and language usage, and an expectation of making it 'sound good' are fundamental.

4 Particular problems

The topics discussed in this section are different. All the previous teaching procedures were related to the designing of individual lessons. Teachers have to interweave the recommendations from several sections into the planning of a lesson for a particular child.

In this section brief consideration is given to several groups of children whose diverse behaviours may call for specific modifications to early intervention lessons. These are things that teachers might have to consider for some exceptional children, but not for the majority of their early intervention students. We are probably talking here about one child in ten.

Usually this section would only be relevant after the teacher has tried other procedures, after she has adjusted her teaching to the child's needs, and after she has consulted colleagues and Reading Recovery professionals for a period. *A teacher who intends to adopt any variations to typical Reading Recovery teaching, such as those recommended in this chapter, should first discuss such changes with a Tutor, Teacher Leader or Trainer. This is challenging territory and two heads will be better than one.* *

Collectively these professionals may conclude that some essential feature of reading or writing seems to be threatening the progress of a particular child and 'something extra' is needed! We must assume that teachers will have access to other professionals for discussions about such children when appropriate.

During the 12–20 weeks of early literacy intervention lessons we do not, at any time, suggest that this child is unlikely to learn to deal with the written code.

> *If the child is a struggling reader or writer the conclusion must be that we have not yet discovered the way to help him learn.*

When a child is not making accelerated progress the teacher should take a closer look at what she is doing because some important aspect of learning to deal with written language needs to receive close attention. Despite good teaching and regular attendance, and signs of responding to the teacher's efforts, something seems to be blocking the child from moving effectively to more independence and greater challenges. Invariably the child is finding some part or parts of the reading and writing process difficult. However, what that difficulty is may be buried in the complexity of the tasks, and therefore very hard to observe.

Discussion of these problems with colleagues is essential because it is one of the roles of these professionals to help the teacher to narrow her focus and

---

* My interest in exceptional children arose from my work as a special class teacher, a school psychologist and a university teacher of child psychologists from 1950 to 1990.

direct very specific attention to a particular process. Usually tutors and teachers can talk this through and find a different way to get the learning done, with the help of some of the things described in these last sections.

The intent is not to find an excuse for the lack of progress, or a label to explain the child's difficulty, or to state what was wrong with the child's past experience at home or at school. The intent is to find a way to get around the road block and re-establish accelerated learning.

Two groups

So we are talking about particular children who are not responding to the range of opportunities with which the trained Reading Recovery teacher is familiar.

Some teachers will predict quite early in the lesson series that they do not expect these children to complete their programmes. That *lowered expectation immediately produces detrimental effects*. We must keep trying. Certain transitions must be made if this child is to become literate. Often a marked change of approach is required. This child's time in Reading Recovery may be his one big opportunity for literacy learning. Do not give up on him.

In addition to those children there is another group of children to be considered, and they are children who have been *identified by other professionals (such as medical advisers or language specialists) as likely to have difficulty with literacy learning. Often a prediction has been made before the child has entered a Reading Recovery programme.* To be admitted to Reading Recovery such children should qualify on the general criteria of being in the lowest 20–30 percent of the age cohort after a period in school, and then they should be given the opportunity of up to 20 weeks of diagnostic teaching.

In the experience of Reading Recovery professionals many of these children will follow the typical path of good Reading Recovery progress. Obviously, however, that prior diagnosis by another professional will correctly identify some children who do find literacy learning particularly difficult. Such children may present an unusual profile of entry scores on the Observation Survey tasks when they enter Reading Recovery.

I am not referring here to children given a vague diagnosis like some hint of learning disability or inherited potential for becoming dyslexic if such labelling was done before the child had the opportunity of good first teaching in formal instruction.

Here are three illustrative examples.

> One little boy who had been developing normally was in an automobile accident at the age of four and a half and lost the use of his dominant right hand and arm, and had a very weak left arm. The school's Reading Recovery team asked for some direction as to which activities they should or could change in his programme.

The parents of another child were asked by a nursery school principal to seek medical advice about extreme clumsiness. The doctor told them that the child had poor ability to manipulate objects (dyspraxia, a term not used very often today) and advised some special training by an occupational therapist. The parents brought the medical report to the Reading Recovery teacher who wanted to take any possible effects of this condition into account from the beginning of her teaching.

Yet another example is provided by a group of children who had already been identified as learning disabled by persons trained to make that diagnosis of children before they have begun formal literacy instruction (described by Lyons, 1994). Reading Recovery can provide a period of diagnostic teaching which tries to have the child learn to read and write and the diagnosis will be negated or confirmed after 20 weeks of instruction.

Fortunately, there is an active research interest in variables to be considered when explaining extreme difficulty in learning to read. Two such variables are phonological awareness and speed of naming letters or objects and research on these variables has influenced some of the general teaching procedures described in earlier sections.

Phonemic awareness receives explicit attention in every Reading Recovery lesson in writing activities (where special attention is given to hearing and recording sounds in words). What is learned in writing is also used when the child is taking words apart while reading and when working with words in isolation at the magnetic board. Those procedures have been an important part of the lesson since 1976 (although critics of Reading Recovery have often missed that fact). Reading Recovery instruction must also develop a child's awareness of other phonological breaks between syllables and words that are run together in normal speech.

The speed of recognising letters and words is stressed throughout the Reading Recovery programme. If something is dealt with by the child correctly but with a slow and thoughtful response, it is necessary to speed up that processing. Ultimately, an increase in speed of processing will result in fluent reading. The emphasis and opportunity to increase speed of responding has existed since the beginning of Reading Recovery, but recent research suggests that we should increase the importance we attribute to it.

If children have low scores *in both these areas* researchers predict that the double handicap will cause extreme difficulty in learning to read. A recent doctoral research reported on the outcomes of Reading Recovery programmes for 59 pupils. By the end of their lesson series they divided into a larger group who completed their lessons series successfully and a smaller group who were predicted to need a longer period of special help. The outcomes for this smaller group varied! (See Further Reading opposite.)

- One group of children did not have low scores on either of these two tests on entry but did not respond well to Reading Recovery and could not be expected to function well in their classrooms.

- Two separate groups who did not complete the programme successfully were low in either phonemic awareness or speed of naming.

- A small group who did not complete and who made really slow progress were those who had the double disadvantage.

To have the double deficit is not good news, but a Reading Recovery teacher can address the problem with Reading Recovery lessons and will bring a majority of such children into the successful completion group.

There was also good news from this research.

- A large number of children with low scores on either phonological awareness or naming speed, or both, on entry to Reading Recovery did successfully complete the programme.

- Their performance on all measures changed significantly between entry and exit, and we have to presume that it had something to do with the activities the teachers designed for them in Reading Recovery lessons.

- They retained the good scores in a short-term follow-up study.

Teachers were able to work effectively with such children and at exit from the intervention many children no longer qualified for the label 'deficit'.

Another research study, published in 2003, reported a large-scale re-analysis of 49 independent studies of rapid naming, phonological awareness and reading and concluded that the importance of rapid naming and phonological awareness measures in accounting for reading performance has been overstated.[53] The search for better explanations continues.

Further reading:
Litt, D.G. (2003). An exploration of the double-deficit hypothesis in the Reading Recovery population, doctoral dissertation.
Lyons, C.A. (2003). *Teaching Struggling Readers*. Note especially the section 'Teaching LD and AD(H)D Students', p. 109.
Lyons, C.A. (1994). Reading Recovery and learning disability: Issues, challenges and implications, *Literacy Teaching and Learning: An international journal of literacy learning*, 1, pp. 1–42.
Jones, N., Johnson, C., Schwartz, R.M., Zalud G. (2005). Two positive outcomes of Reading Recovery: Exploring the interface between Reading Recovery and Special Education. *The Journal of Reading Recovery*, 4, 3, pp. 19–34.
Clay, M. (1987). Learning to be learning disabled. *New Zealand Journal of Edcational Studies*, 22, 2, pp. 155–73.

15 Children who know little about stories and storytelling

Introduction

I am convinced that children who have listened to stories told, and who can retell stories in their own way, with or without a book to support them, have been given something that helps them through their first steps in literacy learning. This is good news for preschool caregivers who read books to children and let them retell stories in their own words. In studies involving children who are listening to stories one can often find much discussion of the storybooks by the children.

A teller of simple stories at five or six years of age has a constructive control of oral language, will be able to compose a simple story for his writing task, and will not find it so difficult to reconstruct the author's story he is reading. I have recently heard researchers discussing the possibilities of studying these ideas. Results from the 'Tell Me' task in the New Zealand school entry tests point to a link between entry scores and subsequent progress.

> Long before Jennifer knew how to decode written language she was familiar with the activity of reading a book. Her grandmother had read her a story about a lion. Later she sat down beside her father on the front steps and said, 'I [will] read a book, Daddy.' She had a leaf in the palm of each hand, and she started 'reading' in a dramatic voice.
>
> J: A big bear *(pause)*
>   went into the woods and saw a big lion *(pause)*
>   and she chased a big lion *(pause)*
>   and she caught a big lion *(pause)*.
> F: And then what did the big bear do?
> J: Then the big bear went home to her mommy.[54]

Reading Recovery procedures

If a Reading Recovery teacher recognises that holding a storyline or anticipating where the story is going is difficult for a student (and this would include children with limited control of English) then this will be an area of learning that early lessons must develop. This particular competence is not fostered by increasing the attention and time given to letter shapes and patterns or phonology.

A Reading Recovery tutor tried (and recommends) a temporary procedure to be used for a few weeks with a small number of students near the *beginning of their lesson series*. When the new book for the day is first introduced try this variation to emphasise the importance of the 'story'.

Find readable texts. You might write down a very simple story, or make a simple book about this child's own experiences, or a simple account of something in his culture, or use an easy published text.

15

Then select one of these three ways of providing additional support. Make a careful judgement whether you need to read the new book to a particular child - once, or twice, or three times.

Once

- First, read the new book (Book 1) to the child (oral input).
- Then introduce Book 1 in the usual way.
- Then have the child read the new book.

    (Take a Running Record of Book 1 next day.)

Twice

- Do a normal book introduction for Book 1 that you read to the child yesterday.
- Then have the child read Book 1.

    (Take a Running Record of Book 1 next day.)

- Read tomorrow's new book (Book 2) to the child.

Three times

- *Share the reading of Book 2 that you read to the child yesterday.*
- Introduce Book 1 that you have both read and shared with him over the last two days.
- Then have the child read Book 1.

    (Take a Running Record on Book 1 next day.)

- Read a new book (Book 3) to the child.

The teacher must make a judgement. Does this child need to hear the story once, or twice, or three times before he tries to read it? Then she must begin to taper off the support she has offered. This slight alteration provides more input for the child at the beginning of his tuition and may facilitate progress through the first book levels up to about Level 3. (This procedure was developed in careful trials by a Reading Recovery Tutor in consultation with a Trainer.)

See also section 22 (pp. 182–83).

Further reading:

Butler, D. (1980). *Babies Need Books*, Wellington: NZCER.

Paley, V. (1981). *Wally's Stories*, Cambridge, MA.: Harvard University Press.

White, D.N. (1984). *Books Before Five*, Portsmouth, NH: Heinemann.

McNaughton, S. (1998). Tell Me, *School Entry Assessment*, Wellington: Learning Media.

16 Teaching for a sequencing problem

Introduction

Perhaps the skilled reader does not appear to attend to the details of print in a strictly left-to-right order but that is how our written code is organised and young children have to learn to do this. Most children gain this directional control within weeks of beginning formal literacy instruction.

David's problem was hard to solve because he had allowed himself to practise being flexible and approaching print in several other ways for a long period of time. The teacher's talk did not sort out David's problem. (See David's exchange with his teacher, Appendix, p. 209.)

The revised procedures for 'Learning to look at print' in this book *recommend close attention early to establishing a systematic left-to-right approach to lines of print and letters in a word*. If the problem persists then I recommend that you do not try to teach this by talking about it. (David's teacher had not learnt this!) The position of the child, sitting or standing to the left of the teacher, is important. He can watch the teacher's careful demonstrations of the left-to-right assembling of words. She can control his construction of words by passing him magnetic letters in the correct order. Left-to-right scanning must become the habit, the default position. The sooner this happens the sooner other things will fall into place. Reading may slow up as the child begins to become more thoughtful about direction. Get the new learning firmly established before you try to speed it up again.

Lapses are important: they should be dealt with. Ignoring David's problem once he has revealed it would be disastrous. By this time it is not likely to 'cure' itself!

A few children may have difficulty with this little piece of learning for quite different reasons.

- A sequencing problem may be caused by being unaware that direction is important.
- Some find it very difficult to control a steady letter-by-letter analysis by their eyes, so they adopt a haphazard approach because it is easier.
- Others could exercise the required control but they prefer a more varied approach and resist the attempt to confine their processing to a fixed habit.
- It may be related to a more general pattern of not very good motor control.

Finger-pointing behaviours may give you some clues about what the child attends to in what order. *There is no way you will be able to accurately observe where the eyes are fixating, or whether the eyes are scanning left to right, or what the brain is attending to.*

16

Hand dominance is not relevant. Whichever hand is used the directional schema requires a left-to-right sequence. It is the scanning with the eyes, and, ultimately, by the brain that must be so well learned that its default position for attending to print in English will always be from left to right.

Activities with letters and words in isolation often allow children to do what David did — approach print in a variety of ways. It is clear that most children can be flexible about identifying letters and words from all kinds of angles and still be able to regularly approach their books or any text in a standard way.

Research is pretty clear that children who are learning literacy in two languages at the same time, say English and Hebrew, can learn two different directional attacks and apply each in the correct context.

If a varied approach to scanning print goes unnoticed then the child might be habituating his attention to print daily to allow himself to practise alternatives to a left-to-right direction.

Once the child with a possible sequencing problem begins Reading Recovery lessons attend to this sequential picking up of information systematically on all word work, text reading and text writing.

If you did not pay enough attention to this during early lessons then, yes, you should have done. It will now take more time, more attention, more ingenuity, and some vigilant behaviour observation to re-establish appropriate sequencing behaviours.

Further reading:
Clay, M. (1979). *What Did I Write?* (The Directional Principles), Portsmouth, NH: Heinemann.
Clay, M. (1991*). Becoming Literate*. Auckland: Heinemann.
Lyons, C. (2003). *Teaching Struggling Readers*, Portsmouth, NH: Heinemann. Chapter 2, Attention, movement, and learning, pp. 26–42.

Reading Recovery procedures

Reread sections 1, 2 and 3 (pp. 3–20) of the procedures plus section 5 d), 'I can take words apart', p. 42, when you study this section.

Have the child sit or stand to your left.

1 Have the child suggest a word he wants to learn (or make a suggestion).

2 *Construct a word with magnetic letters on the magnetic board placing the letters deliberately from left to right. Have the child read the word.*

3 Break up the word, jumble the letters and have the child construct the word. Or pass him the letters one by one. Say 'Read it.' Encourage (motivate) several repetitions.

4   Have the child write the word(s) in his unlined book.

5   Say 'Once more, as fast as you can', controlling for correct and fluent performance without lapses.

6   Repeat these procedures often for at least six days (practising a few words that are becoming very familiar).

No matter where he starts the construction it must be from left to right. Revisit and rehearse the word when it turns up in writing or reading in the near future. Ask him to search for the word in a new context. Have it turn up in 'breaking of words into letters', or any study of words in isolation. Do not allow any scope for lapses from a strictly left-to-right approach. Over-emphasis is appropriate for a longish period until a new habit has been established.

Another opportunity to practise constructing this word, letter by letter, may occur in Hearing and Recording Sounds in Words.

> See section 7, pp. 69–80, and note the exception to a left-to-right sequence.

It is very useful to encounter this new learning again in a different context, such as the cut-up sentence.

As this learned pattern becomes very familiar on a few known words you may extend your prompting to:

What can you hear at the beginning?
What can you hear after that?

Articulate carefully letter by letter for the child. Lengthen the sound of the particular letter he is working on.

Take opportunities to show the child that the left-to-right survey applies

- to lines
- to phrases
- to words
- to small segments like syllables and endings ('jump-ing')
- or to common consonant clusters ('spl-')
- or to onset and rime clusters ('l-ook', 's-and').

The challenge is to maintain sequence despite the necessity to attend to other detail. You may be able to allow other children to be flexible and jump around, to sometimes even solve the end of the word before the middle, but do not allow this when there has been a sequencing problem or a letter-reversal problem.

Keep some masking cards handy so that you can control visual attending and correct sequencing. Use these on text as the child reads or after the child has read a page where this word occurred.

Stress the left-to-right scanning with the eyes.

17 Strong skills that block learning

Introduction

We are more likely to encounter this kind of problem in the child who had been in formal instruction before entering early intervention — at home, preschool, or school. He may have worked hard at the prior learning he brings to his Reading Recovery lessons.

Learned errors   Sometimes the child learns an error response to text reading because he repeats it again and again. (He forms a rapid neural response.) Or he writes a letter or a word incorrectly and builds up more memories of the errors than of the correct word. What seemed like a helpful approximation quickly becomes a bad habit. The problem is that the wrong response will become stronger the more frequently it occurs. It becomes a barrier to a more flexible approach to the possibilities in reading English text.

An invisible boundary exists between approximate attempts that support further learning because they are 'almost correct', and behaviour that gets in the way because in the neural circuits of the brain the wrong response comes to mind first. Tutors or Teacher Leaders need to talk with teachers about examples that could become barriers to progress. Children should not be allowed to repeatedly produce miscues in reading and writing on the same words day after day, week after week, because they are consolidating records in their brains that are very difficult to erase.

Old error patterns obstruct the development of new skills. A child's teacher should be concerned about the ease with which he invents words without thinking. Discuss with colleagues examples of children who are making very poor progress in the classroom and who make these practised errors.

Strong versus weak skills   More problematic than learned errors are the cases where the child has considerable strength in one skill (say, in oral language, or memory for stories). It is a natural response for us all to solve a problem by using our strengths in everyday life. We commonly solve problems by way of our strengths and avoid the things we find hard to do. We sometimes resist putting energy into visually scanning and searching for the exact wording of the author. This happens both consciously and unconsciously.

So if the child's Observation Survey results produce a profile of stanine scores with high peaks for some skills and low troughs for others, then the teacher must continually bear in mind that the child could be avoiding the things he knows little about or finds hard to do. And he may not be aware of this.

Some of these strong-weak contrasts occur because of individual differences in physical characteristics and personality factors. A child who finds it difficult to control his muscular system and body movements, who is not as good as most other children at using a pencil or learning to walk and jump and skip, might be fine when it comes to learning literacy, or he might have problems. This surprises teachers until they realise that the whole directional schema depends upon knowing where one's body is in space. Both scanning visually, and distinguishing the difference between two letters because of their orientation, depend on motor skill. (Think about a letter that becomes a different letter when reversed or turned upside down.) Producing writing also involves movement and spatial orientation.

So a child for whom motor coordination is difficult may avoid writing. While most children can use movement to support other learning a few are doubly disadvantaged. They cannot read and write without learning these essential movements, but their existing motor skills do not support their learning to read and write very well.

Dominated by a learned strength   Another source of difficulty occurs when something the child has learned to do helps him to survive in his day-to-day world at home or in school but gets in the way of new literacy learning. A child with a limited control of the English language is likely to place a lot of weight on visual analysis. Another child who has strong oral language skills and a brain that is eager to know more about the world may try to avoid the tedium of the careful analysis of print in reading or attention to detail in writing. And their avoidance behaviours require astute detection.

I saw a streetwise little girl with great conversational skills divert the conversation with a 'tale to tell her teacher' each time she became aware of a difficulty further along the line of print in her reading or writing. When I observed closely and saw the pattern being used again and again it helped the teacher to work around that problem.

And, sadly, it may even be true that school experiences with a particular curriculum and very strong teachers may have created strong responses that obstruct some literacy learning. The longer children have been at school the more likely it is that they will bring to their Reading Recovery lessons some imbalance of behaviours fostered by the curriculum.

Children taught by a good teacher on a published programme, for example, may sound out each letter in a word. The Reading Recovery teacher may be trying to establish a range of tentative, flexible problem-solving behaviours and encouraging self-correcting words and phrases. The segmented sounding of letters might help, but it can easily get in the way of fluent reading. Occasionally necessary, it is not a routine response used by an efficient reader.

Cognitive and emotional learning   Carol Lyons (2003, *Teaching Struggling Readers*, p. 95) provides us with some interesting examples of learning being blocked. Her writing shows us that cognitive and emotional dimensions of learning are two sides of the same coin. One depends on the other. If children are distraught, there is no interest, no motivation, no focused attention, and they will not engage in thinking and learning processes.

- Matthew's emotional response to a mistake was so strong that he had difficulty recalling previously acquired skills, which prevented him from attending to the remainder of the lesson.
- Or a child's hyperactivity or impulsiveness may lead to his attention flitting from one thing to another without paying close attention to detail.

Further reading:
Lyons, C.A. (2003). *Teaching Struggling Readers*, pp. 91–95.

In each of the above examples   When a child fails to respond to your typical teaching approaches within a few days you could do any of these things:

- become a very careful observer of what, specifically, is creating the resistance.
- think of the child's everyday environment and experience, and ask whether the behaviour you are trying to get rid of is perpetuated by some counteractivity involving parents, teachers or peers.
- plan what you will need to do to build the alternative behaviours into the child's processing system.
- review the way you prompt the child and ask yourself whether your prompts are tuned to your teaching aims.
- invite your Tutor/Teacher Leader to come and observe this pupil.

Further reading:
Take note of carefully reported case studies that you find in the literature and discuss with colleagues the conditions that occur rarely which call for some minor adaptation of a child's Reading Recovery programme. Talk about the downside of any changes that could have been made and how the changes might reduce the opportunities to learn.
O'Leary, S. (1997). *Five Kids*. Bothell, Washington: The Wright Group.
Lyons, C.A. (2003). *Teaching Struggling Readers*; check the Index of Illustrative Examples, pp. 191–92.

Reading Recovery procedures

Most of the hard-to-teach problems are unique, specific to a particular child. They will not match the particular examples I can provide. But the examples below may start you planning for a solution to the particular problem you are facing. The common approach is this. Ask yourself, how can I

- decrease the occurrence of the unwanted behaviour and
- increase the occurrence of the wanted behaviour?

Example 1   A trainer described to me the behaviour of a child who looked up and away from the text each time he came to a difficulty in his reading. Observers will often say 'The child is thinking.'

Perhaps children are mimicking thoughtful children but they cannot pick up the relevant information they need to get from print if they do this. A research study of various movements made by children learning to read described something like this as 'wandering eyes', a common occurrence in the earliest stages of reading instruction.

There could be quite a different explanation for older children continuing to do this: it may lead to getting help. A teacher or another child in the classroom may come to the rescue and supply the word. This seems to the child a 'positive way out of the problem'. Look away and it gets solved, because other people get tired of waiting.

Example 2   Another source of blocks to efficient processing are the letters or words that children have 'learned to confuse'. Two or three alternatives compete with each other every time they occur. In this case the learner is consistently teaching himself that either response will do! You must help him to learn what is okay and what is *not okay*!

Example 3   What about classroom instruction that has some strong emphases? Take the example from above of children taught to sound out words letter by letter from left to right. Competent children learn from the instruction but they also learn to give that approach away when it does not work. Or they find it more efficient to work with chunks, clusters and syllables.

A child may learn to sound out words letter by letter, and fail to move on to more varied and flexible processing. Probably the teacher does not think of this as an inefficient activity. In a repertoire of behaviours it can be justified but it blocks the path to fluent reading. Good readers are rarely heard to use this approach.

Example 4   Sometimes children focus on one kind of information in the text and ignore evidence that does not fit with the response they have chosen. There are several kinds of information in print, and the reader cannot afford to ignore any of them.

The struggling reader may be able to use one source of information at a time but he may not be able to work with three or four different kinds of things (the look, the sound associations, the structure of the sentence, and the meaning of the message). He finds it difficult to pull all the information together. We say that *the child cannot integrate information from several sources*. In Reading Recovery lessons this may be solved in the first few weeks, or it may take eight to ten weeks. During this time teachers must observe and record carefully. This is a time when the child's particular strengths are likely to establish their dominance. Something weaker might get left out. The teacher's prompts are particularly important for getting children to pull two or more pieces of information together.

We cannot prescribe specific ways of attacking each of these problems but some general principles for changing the learner's habits and misunderstandings of the task should be explored.

- As you teach anticipate what the child might do. Try to be one jump ahead of your student. Prevent the inappropriate behaviour occurring whenever possible. Watch closely for the possible appearance of the erroneous response. Interrupt it, sharply if necessary. Don't be polite about it. Don't let it occur. Control the possibility of the unwanted behaviour occurring. If the child is clearly leaning on his language strengths and not looking at the print, butt in with a demand before he utters his response.

- Penetrate an old pattern of responding by splitting it apart. You have met this before in my recommendations about confusable letters and words. Keep the letters and words that could be confused away from one another: separate them in time (don't give them the opportunity to occur one after the other), or in the same place or space. Establish a strong control of the easier response first, and, later, teach how the confusable letter or word has to be distinguished. Never teach them side by side because that is harder. (Adults find this side-by-side placement easier, so unfortunately they do what would work for them with novice readers!)

- Trick the learner into paying more attention to the problem by using exaggeration. This includes shouting, stress, elaborate acting, even singing, varying the size and colour of print, using sand-trays and whiteboards, and disappearing writing (with a wet brush) to get an important item learned, or re-learned correctly. Use any props temporarily until better responses have replaced the unwanted ones.

- Bring the hands and eyes back together into the reading, temporarily. In writing encourage large movements again before returning to more normal writing size.

- Chatting about the problem will do nothing! Slowing up is insufficient. Aim to get alternative processing established!

- Move cautiously towards fluency. At first the child may manage to control a new response by thinking about it, even talking about it. Although this makes for slow responding, it may allow him to control the old rapid, unthinking response and that can be very useful. But the teacher will also have to help the child put aside the thinking and talking responses because they make for very slow learning.

- The child should know which particular behaviour you are applauding. Confirm for the learner each occurrence of successful processing. Be very clear about how you signal right and wrong. It is okay to be negative about unwanted responses, but be 'charmingly' negative.

17

- Ask a colleague to observe your teaching. Are you unwittingly rewarding the child for the unwanted behaviour? Or are you failing to support the child when he is trying to break new ground? Is your prompting working? Are you getting the changes you are trying to bring about? What does your colleague think?

So we are talking about designing a crisp, effective little routine that goes into action every time the unwanted response looks like it might return. The teacher must be alert. That unwanted response is likely to lurk around even after the child has finished his lesson series.

18 When it is hard to hear sounds or see letters

Introduction

Refer to earlier sections on seeing letters and words, and hearing sounds and words. The text below is intended to supplement those sections.

Using the ears: if the child finds it difficult to hear sounds or if the child finds it hard to go from sounds to letters

In the 'red' example (below) the teacher provided an opportunity for the child to make a transition from hearing final sounds to hearing beginning sounds. It happens quite early for most children. However, despite such opportunities some children find that final sounds remain dominant for them. Special efforts may have to be directed to shifting attention to first-to-last sounds.

Check whether the child always knows where to look for the first letter of a word. Nothing will match unless he knows this.

Pay special attention to hearing sounds and going from sounds to letters during writing, hearing sounds in words and in the cut-up story.

Get the child to articulate slowly a word you know he can write. This will stress the sound-to-letter connections. When he can do this quite well you can get him to articulate words he does not know how to write (pushing counters into boxes if necessary for each sound he can hear). This is described in section 7.

Think about his performance on taking words apart in reading. A child may focus on letters in reading and be able to remember the sounds they make, and yet he may find it difficult to go from hearing the sounds in words to producing the letters that can represent those sounds in his writing.

T:	These letters make 'red'. It says 'red'.
C:	'Red' *(he says, looking at it).*
	I'm hearing it. I hear the 'd'.
T:	Mm 'd'. *(she gives credit for this achievement)*
C:	*(moves his finger under the end letter)*
T:	But here's where you start!
C:	*(does nothing)*
T:	What sound do we need to start with?

Using the eyes: if the child's letter knowledge is not secure and/or he finds it hard to go from letters to sounds

Find out how well the child knows his letters and also how the child breaks up words in isolation on the magnetic board. The next statement sounds obvious but it is important. If he 'knows' only half his letters then he will be able to use only half the letters in his books: the remainder will not signal anything to him.

A child may learn the sounds of letters he is writing and he may work well with word boxes and yet he may not be able to use letter-to-sound associations to help him eliminate miscues in his reading. Pay attention to this during reading. Take the same approach as recommended above. Get the child to do the letter-to-sound analysis using words he knows. When he understands how to do the task, shift to easy words he does not know.

Reading Recovery procedures

Use his own written stories

- Increase your attention to sounds from stories the child has written that have been rewritten on light cardboard and cut up (section 8). The sounds of the story are already in his head and he can use these as a guide to finding the words he has written.

- Ask the child to clap syllables. Show him how you can cut a word into two syllable parts. Then get him to remake the story.

Work on his reading book

- When the child comes to a problem word in the text, sound the initial letter for him to help him to anticipate what the next word might be. (Check: does the child move from left to right consistently?)

  Then transfer this sounding task to him by getting him to attend to the first letter(s) and to get his mouth ready to say it (them). The aim is to make him more conscious of a strategy that will help him to eliminate words that fit the context but not the first-letter cues.

- If he has mastered sound-to-letter analysis but does not independently attempt some analysis of simple words in text, write them letter by letter for him (or construct them with magnetic letters), or reread the text for him up to that point and get him to articulate the accumulating letters until the word that would fit the context comes into his head —

  s   sp   spl — ash!

Make this activity more explicit

Check on some words he read accurately with questions like

How did you know?
Were you right?

During text reading this invites the child to examine his own behaviour after he has successfully applied the necessary operations to his reading. Here is an example.

> The child read 'from' as 'for' in a sentence and corrected himself.
> The teacher asked 'Is it "from"?'
>
> The child replied 'It starts with "f".'
> The teacher said 'So does "for".'
> The child said 'It ends with "m".'

It is legitimate to encourage a child to verbalise these operations from time to time when you need to check on what he is doing. BUT verbalising can be overworked, and it can lead to slowing up the reading so we do not get the fast responding that is required for fluency.

We work with a child's strengths but we must remember to strengthen the processes he finds difficult by returning to some practice with 'seeing' or 'hearing' from time to time.

19 When it is hard to remember

Introduction

Turn back to page 102 and reread Dr Larry Squire's advice.

The teacher is trying to help the child develop a range of strategic options that allow him to go in search of alternative responses from which he will select an appropriate one. It is about decision-making on a complex task. It is more than just recalling something that the teacher forced him to attend to.

Some children have particular difficulty with calling up an association or a label for a word, or a name for a letter or the names for story characters. I refer here to children who have difficulty with recall on most occasions, not merely a temporary lapse. Poor recall must be overcome; otherwise linking the earliest, easiest and most basic learning of oral language with print will be very difficult for this child. And a poor foundation for later learning will be laid.

Make an early check on your teaching. Do your introductions to new words allow the child to use something which is already very familiar to him? Notice how helpful it is, if the child is very familiar with his own name in several forms — written, spoken, shortened, abbreviated! It is much easier to learn about the unknown from the very well known.

> *Further reading:*
> Lyons, C.A. (2003). *Teaching Struggling Readers*, chapter 4, 'Emotion, memory and learning', pp. 58–74, and in chapter 7 look at 'Developing strategies for remembering', pp. 104–5 and the account of Alex's learning 'the' on p. 106.

Reading Recovery procedures

Do not aim to train memory in general. Work on items that are essential for a next step in literacy learning. The preliminary step is to capture the attention of the child's brain! What it has attended to (and acted upon) is what that brain is likely to remember.

Involve several modes of learning

Create learning opportunities that involve looking, hearing, saying, manipulating, moving, changing colour, changing pens and pencils, changing textures, changing surfaces (horizontal and vertical), changing books, and so on. The more senses you involve on the tough-to-remember problem the more chance you will hit the jackpot and catch the brain's attention. So watch carefully. When you get that attention remember how it happened, and try that approach next time.

Use the child's association (not what helps you)

When Paul knew very few letters he had no difficulty with recognising, sounding and naming the letter 'O' because he knew what an oboe was, and that was his particular association. For him that was easy; for another child it would have been impossible.

Mark had trouble with 'G'. After several weeks his teacher found an appropriate meaningful association that triggered the letter name. By calling part of the symbol a saddle she taught Mark to say *'A saddle for the gee-gee [horse]'* — not the best link for most children but it worked for Mark.

Arrange for repetition

Increase the opportunities to recall, that is, to use strategies for remembering, on a few very important items. Practise recall on known items.

Arrange for over-learning

This refers to the practice we continue to have after something has been learned. We continue to practise as an insurance against forgetting. Continue to provide opportunities for further practice long after the labels or names seem to have been learned.

Use games

Sometimes a game like Snap (pairing matching cards) is useful for providing practice, attention to detail, and the expectation that one has to remember. Do not move too far away from what has to be learned because the child may not then make the connection.

Revise

As a matter of routine go back and check on old difficulties. You may think the memory must have been established by repetition but it may also have been short-lived. Check more rigorously than you would with most Reading Recovery children.

19

Teach for flexibility

- Use different responses like singing, shouting, or role-playing suitable actions, as for oboe, or gee-gee (but when the learning is stable do away with the props).
- Use different things such as magnetic letters, chalk, felt-tip pens, paint, cards, toys, sand-tray — anything for variety.
- Find the items to be remembered in many different locations; experience them at different times.

Extend the known set, selecting items which are unquestionably examples of what you are teaching and avoiding any which are questionable.

Have several cards of all the letters and words that the child recognises plus the ones that are half-known plus one or two that have just been taught. Run through these, making 'your pile' and 'my pile' of the known and not known words.

Games in general have little value, but designed specifically for a particular child and used for a brief period of time they may help to increase the items that a child remembers. For example, the teacher makes several cards of each of the words that the child knows with upper- and lower-case first letters. The game is to form pairs by asking your partner if he has a word that you have in your hand.

> *Do you have 'go'?*
> *Yes* (he hands 'go' to the teacher) or
> *No* (the teacher picks one from the centre pile).

Develop a way of studying words

A child may have some reading skill but may show little skill in accumulating new words or profiting from instruction given only the day before. It is as if he cannot 'hold' the experience and store it for future use.

Help the child to develop a consistent approach to remembering words. Adapt it to suit the strengths and weaknesses of each child. Explore several ways of 'inputting'. Find out which ways suit this particular child. What helps him?

- Ask the child to look at the word written on the board or with magnetic letters or in large print. The teacher can say it slowly and run her finger under it.
- Ask the child to say it slowly and/or run his finger across it.
- Ask him to close his eyes and see it, 'the first bit and the next bit' because we do not usually visualise all the parts of a word at the same time.
- Ask him to look again, scanning it without help, and saying it in parts. (Perhaps he does not search the letter outlines or the letter sequences with his eyes. This could take you back to a left-to-right scanning problem.)

- Ask him to write the word, or parts of it, without copying it. (Do not be too strict on this point for young children.) Have him say it slowly as he writes it.

Now present the word again in a different place but call for exactly the same correct response that the child gave you in the first setting.

Practise word reconstruction

- Make the word out of magnetic letters. Get him to break it. Remake it one or two times then ask him to do the remaking. Move him to fluency on this.
- Write the word on the board in large print. Demonstrate how you can use verbal instructions to yourself as you write each letter.

Introduce tracing; it will probably help, temporarily

If visual analysis and word reconstruction do not produce good results, introduce tracing and add the feel of the movements to the child's sources of information.

- Ask the child to trace the word with finger contact saying the part of the word as he traces it. Finger contact is important.
- Find other places to use the finger to explore the shape — in a sand-tray, on magnetic letters, use see-through tracing paper just for the novelty.
- Repeat this process as often as is necessary until the child can write the word without looking at the copy.
- Write the word on scrap paper as often as is needed to reach fluency.

Other activities

- Encourage the child to include the word in his written story.
- Choose books that include the new word.
- Establish fluency with a vocabulary of known words.

A way of remembering

When a child has used these rather laborious strategies for establishing his early visual memories for a small vocabulary of words or list of letters he usually arrives at the stage where he can take short-cuts. An early researcher of reading difficulties, Grace Fernald, directed attention to this shift.

> … one of the most interesting things to be found in our non-reading cases was that the child, who had to trace each word many times at first, eventually developed the ability to glance over the words of four and five syllables, say them once or twice as he looked at them and then write them without a copy.

> *Further reading:*
> Fernald, G.M. (1943), *Remedial Techniques in Basic School Subjects*, pp. 21 ff.

The child is then able to learn from the printed word by merely looking at it and saying it to himself before he writes it. He may use one of several strategies — silent articulation, visual scanning, or some other aid.

> Dale was certain about his visual memory for some words. The teacher said, '*Have a look at "come", a really good look, and then write it down there.*' Dale replied, '*I don't have to look.*' He covered his eyes and wrote the word. But his final comment was interesting. He said, '*Then you aren't looking and your eyes help you.*'

From his comment we can tell that Dale is able to monitor something about how he learns.

Relating new words to old

If something is completely novel it requires a great deal of effort to learn about it. If we can relate the new item to something we already know it is easier to master. Expanding out from a known procedure will be easier than learning a novel procedure.

To make the child an independent reader the teacher must encourage him to search for links between new words and words he already knows.

Word making and breaking activities help to build such habits of search. Questioning during book reading can also foster a search for relationships.

20 Children diagnosed with different problems

Introduction

As a preventive intervention Reading Recovery does not discriminate when selecting children for extra help. A prior classification or diagnosis of emotional problems, learning disability, attention deficits or double deficit problems would not exclude them from selection for a period of diagnostic teaching. If they are in the lowest 20 percent of the age cohort who entered school with them, then the first step in a sequence of help is to work with them to try to develop a reading and writing process that could help them to work in ordinary classrooms. If this can be achieved in 12–20 weeks then the condition may have disappeared but if not, then a foundation for literacy learning may enable their participation in the classroom programme with a reduced need for specialist help for the literacy tasks of the curriculum.

That is a conclusion that maximises the educational and psychological facets of the problem: administrators may come to a different conclusion based on resource and funding issues.

I recommend that you read 'Bobby's Story' in *Teaching Struggling Readers*. Carol Lyons wrote: 'It took Bobby three times as long to develop a program of action to form and recognise letters quickly and to learn how to attend and control impulsive actions.'

I particularly like his comments when he failed to match his writing to his verbal directions to himself. Writing 'B' for 'Bobby' he said, 'Let me do it myself! Down, up and around.' The teacher asked, 'Were you going around when you said around?' 'No,' said Bobby, 'my words are too fast and this board is too slow.' Nevertheless, his programme was successful!

Children with more than one problem area

Children who have particular difficulties often have problems with two or more aspects of the literacy tasks (such as the double-deficit hypothesis described on pp. 160–61).

If children have little phonological awareness to draw on and they have low letter-naming scores how should the teacher approach her task? In this case the teacher will have to work even more thoughtfully than she would normally.

- What little knowledge does the child have that the teacher could draw upon? Watch for small increments in learning on the first steps of each of the lesson activities.

- Make sure the child is secure and that you are teaching him to solve problems using things he does know. He will not learn how to problem-solve on the new things you introduce.

- Take enough time (and I know how precious time is) to really establish rapid processing control of that first group of sounds the child can hear or the first group of letters he really knows.

Some activities we already work with in Reading Recovery lessons are designed well for children with special needs. Litt (2003) considered the following list relevant for children with low scores on the speed of naming tests.

- Rereading familiar text; three or four little books each session.

- Sorting activities with magnetic letters leading to increased speed and accuracy in letter recognition.

- Writing high-utility *words* fast until an automatic response is developed.

- Practising writing *letters* fast to develop an automatic response.

- Masking a text to reveal a target word clearly and require fast automatic response.

- Directing instruction in phrasing and grouping words together.

- Expecting fluent fast reading on readable material.

In all the above activities the teacher must remember one thing: the aim is to encourage the child to make the brain search rapidly through all its networks and make a fast but sound decision. Whenever possible avoid making the child's brain attend to unnecessary things — like teacher talk and pictures and what he did last week. Those detours do not encourage the brain to rapidly gather up the stored information it has and use it to confront the information coming in through the eyes. It may foster a thoughtful approach but not speedy perceptual recognition.

See section 15 (pp. 162–63) for 'reading to' in the case of deaf or hard-of-hearing children. And for such children another minor adaptation occurs in composing the sentences to be written. The teacher would take opportunities to shape the child's composed sentence, adding in some features of simple English grammar or structure that the deaf child does not yet use.

> *Further reading:*
> Lyons, C. (2003). *Teaching Struggling Readers.* Chapters 5, 6 and 7 are particularly helpful.

21 Children who are finding it hard to accelerate

Introduction

The patterns of progress made by children will be very different from child to child. For hundreds of children selected annually for Reading Recovery, *acceleration is an outcome of sound teaching in the first few weeks of the lesson series.* As the child gains control of the various components of the reading process the observant teacher begins to realise that a faster pace up through text difficulty levels is now possible. However, for some children and some teachers this does not seem to happen.

There is only one position to take in this case. The lesson series has not been appropriately adapted to the child's needs, whatever they were. It is time to take a close look at possible reasons for this, to back up, to return to an earlier level of competence and to teach more carefully building in whatever skills are not yet working for the child. Colleague comment and Tutor/Teacher Leader comment is what the teacher should seek.

Steps to take

Has your teaching got in the way of these children developing ways of extending their own knowledge?

Consult and work closely with your Tutor/Teacher Leader with challenging children, even in the first weeks of instruction. Notice the poor progress early. If you do not call for help early there will not be enough time in Reading Recovery for this child to become a successful reader. Start to adapt your teaching early. Rework the early basic learning. Build a secure foundation before you begin to stretch the child's pace of progress. Then there will be a much better chance that you will be able to discontinue this child.

Ideally consultation would occur after 'Roaming around the known' and not more than 10–15 lessons later.

1   *First check up on yourself as teacher*

- Have you made some assumptions about the child that could be wrong?

- Are you operating the programme as required?

- Is your programme addressing this child's strengths and weaknesses that were revealed in the Observation Survey?

- Is writing receiving attention? Or enough attention?

- Have you taught in such a way that the child has learned to depend on you and does not feel the need to take the initiative?

- Did you start the child at too high a level, assuming competence, when he was shaky at a more basic level? Were you fooled by a good talker? a bright personality? similarities with someone else you had taught? and so on.

2   *Now check up on your records of the child's progress*

- Look at the first Observation Survey, particularly at the low scores. Which parts of the programme would be difficult because of these?

- Look over your Lesson Records and describe what the succession of learning and failing to learn has been in particular areas. What have your records to say about the things that this child has found difficult?

3   *Now set about observing the child's literacy behaviour very closely*

- Ask yourself questions about why he might be finding parts of the task difficult.

Take stock of what you have found in these three areas. Reread the appropriate parts of your supporting texts, using the index. Then talk out your problems with some Reading Recovery colleagues.

- You may decide that you have to work out some new ways of getting the child to do the 'reading work' in the areas in which he is opting out. Use all your ingenuity. Ask others to watch you and the child at work and check out what is happening.

In general, when the child is hard to accelerate he is finding some part or parts of the reading process difficult. Ask yourself, which parts? Often he has learned to do something that is interfering with his progress, and he may have learned it from the way you have been teaching.

Another reason for the child finding it hard is that some important aspect of the reading process has not received attention; it has been left out of the construction of the reading process.

For most children, whatever the problem, it is wise to drop the level of text difficulty, as a first step. This seems in conflict with the aim to accelerate the child. However, it is the child who accelerates, and in one sense the teacher merely matches the texts to the child's rate of acceleration. So, returning to an easier text level, the child will need to orchestrate the whole process in a more satisfactory way before moving up the difficulty sequence.

Things to check are:

- your own teaching behaviour,
- your analysis of the child's difficulties,
- new explanations that might apply,
- the intactness of the reading process on easier material,
- whether the child's writing behaviour is improving.

You are likely to have some blind spots in these areas, and the opinions of colleagues could be most useful for the readjustment of your programme. It has been one of the values of the professional development training sessions that teachers have been able to pool their collective wisdom on their most puzzling students.

Further reading:
Lyons, C. (2003*). Teaching Struggling Readers*, chapters 6 and 7.

---

22 Children aged five to nine schooled in another language, who need to make accelerated progress in English

Introduction

It has been the practice in Reading Recovery to take into the programme the lowest achievers in reading and writing in the first or second year at school.

A speaker of another language recommended for Reading Recovery in a school where early literacy instruction is in English is subjected to only one rationale for exclusion — the child is unable to understand the teacher's instructions on the Observation Survey tasks. If they follow the instructions and attempt the tasks, even though they fail most of the items, a series of lessons can be designed for that individual child.

At the conclusion of the lesson series the child is still in need of rich opportunities for further development in the language of instruction. His exposure to English vocabulary and grammar has been limited, and many of the concepts he encounters in his classroom reading will be unfamiliar. However, after a series of Reading Recovery lessons the child then has three complementary routes to that further language learning, via oral language, writing and reading.

Longitudinal research results from the United States, England and New Zealand are consistent in their findings. The children's success rates compared favourably with those of the total population involved in this intervention, and they achieved scores within the average range of a cohort of their peers, and they did this within the normal time available to Reading Recovery students.

In a few instances schools set up Reading Recovery programmes mainly to serve new immigrant children during a period of transition into a new country. They have used Reading Recovery with those children at the lower age or class levels when an accelerated rate of learning would facilitate adjustment to the child's new school. In special cases it is also appropriate to work with older children aged seven to nine if they need foundational instruction in English reading or writing.

Some critics have recommended that children who were learning English as a second language should be excluded from Reading Recovery. This is contrary to practice in five countries where we monitor the progress of those children on a daily basis while they are in Reading Recovery. This group of children derives benefit in subsequent years from having had this supplement early.

Language was the major block to their learning and in Reading Recovery they were given 30 minutes every day with a teacher who increased the time they spent talking, who personalised their instruction, and who also taught them to read and write. This gave them access to two new routes to language expansion.

Read section 15 (pp. 162–63) and note the discussion of reading the texts to some children as a first step towards them reading those texts for themselves. This should be a teaching practice used sparingly, but it is obviously sensible to use it for, say, a hard-of-hearing or deaf child or for the earliest stages of learning English.

22

Further reading:

All these articles are in *Literacy, Teaching and Learning*, Vol. 2 (2), pp. 21–39; Vol. 4 (2), pp. 81–107; Vol. 5, (1), pp. 29–42. (See References pp. 221–24.)

Hobsbaum, A. (1997). Reading Recovery in England.

Neal, J.C. and Kelly, P.R. (1999). The success of Reading Recovery for English language learners and Descubriendo La Lectura for bilingual students in California.

Ashdown, J. and Simic, O. (2000). Is early literacy intervention effective for English language learners?: Evidence from Reading Recovery.

Appendices

Appendix 1

CALCULATION AND CONVERSION TABLES

Box 1

Count the Running Words
150

Box 1: Count the words in the text, omitting titles.
Box 2: Count the errors, and enter the Error Ratio.
Box 3: Use the conversion table to find the Accuracy Rate.
Box 4: Work out the Self-correction Ratio.

Here is one way to think about self-corrections. There were 15 errors in the 150 running words of text and the 5 self-corrections represent an extra 5 potential errors. Altogether the child made 5 self-corrections in 20 chances to self-correct.

Box 2

Ratio of Errors to Running Words

$$\frac{Errors}{Running\ Words}$$

$$\frac{15}{150}$$

1 : 10

One in ten

Conversion Table

Error Ratio	Percent Accuracy	
1:200	99.5	
1:100	99	
1:50	98	
1:35	97	
1:25	96	Good opportunities for teachers to observe children's processing of texts
1:20	95	
1:17	94	
1:14	93	
1:12.5	92	
1:11.75	91	
1:10	90	
1:9	89	
1:8	87.5	
1:7	85.5	The reader tends to lose the support of the meaning of the text
1:6	83	
1:5	80	
1:4	75	
1:3	66	
1:2	50	

Box 3

Accuracy Rate

$$100 - \frac{E}{RW} \times \frac{100}{1}$$

$$100 - \frac{15}{150} \times \frac{100}{1}$$

$$= 90\%$$

The four boxes provide the calculations corresponding to the steps outlined above. The conversion table provides quick access to accuracy rates.

Box 4

Self-correction Ratio

$$\frac{SC}{E + SC}$$

$$\frac{5}{15 + 5}$$

1 : 4

One in four

OBSERVATION SURVEY SUMMARY SHEETS

Name: _____ Date: _____ D. of B.: _____ Age: _____ yrs _____ mths

School: _____ Recorder: _____

Text Titles		Errors Running Words	Error Ratio	Accuracy Rate	Self-correction Ratio
Easy	_____	_____	1: _____	_____ %	1: _____
Instructional	_____	_____	1: _____	_____ %	1: _____
Hard	_____	_____	1: _____	_____ %	1: _____

Directional movement _____

Analysis of Errors and Self-corrections
Information used or neglected [Meaning (M), Structure or Syntax (S), Visual (V)]

Easy _____

Instructional _____

_____

Hard _____

_____

Cross-checking on information (Note that this behaviour changes over time)

_____

How the reading sounds	Easy Instructional Hard			
			Raw Score	Stanine
Letter Identi-fication				
Concepts About Print	* Sand Stones Shoes Moon			
Word Reading	* List A List B List C Other _____ (Enter test name)			
Writing Vocabulary				
Hearing and Recording Sounds in Words	* A B C D E			
Other tasks	Writing sample Story Spelling			

* Circle whatever was used

An Analysis of the Child's Strategic Activity

Useful strategic activity on text:

Problem strategic activity on text:

Useful strategic activity with words:

Problem strategic activity with words:

Useful strategic activity with letters:

Problem strategic activity with letters:

Summary statement:

Signature: _____

WEEKLY RECORD OF KNOWN READING VOCABULARY

Name: _____

Date of Birth: _____

Initial Testing: Date:	Week: Date:	Week: Date:	Week: Date:	Week: Date:
Week: Date:	Week: Date:	Week: Date:	Week: Date:	Week: Date:

CHANGE OVER TIME IN TEXT LEVEL

Name: _____

Date of Birth: _____

Text Level	Enter examples of titles here
: :	
: :	
24	
23	
22	
21	
20	
19	
18	
17	
16	
15	
14	
13	
12	
11	
10	
9	
8	
7	
6	
5	
4	
3	
2	
1	
0	

Gradient of Text Difficulty (Teacher Devised)

Date

Weekly Observations

90% accuracy or above

below 90% accuracy

WEEKLY RECORD OF KNOWN WRITING VOCABULARY

Name: _____

Date of Birth: _____

Initial Testing: Date:	Week: Date:	Week: Date:	Week: Date:	Week: Date:
Week: Date:	Week: Date:	Week: Date:	Week: Date:	Week: Date:

CHANGE OVER TIME IN KNOWN WRITING VOCABULARY

Name: _____ Date of Birth: _____

Number of words the child can write

| 52 |
| 50 |
| 48 |
| 46 |
| 44 |
| 42 |
| 40 |
| 38 |
| 36 |
| 34 |
| 32 |
| 30 |
| 28 |
| 26 |
| 24 |
| 22 |
| 20 |
| 18 |
| 16 |
| 14 |
| 12 |
| 10 |
| 8 |
| 6 |
| 4 |
| 2 |

Weeks of instruction

First Entry

Date:

Last Entry

Date:

OBSERVATION SUMMARY FOR MULTIPLE ASSESSMENTS

Name: _____

Date of Birth: _____

School: _____

SUMMARY OF RUNNING RECORD

Text Titles	Errors / Running words	Error Ratio	Accuracy Rate	Self-correction Ratio

Initial Assessment   Date: _____

1. Easy _____   _____   1: _____   _____ %:   1: _____

2. Instructional _____   _____   1: _____   _____ %:   1: _____

3. Hard _____   _____   1: _____   _____ %:   1: _____

Reassessment   Date: _____

1. Easy _____   _____   1: _____   _____ %:   1: _____

2. Instructional _____   _____   1: _____   _____ %:   1: _____

3. Hard _____   _____   1: _____   _____ %:   1: _____

Further Assessment   Date: _____

1. Easy _____   _____   1: _____   _____ %:   1: _____

2. Instructional _____   _____   1: _____   _____ %:   1: _____

3. Hard _____   _____   1: _____   _____ %:   1: _____

ASSESSMENT	L.I.		C.A.P.		Word Reading		Other Reading	Writing Vocabulary		Hearing Sounds in Words	
	54	Stanine	24	Stanine	15	Stanine	Test Score	No.	Stanine	37	Stanine
Initial assessment Date:											
Reassessment Date:											
Further Assessment (1)											
Further Assessment (2)											

RECOMMENDATIONS (for class teacher, or for review, or further teaching, or further assessment):

RECOMMENDATIONS FOR DISCONTINUING BEFORE FINAL ASSESSMENT

Name: Date: School:

1 SETTING (Same class, new class, book level, teacher's reaction, size of group etc.)

2 SURVIVAL (Detail what behaviours will ensure coping in group instruction)

3 RUNNING RECORD ANALYSIS (Detail information used and information neglected)

4 WRITING ANALYSIS

5 COMMENTS ON IMPROVEMENTS SINCE PREVIOUS SUMMARY AND PREDICTIONS

RECOMMENDATIONS (for class teachers, or further teaching or further assessment):

Signed: _____

DAILY LESSON RECORD SHEETS

NAME: _____

DATE: _____

FAMILIAR READING	NEW TEXT	STRATEGIC ACTIVITIES ON TEXT		LETTER WORK. BREAKING, WORD WORK AND ANALYSIS
		Observed	Prompted	

over

WRITING		CUT-UP STORY, SPACE, CONCEPTS, SEQUENCE, AND PHRASING	COMMENTS ON ANY PART OF THE LESSON
MESSAGE COMPOSED	CONSTRUCTING WORDS, GAINING FLUENCY		

Appendix 2

Topics for discussion in professional development

1 Mother is baking

From *Becoming Literate: The construction of inner control*, pp. 118–19, in a section emphasising that the left-to-right serial order has to be learned.

Suppose a teacher has placed an attractive picture on the wall and has asked her pupils for a story about the picture. They offer the text 'Mother is cooking' which the teacher alters because she wants an opportunity to work with the letter and sound 'b'. She writes

> Mother said,
> 'I am baking.'

If she says 'Now look at our story', 30 percent of the new entrant pupils will attend to the picture. If she says 'Look at the words and find some you know', between 50 and 90 percent will be searching for letters. If she says 'Can you see Mother?' most will agree that they can but some will see her in the picture, some can locate 'M' and others will locate the word 'Mother'.

Perhaps the children read in unison 'Mother is …' and the teacher tries to sort this out. Pointing to 'said' she asks, 'Does this say "is"?' Half agree it does because it has 's' in it. 'What letter does it start with?' Now the teacher is really in trouble. She assumes that children know that a word is built out of letters but 50 percent of children still confuse the concepts of a word and letter after six months of instruction.

She also assumes that the children know that the left-hand letter following a space is the 'start' of a word. Often they do not. She says, 'Look at the first letter. It says s-s-s-s', and her pupils make s-noises but we cannot assume that they are all looking at the 's'.

The teacher continues. 'What do you think Mother said? Look at the next word and tell me what it says.' That should be easy because most children learn 'I' early, but for a child who does not yet know the difference between a letter and a word 'the next word' selected will often be the second letter in 'said'. For other children who have not yet established left-to-right movements with return sweep the next word may be 'gnikab' because they are returning right to left along the second line. Still others may be conscientiously striving to decode the comma or the inverted comma before they get to the 'I'.

The lesson continues and the class makes a final unison statement,

> Mother said,
> 'I am cooking.'

Many have focused on the quaint letter 'k' in the middle. The teacher says, 'Does it say cooking? Look carefully. Look at the beginning. Tell me what the first letter says.' Many children may not yet be able to locate the first letter.

'Does it say c-c-c-c?' Any child with an intuitive knowledge of the sound of the letter 'k' will agree heartily. The teacher has now reached the new piece of knowledge for which she designed the lesson. 'It says b-b-b-b for baking.' Some of the class will be surprised to find that the 'k' they are focusing on says 'b' and others gain the impression that the whole word 'baking' says 'b'.

An earnest child might be found reading the story to himself the next day. Cleverly matching the number of word impulses he says to the number of word patterns he sees, we might hear him reading to himself 'Mother is cooking some cakes', and he might be very satisfied with his efforts.

It is not easy to talk with children about these essential directional rules for attending to a language while they are coming to terms with all the new signs and movement restrictions that apply to written language.

2   Early transitions

In the first weeks of formal literacy instruction children are expected to read and write. Society and the laws about school entry have decreed that now all children will actively engage with reading and writing. All their preschool experiences have, individually, been very different and their personal strategies for learning so far have been developed by a unique set of events in their homes and cultures. Therefore the short list that follows simplifies drastically the amount of challenge children face.

- They link oral language systems to the visual code.
- They develop ways of telling stories.
- They learn to compose messages to write.
- They learn to recognise a few letters and a few words.
- They master the directional schema for print, but this takes time.
- They work out how to pull together knowledge of several kinds to make one decision (like solving a new word).

We are not surprised that some children have difficulty making transitions like these in a satisfactory manner. They make the shifts on different time schedules and some become confused.

Much of this earliest learning is involved in seeing the symbols and the patterns of symbols in print and attending according to the directional rules of English. This involves motor learning and visual perception learning that soon moves from explicit deliberate processing by the brain to implicit processing that demands no conscious attention. Two things, the recognition of letters, and attending according to the directional rules of the printer's code, would help the child with both reading and writing. Such perceptual and motor learning would facilitate the cognitive decision-making that has to be done.

Excellent literacy learning results have been achieved with children in the lowest 20 percent of the six-year-old age group across the world in Reading

Recovery. Despite this, we can still be concerned that between one and five percent of children in early intervention do not become independent readers even when they receive individually delivered and individually designed instruction.

I want to call special attention to the fifth bullet point above. In classrooms we invite children to read and write without stressing left-to-right survey of print unduly. For children who have individual lessons in an early intervention programme following their experience in classrooms we have to guide children to the habit of left-to-right scanning of print in our shared activities and demonstrations. I recommend that we teach as if this was a very important transition to facilitate from the first week of a child's lesson series.

It would be a viable hypothesis that the limited progress of our slowest children is related to one of those transitions listed above. For example, a problem may arise, not in the learning to know letters and words and letter-sound relationships, but in failure to learn to survey print according to the directional rules required for recording English, which in turn slows their visual recognition processing, and their decision-making in word-solving.

With this possibility in mind I reviewed two of my research studies published in 1970 and 1974. I also reconsidered the highly stable results over decades of two items on the Concepts About Print test that require a child to reveal 'just one letter' and 'just one word' across a line of text. Correct responses to these items can be surprisingly late achievements.

Typically early intervention placement is only made after a child has spent about a year in school. That is time enough for inappropriate scanning of print to have become habituated. I am confident therefore that it is unwise to wittingly allow Reading Recovery children to continue to identify whatever parts of words they can as a first step rather than insisting on a left-to-right survey of words by the eyes across a line *and across the letters in a word.*

This emphasis should occur from the earliest days of intervention instruction. It becomes a responsibility of the teacher to demonstrate appropriate moves across words, and to observe and work on any lapses from the first days of intervention lessons.

Flexible teachers may be reluctant to fuss about this learning with children who are already having difficulty with many aspects of beginning reading. We know the child knows very little, and we want him to have the opportunity to use anything he knows as he reads. But if those teachers are consistent in the way they work at the magnetic board, across the books and in their demonstrations of writing or reading, their pupils will quickly catch on to the left-to-right habit. Teachers do not have to talk at length about it.

It is appropriate for Reading Recovery instruction to emphasise left-to-right movement during early lessons,

- across a line of text,
- when reading word by word,

- and when writing words letter by letter,
- and when analysing a new word.

The teacher can model the behaviour, condition the approach almost without words or instructions, and try to encourage the child to scan with his eyes from left to right. Psychologists established long ago that learning to read and write does condition a reader to move the eyes from left to right (or from right to left for some languages) when scanning print but not necessarily to move within these constraints when looking at other phenomena.

I am very impressed with the differences that I reported from my study of identical quadruplets in *Visible Language*, 1974. I plotted their finger-pointing and hand movements on print in monthly observations during their first two years at school. Consistent success 'using either hand on either page of a reading book without lapses' was defined as satisfactory performance. The correlation of achieving directional control and becoming a reader of small books was perfect on this set of identical siblings: about the time I recorded the directional control in my observations each girl began to read her little reading books with marked success. The first to gain directional control was six months ahead of the last.

Another published study has influenced this decision. I reported a longitudinal replication of an experiment in which randomly chosen children from classroom programmes in five schools read lists of 15 easy words in normal, reversed and inverted orientation at five and a half, six, seven and eight years of age. Of 100 children studied for a year from their fifth to their sixth birthday there were 87 available at 8:0 years (21 or 22 children in each of four progress groups measured at 6:0).

Here is a simple report of the findings. High-progress readers were very disturbed by reversed print after six months of school. They had already learned to anticipate letters in normal orientations. All readers were disturbed by reversed print after two years. Although all the words read were easy words, at eight years of age the lowest-progress readers were no more accurate on normal print than they were on inverted print. Was this because they had persisted with a non-standard survey of print throughout their first three years at school? That is a possibility. At eight years the children in the lowest quartile did not have the same print expectations of the five-and-a-half-year-old high-progress children.

When the test words were written in the reversed condition, facing back to front, only five letters (b, d, p, q, g) might be read as another letter, but when the words were written in inverted print, 15 letters could be readily identified as other letters (b, d, f, g, h, k, m, n, p, q, r, t, u, v, w). There were many opportunities to confuse letters if you adopted a flexible approach to letter forms. This study is not conclusive. It leads me to suspect that early control over directional orientation and the survey of print from left to right was associated with high progress. The order in which we scan print governs the order in which we pick up information in print.

I recommend to Reading Recovery teachers that a consistent emphasis on the left-to-right scanning of print from the beginning of a lesson series is warranted. This will not alter the sequence of teaching in Hearing and Recording Sounds in Words in Reading Recovery. In fact, allowing the child to record the last sound in the Elkonin box on the right is not inconsistent with what I am recommending above. It provides a practical example of the 'brain work' the child has to do to shift his attention to the beginning of a word.

3   A collection of prompts for reference

Prompts are not just talk! Short prompts give a maximum of information to the child using the fewest words. 'Too much teacher talk' interferes with solving a problem. Conversations in the lesson should be warm and friendly, but when the child must attend to something, or must pull several things together, the prompt should be short, clear and direct. What is the next most helpful thing this child could do?

Contrast the next two examples.

> *I really liked how you were noticing when you got here that it did not say 'put it on' and you went back and fixed it up. You did some good thinking. On this page when you were trying to figure out 'lion tamer' I saw you checking the picture. Does it start right for 'tamer'? Would you expect to see that 't' there?*

Good teaching would have sounded more like this.

> *Good thinking! Show me 'lion'. Now look at what letter comes next — the first letter of that new word!*

It is imperative to prompt clearly. It is not imperative to use any particular prompt in the guidebook. Teachers have asked for more alternative prompts, and I have provided some suggestions. Vary your prompting to maximise the progress of individual children.

Some of the prompts scattered throughout the teaching procedures are listed below under headings that suggest why the prompt might be used. Most of them come from sections 10, 12 and 13. However the same words might prompt different responses, depending on the reading or writing context. The list is illustrative, not exhaustive.

Be clear
> *Do this.*
> *Don't do that.*
> *Cover the end.*

Open-ended (*used more in later lessons*)
> *What did you notice?*
> *Try that again.*

Were you right?

How did you know it was …?

Look carefully and think what you know.

Was that okay?

How could we finish it?

Why did you stop?

Think what you know that might help.

How did you know?

How did you know it was right?

How did you know it said 'was'?

To locate

Read it with your finger. Did it match?

Were there enough words?

Did you run out of words?

Point to each letter/word.

Use the pointer and make them match.

Try that again with your finger.

Can you find the tricky word?

What do you expect to see at the beginning?

   … at the end?

   … in the middle?

Where is the hard bit?

Why did you stop?

What did you notice?

Run a finger under it while you say it slowly.

To look

Would X start like that?

I liked the way you were using your eyes.

Does it look right?

Do you think it looks like 'went'?

Use your eyes and think about it.

Look for something that would help you.

What can you see that might help?

Do you know a word that looks like that?

Can you see what might help?

See this letter.

Look at this letter/word.

Does this help? (pointing to a helpful cue)

You know a word that starts with those letters.

Make another word that looks like that.

Make another word that ends with that pattern.

To hear sounds and words

What is the first letter?
Let's go to the board. You write the first letter.
What's the first letter in 'look'?
We can take the first part away (to the left).
Where is the first letter?
Where do we start?
What is a word that starts with that letter?
What is a word that starts with that sound?
Make another word that starts like that.

To find first letters

Can you hear this letter?
You said … Was that right?
Can you hear the last part of 'looking'?
What sound does it make?
What is its name?
Make another word that sounds like that.
What sounds can you hear in that word?
Does that sound right to you?

To attend to meaning

You said … Does that make sense?
Would X make sense?
Would that make sense?
Would 'went' fit in there?

To attend to structure

You said … Can we say it that way?
Is that a little letter or a big one?
Is that a capital letter or a small one?

To think about processing

What could this word be?
You solved the puzzle. How did you do that?
You said, 'I think we shall go and find him.' Is that what the rabbit said?
And here Mother Bear is asking a question. How would she ask a question?
Was that okay?
How did you know?
What do you think?
Which is it? What do you think?
You found out what was wrong all by yourself.
You made a mistake on this page. Can you find it?
How did you know?
How did you know it was right?

To attend to fluency, and/or phrasing

Let's put this together.
Let's put 'here comes' together.
Are you listening to yourself?
Did it sound good?
Can you read this quickly?
Put them all together so that it sounds like talking.
How would you say that?
Make it sound like a favourite book.
Make it sound like a story you would love to listen to.
Read up to your finger.
Read it all smoothly.
Make your voice go down at the end of the sentence.
Change your voice when you see these marks on the page.

To seek help from writing

You're saying 'said' for a word you know.
Write this word.
Write it quickly. Good job. What is it?

Prompt to remember

You need to know that word tomorrow. Have you got it in your head?
How could we finish it?
I liked the way you did that [searched memory].
You tried to think of that word. That was good.
What is another letter that looks like that?

Prompting to check

Check it.
Were you right?
What could you check?
Does it look right and sound right?
It has to make sense and it has to sound right.
What would make sense, and sound right and look like that?
You made a mistake on that page. Can you find it?
What's wrong with this?

Comprehension — to think about the message

You said … Does that make sense?
What did he do that was nice?
Does the pot look too small to you?
How did Mum trick Greedy Cat?
Would you like to have Jake for a brother?
What do you think Dad is going to do now?

General

Try again.

Try that again.

Try that again and think what could make sense.

Try that again and think what would sound right and look right.

4   What is special about instruction that is individually designed and individually delivered?

Reading Recovery has a framework for lessons that critics have mistaken for prescriptive teaching. Each required segment of the lesson is a 'task with scope'. Teachers create a learning opportunity for a particular individual, at a particular moment in time. Learners are coming to complex learning from different directions. In every lesson a child

1   reads familiar books,

2   rereads yesterday's book,

3   does a few minutes of work with magnetic letters, breaking up words, and constructing words,

4   composes and writes a story,

5   reassembles that story as a puzzle from its parts,

6   is introduced to a new reading book and

7   reads that book for the first time.

What occurs in each slot of the lesson increases in difficulty on an individual schedule until the activities are as advanced as those completed by most children in the learner's classroom. The tasks can remain 'whole' because the teacher shares any part of the task to support the learner's participation, and sometimes completes some part of the task. It would be possible to use this framework prescriptively but the Reading Recovery teacher does not do that. She designs the task to provide scope for an individual learner to act.

Each day the teacher observes the learner completing tasks of increasing difficulty; she slows the child down, momentarily, asking him to look and think again, and then prompts him to fine-tune his decision-making. Her theory is that this learning is complex, and at any one time on any one day the individual learner's challenge will be idiosyncratic. Her task is to elicit effective performance that could lead to vague awareness, and over time the learner may become able to verbalise what he does but not at the time he is learning to do something new.

The child's progress can be described and recorded in some detail within a constructivist theory that allows for an adult to share the complex task. Gradually the teacher will become less helpful as the learner locates more of the information in print, and takes on more of the processing and problem-solving. The reader shifts from meaningful acts to cognitive awareness of how these things can work together, and how to use new learning from this task in another context.

The tasks in the Reading Recovery lessons provide scope for performance at easy to challenging levels. They can be analysed for the aspects of literacy learning that they foster. Two examples may illustrate this. At the beginning of each lesson children reread familiar texts which still present processing challenges to the learner. Comprehension of messages is best assessed on this material when the orchestration of smooth decision-making and fluent reading aids comprehension. Rereading familiar texts allows for greatly increased volume of reading, and that is hard to achieve for beginning readers who find the task difficult.

A second example occurs in the writing segment of the lesson for which children compose a short message. This is where the teacher shares the complex task so that the whole message gets written. Inevitably in writing the child must construct words letter by letter, and work with phonemic awareness, orthographic awareness, known words and new words. The teacher can allow the child to take risks and attempt new things with teacher support, working by analogy from what he already knows.

Reading Recovery lessons are individually designed by teachers who have additional training over and above their classroom expertise. They can use a wide range of alternatives for working with the limited response repertoires of the children. They can start at lower levels than the classroom teacher, pursue a difficulty for longer, and carry the child to higher levels than the classroom teacher would think of doing. These adaptations result in learning at a faster rate than classmates, producing the necessary accelerated progress needed to catch up to them. The teacher's daily records of child responses 1) demonstrate the idiosyncratic paths to success, 2) can be used by a school's Reading Recovery team to track the effectiveness of the lesson series so far, and 3) are available for research analysis.

Some of the changes in a Reading Recovery teacher's responses to children were described in research by Wong, Groth and O'Flahavan (1994).

> … teachers changed the nature of their scaffolding as a function of text familiarity. As students reread familiar texts, for example, teachers became less directive and began to coach the students' attempts to read. … In contrast, when students read new texts, these teachers responded by increasing their modeling, prompting, and discussing comments. They (modeled) fluency, prompted students to attend to visual and meaning cues, and discussed the story line. (p. 22)

5   Teaching with diversity in mind

We consider human variability and divergence from normality when it comes to superiority: sporting prowess, high intelligence, giftedness in art, music and figure-skating. We accept differences in personal attributes like looks, physique, reaction time, need for sleep, visual perception, auditory perception, sight, hearing, muscle power, singing ability. Yet we grossly underrate how different each child's prior history of learning opportunities has been. Education has typically responded to diverse learners by slowing down the pace of learning and simplifying the content, but diverse learners do have to learn complex things.

In literacy learning this means helping individuals in different ways to perform the complex activities so that they move up a steep gradient of difficulty being continually successful. We need to know what successful learners learn to do as they move up a gradient of difficulty in texts in order to know what shifts diverse students need to make.

Reading Recovery teachers

- find each learner's starting point,
- observe how children work on easy tasks when things go well,
- respond to children's initiatives,
- interact with their thinking,
- observe how they work on novel things,
- applaud what is correct in a partially correct response
- and identify strengths as 'firm ground' on which to build.

The emphases in tomorrow's lesson will arise out of today's observations. All the activities listed above would be realised differently with each of the four to six pupils taught on a particular day.

Reading Recovery teachers draw upon four large bodies of theory:

- theory about the psychological competencies needed for effective performance, including both language learning and perceptual learning;
- theory about the influence of social contexts on learning and particularly on teaching interactions;
- theory about designing instruction for diverse learners;
- and theory about implementing effective programmes in education systems.

The vast repertoire of alternative teaching moves that Reading Recovery teachers need calls for more training than that required for quality classroom teaching. Faced with a puzzling pupil, teachers brainstorm possible ways to work with a child, maintaining a peak level of tentativeness and flexibility. These are bywords of Reading Recovery instruction. Teachers need to be tentative in their judgements and must easily and quickly change the emphases of the instruction in response to interactions with learners. Therefore Reading Recovery encourages networks of teachers, schools, Tutors/ Teacher Leaders and Trainers to critique and support each other's problem-solving. The search for solutions has no end.

Appendix 3

Cases from teachers and observers: they could be discussed in teachers' training sessions

1   David was receiving help in individual lessons

Finding one's place while reading often involves locating and holding that place with the finger or hand, turning the head, scanning with the eyes, and locating with the finger. It is a coordinated set of movements in two-dimensional space. This pattern of behaviour is observable in most preschool children as they look at books. When they come to read the printed messages of books they must control both this set of behaviours and the directional rules.

If a child learns to be flexible about these inflexible rules for writing English he will have the problem of relearning the inflexible rules, as David did.

David wrote 'I am a dog.' His teacher wrote out the sentence on paper, cut it up into words and asked David to put the sentence together again. She cut 'dog' into separate letters to increase the difficulty of the task. David placed the cards in this order:

```
dgo   a   am   I
654   3   2    1
```

and the teacher began this interesting interaction.

T: Oh! Can you read that to me?

C: I am a dog. *(moving a finger across the print from right to left)*

T: But you read it that way. *(pointing right to left)*

C: I know.

T: But you can't do that.

C: Why?

T: Because we always read that way. *(pointing left to right)*

C: Why?

T: Because it's a rule.

C: Why?

T: Well, if we did not make a rule about reading and writing no one would know where to start and which way to go and we would get mixed up, wouldn't we?

C: How?

T: *(picking up the book)* If I did not know that the person who wrote this book kept to the rules and wrote this way I might read the top line like this: 'engine fire the at Look'.

C: *(solemn, takes a long look)* Phew.

T: Haven't you always been shown to read this way? *(demonstrating left to right)*

C: Ye-s. I didn't think it mattered.

T: You are absolutely not allowed to go the other way in reading or in writing. Did you know that?

C: No!

T: Well, we will have to remember to go only one way and to stick to it. Okay?

C: Okay.

T: Where do we begin?

C: *(points to the right)*

T: Where is the beginning?

C. *(points to the right and the left and looks questioningly at the teacher)*

T: Where shall we start?

C: I don't know!

To David starting at either end seemed to be legitimate. After that, every lesson began with left-hand touch-down practice. The teacher had observed the problem. In time David could overcome his flexibility, but old habits take a while to unlearn. He had a habit of being flexible.

After all, it is often an advantage in the world of experiences to be flexible about how you react to a problem, but not when reading and writing, and not when driving a car.

David learned to be flexible about these inflexible rules for writing English, and became very resistant to changing. When his teacher tried to talk it through, he argued and was unconvinced by her logical explanation. She had to take very firm consistent action to give him the opportunity to train out his old (unhelpful) flexibility (Clay, 1979, p. 101).

2 Kay, a five-year-old making excellent classroom progress

I selected an illustration of 'acts of processing' from an old research tape made in 1963. It captures some of the earliest processing behaviours observed in that research. Kay entered school on her fifth birthday in February and was not a reader. Like all her New Zealand classmates she was not in a preparatory programme: she was expected to learn to read and write now that she was 'in school'. After a month her teacher introduced her to first level reading books, and in her second month at school she was reading at a higher level of the reading series. (See Randell, 2000, for discussion of the type of reading material.) This is how she read.

Introduction

  Kay: We've got a tape-recorder.

  T: Have you?

Kay: *(reads the title)* Grandma *(pause)* Comes *(pause)* To Stay. There's 'come' there. It shouldn't have the 's' on the end. *(laughs)* I just write 'come'. *(reads)* … comes **to** stay.

T: All right. Go on. Read the book.

Reading the book

p. 1   Kay: 'Here's the plane,' said Father.
'The Viscount,' shouted Bill.
'The Viscount,' shouted Peter.

p. 2   Kay: 'Grandma is in the plane,'
said Father. *(long pause)*

T: Where are you?

Kay: Here. *(pointing, long pause)*

T: What does it say?

Kay: 'Grandma …

T: Yes. Go on.

Kay: … is …

T: Mm.

Kay: … in …

T: Mm.

Kay: … the plane,' said Bill.

T: Mm.

p. 3   Kay: Grandma and Father
are in the car.
'Bill, Peter. Come here,'
said Father.

T: Now would you read the next page with your finger?

p. 4   Kay: *(pointing word by word)*
'Mother. Mother.
Here is Grandma,'
shouted Pe-/Bill.

p. 5   A doll for Sally.
A ca-/a fire engine for Bill.
A car for Peter.
'Oh thank you, Grandma,'
said Bill, Peter and Sally.

p. 6   'Bill, Peter, Sally,
come … to … bed,' said Mother.
Bill and the fire engine *(repeats the line)*
… Bill, *(repeats)* Bill and the fire engine is/are in bed.
Peter *(repeats)* Peter and the car are in bed.

p. 7   The doll is in bed. *(pause)*

T: Where are you?

Kay: Here.

T: What is it?

Kay: Sally is up. *(She moves to close the book but seems to be uncertain.)*

T: Yes. And what about the last part?

p. 8   Kay: *(She turns the page.)* Sally is naughty.

This child was off to a very good start. The record shows a beginner working with information of different kinds on continuous text. She made sense of the story; she studied a word, 'comes', and commented on the 's' she did not expect to see, she lost the thread and read one page slowly, word by word without linking it up. From time to time she paused and studied the print and could not initiate anything until encouraged. Brilliantly, she corrected herself on the run several times — Pe-/Bill, a ca-/a fire engine — and she anticipated the verb 'is', corrected it to 'are' which must have been on visual information, but rolled it very slowly across her tongue, and caught it again a few words later, as if to say 'Okay, you have to look carefully.' She was not satisfied with what seemed to be the end of the story but did not assume that there must be another page. She used several working systems in the areas of story structure, word structure, the sounds of letters, and language structure. She already knew that reading is complex and if you shift gear and work on the text in different ways it can be figured out. After two months at school she was moving into a second level book. By the end of that school year she was in the proficient group for literacy.

3   Profile of a successful writer in Reading Recovery

At entry to Reading Recovery, Jack's 'islands of certainty' were few, with no discernible links between them. The initial Observation Survey showed that his letter knowledge was reasonable. However, he had many, many confusions between similar-looking letters and lots of reversals; he could control basic directionality and *positional concepts* but had no real concept of a word; he sounded out or spelt out individual letters in the word tests; his corpus of written words included his and his brother's name, 'mum', 'I' and 'a'; he accurately heard and recorded six initial or final sounds.

His text reading (Level 1 instructional) was solely driven by meaning and structural information. During 'Roaming around the known', it was immediately apparent that Jack was relying very strongly on his memory for text, to the exclusion of the visual information, and that he could control one-to-one matching only on a single line of text. He was prescribed glasses early in the lesson series and his teacher also discovered he had major hearing problems that required surgical intervention. In addition, spatial awareness and gross and fine motor control were all real challenges to Jack. He was also easily thrown or confused, and so his teacher needed to be very explicit with her talk and her demonstrations. He had a sweet, ingenuous disposition and was always keen to participate. He often reminded the teacher of a young Labrador puppy — all affection and clumsy feet.

He came from a loving, nurturing family who were more interested in sporting activities than literary ones. Although Jack quickly became very proficient at self-monitoring in reading and writing and at articulating his attempts at strategic processing (both successful and unsuccessful), the milestones, such as overcoming letter confusions and reversals, weren't reached quickly or easily. Often, when he had mastered a new concept, or problem-solved independently, or made a link to some prior learning, the joy on his face was overwhelming. It would bring tears to his teacher's eyes and she really thought she could feel her heart sing. To enable Jack to develop strong strategic processing in reading and writing his teacher took responsibility for the more 'item-based' elements to give him opportunities to work from his strengths — a good sense of story and good control of his oral language. For example, his teacher acted as his memory for spatial concepts (like the spacing between and within words, return sweep, and so on). About ten lessons before he discontinued he announced to his teacher 'I don't need you to remind me about spaces any more, Jo, cos I can do that as well as do the writing.'

His teacher had felt it was far more important for him to concentrate on developing the complexity of his writing as she hopes these examples show. (The numbers indicate the lesson number.)

1. I love my family. *(dictated to teacher)*
4. I asked mum to give me a Harry Potter scar.
10. My Grandma's rooster attacked me and hurt my leg.
15. On a school day I was outside with Jo and I did a trick.
20. I dressed up for the parade as a knight in shining armour.
27. My plane does tricks. It does flips and flies around me.
32. When grandpa took us to the fire station we had a ride on the fire truck.
39. Little Bulldozer felt hurt because the fire truck and the big truck said go away.
44. When I went to play at Stacey's house we put sand in each other's hair.
52. The teachers and the big kids made pancakes for the little kids to eat. I had golden syrup on mine.
55. We were doing freestyle, backstroke and floating on our backs at the swimming pool.
60. On Saturday morning, when I went to Auskick, I was given this tattoo.
65. Three days ago I got a bee sting on my foot when I was playing outside.
69. I know how to make sultana slice. You need to use sultanas, flour, milk and a teaspoon of sugar.

In her analysis of the changes that took place during Jack's 69 lessons the teacher recorded the type of help the child required with comments like these.

> The child wrote independently.
> The word was taken to fluency.
> A known word or part was linked to a new word or part.
> The teacher wrote the word.
> The teacher prompted the child to respond.
> The word was analysed using Elkonin boxes.
> She made notes on the sequence of hearing the sounds in a word.
> She recorded which letters and sounds were produced.
> When the child was able to hear sound but unable to record a corresponding symbol, this was recorded.

It is a very complex task to track the changes, and the interchanges, that occur during writing!

4   John — a tale of success in a classroom programme

John was a child with many counts against him, yet he became a literacy star after one year of school. When John entered school on his fifth birthday he scored below the fifth percentile score on a well-known readiness test: that was as low as one could get. He began at once to learn to read and write because this was the custom in his country. His progress was recorded weekly in a research study of 100 children, and by the end of the school year John had propelled himself, with the help of teachers, from the lowest group on a readiness test to the reading group making the highest and fastest progress. As his reading and writing experience increased John became a commentator on the printed code. He showed interest in words and their possibilities, and he made analyses that his school programme would not have taught him to do (although I suspect someone showed him how to 'cover up' parts of words and showed him some tricks). He actively verbalised what he was noticing about print and how he was categorising words. Readers may have read about John and the good progress he was making after about nine months at school. He had become a child who enjoyed commenting on the odd things he discovered in print. On one observation day when he was about 5:9 my record of his reading, scribbled down at a rapid pace, contained this commentary.

> Look!
> If you cover up *painting* you get *paint*.
> If you cover up *shed* you get *she*.
> If you cover up *o* in *No* you don't get anything.
> *I've* is like *drive* but it's *have*.
> That looks like *Will* but it's *William*.

(From *Reading: The patterning of complex behaviour*, Clay, 1979, second edition)

He is in the first year of formal schooling, and is somewhere in the middle of a family of children who did not make good progress in school. No one expected or encouraged John to make anything but slow progress after he entered school.

Look at what John did not know in the first six months at school (from records taken weekly, Clay, 1972).

Feb. 3   John entered school at 5:0 on the first day of the school year, alert, friendly and not well-prepared by his home for school.

Mar. 10   His dictated caption for the teacher to write under his drawing was 'Saw boxing on TV.' He pointed right to left and from bottom to top as he reread the teacher's print under his picture.

Apr. 7   It had been two months before the teacher judged him ready to try to read a book of captions for pictures that he brought to share with me. He could not come up with any response to it and did not seem to know what was required of him.

Apr. 14   One week later he had grasped the essential nature of book reading. He made up the text of *What Goes Fast* and was almost word perfect. He moved his finger across the print controlling left-to-right direction *and pointing with either hand*. He spent the next two months reading one and two line sentences in simple books with helpful picture clues.

Apr. 21   His new book *My Games* is less accurate, direction is under control, he whispers as if trying out the text and is reluctant to point.

Apr. 28   His new book is *Every Day*. There was one lapse with direction when he tried to read the bottom before the top line. The text was not word perfect. *(Was this just a new book or was he opening up his 'processing system' to some new learning?)*

School vacation time

June 9   He was promoted to a new class with a new teacher. (The promotion indicates that someone has recognised he now needs more challenge.) On his new book *Mother and Father* he controls direction, reads the first word in a line carefully, holds a memory for the text and uses picture clues. A Running Record suggested he was using a variety of information to prompt himself.

June 16   Good teaching had brought him to pre-reader level, McKee's *Come Here*. A high error rate of 1 in 2 or 1 in 3 showed he was struggling.

June 23   No better than last week and on the first page he went from right to left! A serious lapse.

July 7   About the same but he is gaining control over some words.

July 14   Read 12 pages of his book with 94% accuracy and two self-corrections. He was now able to coordinate all the behaviours he needed to read the simple book.

July 29   Read *Wake Up Father* (1963 edition) with 90% accuracy, one self-correction in nine errors. He is reading with effort and reacts to the last page with 'Oh! It's a lot of words.' But he sometimes does effective self-correction.

August 4–18   Reads with 95–100% accuracy and reaches the lowest level of the 1963 Ready to Read books.

School vacation time

After seven months at school he was well-prepared for successful reading and had made an unusually fast and successful run through the 12 reading books (levels) in the series, plus supplementary books, and story books. In my observations all readings were 97–100 percent correct. Over the summer vacation there was no drop in level or accuracy *but there was no gain either.*

That illustration by a single case of early literacy learning progress is recaptured in a theory of possible progressions in acts of processing, Table 1, sections 1–3 in *Change Over Time in Children's Literacy Development* (Clay, 2001, pp. 84–85).

5   Jimmy's progress shows how control over direction can fluctuate (in a classroom programme)

This case illustrated how much directional fluctuation can occur, even in a child making excellent progress.

When Jimmy entered school he did not know which way to move across print. From his records I have extracted seven points during his first year at school that report his fluctuating directional behaviours.

1.   Moved right to left and bottom to top.
2.   Used either hand for correct directional pointing.
3.   Was reluctant to point.
4.   Made one lapse going bottom to top.
5.   Used correct direction but not matched word to word.
6.   Made one lapse going right to left.
7.   Used incipient pointing at difficulties.

For the most part Jimmy was reading by eye scan alone. As he worked on a difficult part of the text his hand came into action, remote from the page, fingers moving slightly as if to help the eyes and the brain to mark significant features that somehow his brain was trying to work on. In terms of the Russian psychologists of the 1960s who made a study of such behaviours this is an outward sign of the inner programme for processing that has become a matter of brain attention rather than of hand movement. Learned in action, the pattern has become a recipe for attending but the learner can apparently return to the full action schema if need be.

Endnotes

Endnotes contain information for teachers which is not essential to initial study of the procedures but which they may search out in subsequent rereadings. Sometimes authors in the endnotes are listed again in the full reference list.

1   Hart, B. and Risley, T.R. (1999). *The Social World of Children Learning to Talk*. Baltimore: Paul Brookes. The authors reported on what 100 ordinary American families, all similarly engaged in child-rearing, said to children during their daily activities, when they were asked to do what they usually do at home. Only 94 words were common across all of the parents and their children.

2   Clay, M.M. (2001). *Change Over Time in Children's Literacy Development*, p. 146.

3   Lyons, C.A. (2003). *Teaching Struggling Readers*, p. 160.

4   Ford, J.R. (1982). *A study of young children learning to read and write Hebrew and English simultaneously*. MA thesis, University of Auckland Library.

5   Morris, D., Bloodgood, J.W., Lomax, R.G. and Penny, J. (2003). Developmental steps in learning to read: a longitudinal study in kindergarten and first grade. *Reading Research Quarterly* 38, 3: 302–29.

6   Clay, M.M. (2005). *An Observation Survey of Early Literacy Achievement*, p. 21.

7   White, E.Q. (1964). *No Turning Back*. Albuquerque: University of New Mexico Press, p. 25.

8   Rayner, K. and Juhasz, B. (2004). Eye movements in reading: Old questions and new directions. *European Journal of Cognitive Psychology*, 16, 1–2: 349.

9   See endnote 5.

10 The procedures are written to apply across countries. In countries where children enter Reading Recovery knowing almost all the letters of the alphabet most of the children will be practising fast recognition. In all countries we find some children with very limited alphabetic knowledge, so these procedures begin at that level.

11 Nodelman, P. (2001). 'A' is for what? The function of alphabet books. *Journal of Early Childhood Literacy*, 1, 3: 235–54.

12 Foorman, B.R., Chen, D., Carlson, C., Moats, L., Francis, D.J. and Fletcher, J.M. (2003). The necessity of the alphabetic principle to phonemic awareness instruction. *Reading and Writing: An interdisciplinary journal*, 16, 4: 289–324.

13 The break into onset and rime is a feature of English linguistics; in Spanish the more useful unit is the syllable; and I suspect in French there will

need to be a different analysis again, taking accents and orthography into account.

Recent research has shown that by the time they enter school many children who speak English at home have a useful awareness of two parts in a single-syllable word — a beginning part and a rhyming part. The beginning part is being called by linguists the onset (which is made up of consonants at the beginning of the word) and the second part is called the rime (or the rhyming part at the end of the word). Hearing the rimes they can discover the onsets.

14   Reutzel, D.R., Dawson, P.C., Young, I.R., Morrison, T.G. and Wilcox, B. (2003). Reading environmental print: What is the role of concepts about print in discriminating young readers' responses? *Reading Psychology*, 24, 2: 123–62.

15   Clay, M.M. (1998). *By Different Paths to Common Outcomes* has a chapter entitled 'The Power of Writing in Early Literacy', pp. 130–61.

16   Vernon, S.A. and Ferreiro, E. (1999). Writing development: A neglected variable in the consideration of phonological awareness. *Harvard Educational Review*, 69: 395–415. Also Kamii, C. and Manning, M. (2002). Phonemic awareness and beginning reading and writing. *Journal of Research in Early Childhood*, 17, 1: 38–46.

17   In *Change Over Time* there is a discussion about the extra power of writing in early literacy interventions, chapter 1, pp. 9–38.

18   See endnote 16, Kamii and Manning, 2002.

19   *Change Over Time*, pp. 27–30.

20   See *Change Over Time*, pp. 28–30, about cut-up stories.

21   *Becoming Literate: The construction of inner control*, p. 216.

22   *Change Over Time*, pp. 24–25.

23   Hobsbaum, A., Peters, S. and Sylva, K. (1996). Scaffolding in Reading Recovery. *Oxford Review of Education*, 22: 17–35.

24   Clay, M. and Cazden, C. A. (1990). A Vygotskian interpretation of Reading Recovery. In L. Moll (ed.), *Vygotsky and Education*. New York: Cambridge University Press.

25   Rodgers, E. Language matters: When is a scaffold really a scaffold? *National Reading Conference Yearbook*, 49: 78–90.

26   See endnote 12, Foorman et al., 2003.

27   Joseph, L.M. (1999). Word boxes help children with learning disabilities identify and spell words. *The Reading Teacher*, 52, 4: 348–56.

28   Moats, L.C. (2000). *Speech to Print: Language essentials for teachers.* Baltimore: Paul Brookes.

29   Cut-up stories were first demonstrated to me at a conference in Hamilton, New Zealand, by Dr Max Kemp who was using them with older children

with reading difficulties for achieving some more advanced concepts of how texts work. Probably the use of this procedure in Reading Recovery does not do justice to his original concept but his contribution to many children's success is acknowledged.

30   Sunshine Books, The Wright Group.

31   Sunshine Books, The Wright Group.

32   Story Basket, The Wright Group.

33   Greenfield, S. (2000), pp. 72–73.

34   Greenfield, S. (2000), p. 74.

35   *Becoming Literate*, p. 336.

36   *Becoming Literate,* p. 328.

37   Squire, L., *Your Brain*, The Dana Foundation video, 1996.

38   *Becoming Literate,* pp. 326–27.

39   Ehri and Sweet, 1991. (See References.)

40   *Becoming Literate*, p. 292.

41   This list is repeated, see p. 132.

42   Schwartz, R.M. (2005). Decisions, decisions: Responding to primary students during guided reading. *The Reading Teacher*, 58, 5: 436–43.

43   Kintsch, W. (1994). The role of knowledge in discourse comprehension: A construction-integration model. In R.B. Ruddell, M.R. Ruddell and H. Singer (1994) (eds), *Theoretical Models and Processes of Reading*. Newark, Delaware: International Reading Association, pp. 951–95.

44   Weaver, C.A., Mannes, S. and Fletcher, C.R. (1995). *Discourse Comprehension: Essays in honor of Walter Kintsch*. Lawrence Erlbaum: Hillsdale, New Jersey.

45   Arocha, J.F. and Patel, V.L. (1995). Constructive-Integration Theory and Clinical Reasoning. See Weaver et al., *Discourse Comprehension*, endnote 44.

46   See endnote 45.

47   Goswami, U. (2003). How to beat dyslexia, *The Psychologist (Broadbent Lecture Report)*, 16, 9: 462–65.

48   See also sections 4, 9 and 11.

49   Metropolitan Reading Readiness test, NZCER edition, 1948.

50   Lyons, 1991, p. 209.

51   See Clay, 1979, pp. 60–63, 77; Iverson, 1991; Hatchett, 1994. The section is strongly influenced by research and advocacy about phonological awareness, onset and rime and analogy. Reading Recovery retains its major emphasis of hearing and recording sounds in words in writing. It requires teachers to call for the children to use what they know in writing in their reading, to attend to the building of a foundational writing vocabulary, and to help children approach the breaking of English words in flexible

and tentative ways. Prescriptive teaching is not compatible with the goal of having children reach the highest levels of competence in the fewest number of lessons.

52   Kuhn and Stahl, 2003. (See References.)

53   Swanson et al., 2003. (See References.)

54   McLane and McNamee, 1990. (See References.)

References

Ashdown, J. and Simic, O. (2000). Is early literacy intervention effective for English language learners?: Evidence from Reading Recovery. In S. Forbes and C. Briggs (eds), *Research in Reading Recovery*, Vol. 2, pp. 115–32. Portsmouth, New Hampshire: Heinemann.

Bissex, G. (1980). *GNYS AT WRK: A child learns to write and read.* Cambridge, Massachusetts: Harvard University Press.

Breznitz, Z. and Share, D. (2002). Introduction to a theme of 'Timing and Phonology'. *Reading and Writing: An international journal*, 15: 1–2 (February).

Cazden, C. (2004). Teaching Literacy. *Bank Street Alumni News Digest*, Fall: 18, 25–27.

Clay, Marie M. (1972). *Reading: The patterning of complex behaviour*, second edition 1979. Auckland: Heinemann.

———. (1974). The spatial characteristics of the open book. *Visible Language*, 8, 3: 275–82.

———. (1979 US reprint, 1975). *What Did I Write?* Auckland: Heinemann; Portsmouth, New Hampshire: Heinemann.

———. (1982). *Observing Young Readers: Selected papers.* Portsmouth, New Hampshire: Heinemann.

———. (1985). *The Early Detection of Reading Difficulties,* third edition. Auckland: Heinemann.

———. (1987). *Writing Begins at Home.* Auckland: Heinemann.

———. (1987). Implementing Reading Recovery: Systemic adaptations to an educational innovation. *New Zealand Journal of Educational Studies*, 22, 1: 35–58.

———. (1990). The Reading Recovery Programme, 1984–88: Coverage, outcomes and Education Board figures. *New Zealand Journal of Educational Studies*, 25, 1: 61–70.

———. (1991a). *Becoming Literate: The construction of inner control.* Auckland: Heinemann.

———. (1991b). Introducing a storybook to young readers. *The Reading Teacher*, 45, 4: 264–73.

———. (1993a). *Reading Recovery: A guidebook for teachers in training.* Auckland: Heinemann.

———. (2005, 2002, 1993b). *An Observation Survey of Early Literacy Achievement.* Auckland: Heinemann.

———. (1998). *By Different Paths to Common Outcomes.* York, Maine: Stenhouse.

————. (2001). *Change Over Time in Children's Literacy Development.* Heinemann, Auckland.

Clay, M.M., Gill, M., Glynn, T., McNaughton, T. and Salmon, K. (1983). *Record of Oral Language and Biks and Gutches.* Auckland: Heinemann.

Clay, M.M. and Tuck, B. (1993). A Study of Reading Recovery Subgroups: Including outcomes for children who did not satisfy discontinuing criteria. In Clay, M.M., *Reading Recovery: A guidebook for teachers in training*, first edition, pp. 86–95.

Clay, Marie M. and Watson, B. (1982). The Success of Maori Children in the Reading Recovery Programme. Report to the Director of Research, Department of Education, Wellington.

Dyson, A.H. (1984). Research Currents: Who controls classroom writing? *Language Arts*, 61, 6: 442–62.

————. (1990). Weaving possibilities: Rethinking metaphors for early literacy development. *The Reading Teacher*, 44, 3: 202–13.

Ehri, L.C. and Sweet, J. (1991). Fingerpoint-reading of memorised text: What enables beginners to process the print? *Reading Research Quarterly* 26, 4: 442–62.

Fernald, G.M. (1943). *Remedial Techniques in Basic School Subjects.* New York: McGraw-Hill.

Ferreiro, E. (2003). *Past and Present of the Verbs to Read and Write: Essays on literacy.* Toronto: Douglas and McIntyre.

Gentile, L.M. (1997). Oral language assessment and development in Reading Recovery in the United States. In S.L. Swartz and A.F. Klein (eds), *Research in Reading Recovery*, Vol. 1: 187–96. Portsmouth, New Hampshire: Heinemann.

Glynn, T., Crookes, T., Bethune, N., Ballard, K. and Smith, J. (1989). *Reading Recovery in Context.* Report to Research Division, Ministry of Education, Wellington.

Goodman, K.S. and Burke, C.L. (1973, April). Theoretically based studies of patterns of miscues in oral reading performance (Project No. 9–0375). Washington, DC: US Office of Education.

Greenfield, S. (2000). *Brain Story.* London: BBC Worldwide.

Hatcher, P. (1994). An integrated approach to encouraging the development of phonological awareness, reading and writing. In C. Hulme and M. Snowling (eds), *Reading Development and Dyslexia.* San Diego, California: Singular Publishing, pp. 163–80.

Hobsbaum, A. (1997). Reading Recovery in England. In S.L. Swartz and A.F. Klein (eds), *Research in Reading Recovery*, Vol. l: 132–47. Portsmouth, New Hampshire: Heinemann.

Hobsbaum, A., Peters, S. and Sylva, K. (1996). Scaffolding in Reading Recovery. *Oxford Review of Education*, 22, 1: 17–35.

Iversen, S.J. (1991). Phonological processing skills and the Reading Recovery programme. MA dissertation, Massey University Library, Palmerston North, New Zealand.

———— (1997). Reading Recovery as a small group intervention. Unpublished doctoral dissertation, Massey University, Palmerston North, New Zealand.

Johnston, P.H. (2004). *Choice Words: How language affects children's learning*. Portland, Maine: Stenhouse Publishing.

Jones, N., Johnson, C., Schwartz, R.M. and Zalud, G. (2005). Two positive outcomes of Reading Recovery: Exploring the interface between Reading Recovery and Special Education. *The Journal of Reading Recovery*, 4, 3: 19–34.

Joseph, L.M. (1999). Word boxes help children with learning disabilities identify and spell words. *The Reading Teacher*, 52, 4: 348–57.

Kamii, C. and Manning, M. (2002). Phonemic awareness and beginning reading and writing. *Journal of Research in Childhood Education*, 17, 1: 38–46.

Kaye, E.L. (2002). Variety, complexity and change in reading behaviours of second grade students. Doctoral dissertation, Texas Woman's University.

Kuhn, M.R. and Stahl, S. (2003). Fluency: A review of developmental and remedial practices. *Journal of Educational Psychology*, 95, 1: 3–21.

Litt, D.G. (2003). An exploration of the double-deficit hypothesis in the Reading Recovery population. Doctoral dissertation: University of Maryland.

Lyons, C.A. (1991). Helping a learning-disabled child enter the literate world. In D.E. Deford, C.A. Lyons and G.S. Pinnell (eds), *Bridges to Literacy: Learning from Reading Recovery*. Portsmouth, New Hampshire: Heinemann, pp. 205–16.

———— (1994). Reading Recovery and learning disability issues, challenges and implications. *Literacy, Teaching and Learning: An international journal of literacy learning*, 1: 109–20.

———— (2003). *Teaching Struggling Readers: How to use brain-based research to maximise learning*. Portsmouth, New Hampshire: Heinemann.

McLane, J.B. and McNamee, G.D. (1990). *Early Literacy*. Cambridge, Massachusetts: Harvard University Press.

Neal, J.C. and Kelly, P.R. (1999). The success of Reading Recovery for English language learners and Descubriendo La Lectura for Bilingual Students in California. In S. Forbes and C. Briggs (eds), *Research in Reading Recovery*, Vol. 2, pp. 115–32. Portsmouth, New Hampshire: Heinemann.

Nodelman, P. (2001). 'A' is for … what? The function of alphabet books. *Journal of Early Childhood Literacy*, 1, 3: 235–54.

O'Leary, S. (1997). *Five Kids*. Bothell, Washington: The Wright Group.

Pearson, P.D. (2000). Ohio Reading Recovery Conference address. See Clay, M. (2005), Stirring the water again. *The Journal of Reading Recovery*, 4, 3: 1–10.

Pinker, S. (2000). *Words and Rules: The ingredients of language.* London: Phoenix.

Pinnell, G.S., DeFord, D.E. and Lyons, C.A. (1988). *Reading Recovery: Early intervention for at-risk first graders.* Arlington, Virginia: Educational Research Service.

Randell, B. (2000). *Shaping the PM Story Books.* Wellington: Gondwanaland Press.

Rayner, K. and Juhasz, B. (2004). Eye movements in reading: Old questions and new directions. *European Journal of Cognitive Psychology*, 16, 1–2: 349.

Rodgers, E. (2000). Language matters: When is a scaffold really a scaffold? *National Reading Conference Yearbook*, 49: 78–90.

Schmitt, M.C., Askew, B.J., Fountas, I.C. and Pinnell, G.S. (2005). *Changing Futures: The influence of Reading Recovery in the United States.* Columbus, Ohio: The Reading Recovery Council of North America.

Schwartz, R.M. (1997). Self-monitoring in beginning reading. *The Reading Teacher*, 51, 1: 40–51.

———— (2005). Decisions, decisions: Responding to primary students during guided reading. *The Reading Teacher*, 58, 5: 436–43.

Smith, P. (2005). Self-monitoring and the acquisition of literacy. Doctoral dissertation submitted: University of Auckland, Auckland.

Swanson, H.L., Trainin, G., Mecoechaea, D.M. and Hammill, D.D. (2004). Rapid naming, phonological awareness, and reading: A meta-analysis of correlation evidence. *Review of Educational Research*, 73, 4: 407–40.

Tunmer, W.E. and Chapman, J.W. (2003). The Reading Recovery approach to preventive early intervention. As good as it gets? *Reading Psychology*, 24: 345 ff.

Weaver, C.A., Mannes, S. and Fletcher, C.R. (1995). *Discourse Comprehension: Essays in honor of Walter Kintsch.* Hillsdale, New Jersey: Lawrence Erlbaum.

Wong, S.D., Groth, L.A., and O'Flahavan, J.F. (1994). *Characterizing teacher-student interaction in Reading Recovery lessons.* Universities of Georgia and Maryland: National Reading Research Center Report, No. 17.

Index

Acknowledgements

Acknowlegement to those who helped me with examples:

Billie Askew	Blair Koefoed
Ann Ballantyne	Rosalie Lockwood
Carol Barnhart	Carol Lyons
Christine Boocock	Debbie Magoulick
Courtney Cazden	Michael
Ann Dyson	Natasha
Mary Fried	Emily Rodgers
Susan Fullerton	Sally-Ann
Ellen Hauser	Robert Schwartz
Jo Hillman	Janet Scull
Phoebe Bell Ingram	Pamela Smith
Jenny	Pauline Smith
John	Barbara Watson
Barry Kerr	Keith Williamson

Acknowledgements to the editorial reviewers:

My manuscripts were reviewed prior to publishing by an international set of Reading Recovery Trainers who were asked for critical feedback to assist me in ensuring that these texts are appropriate for an international audience of educators. At my request, the Chair of the Executive Board of the International Reading Recovery Trainers Organization (IRRTO) working with members of the IRRTO Board invited Trainers to read, edit and comment upon the first proofs of the two books. To ensure international representation the following current and former IRRTO Executive Board members and one additional representative of each of the five national implementations participated in the editing activity: Billie Askew, Ann Ballantyne, Christine Boocock, Sue Burroughs-Lange, Andrea Chalmers, Julia Douetil, Mary Anne Doyle, Jann Farmer-Hailey, Irene Huggins, Carol Lyons, and Janice Van Dyke. In addition, several current and former editors of Reading Recovery journals, published by the Reading Recovery Council of North America, were asked to apply their editorial skills to reviewing the texts. These reviewers included Judith Neal, Emily Rodgers, Maribeth Schmitt, and Robert Schwartz. The combined insights and shrewd critiques of this team of readers, their skill with editing and publication, and their knowledge of research were valued contributions to my final revision process. I am personally grateful for every minute of time they gave to this challenging task, but I take ultimate responsibility for all of the content in the final text.

Contents of Part One

LITERACY LESSONS
DESIGNED FOR INDIVIDUALS

PART ONE
Why? When? and How?

MARIE M. CLAY